THANK YOU,

HOLY
SPIRIT

Harlee,

Thank You, Holy Spirit,
is an excellent title for a book
to give to you, my awesome
gift of a daughter, whom God
gave to me. I Thank God for
you everyday.

I love you,
Your favorite mommy

Christmas 2001

Thank You, HOLY SPIRIT

Meditations from

GENESIS *to* REVELATION

MARILYN HECKSHER

Chosen Books

A Division of Baker Book House Co
Grand Rapids, Michigan 49516

© 2001 by Marilyn Hecksher

Published by Chosen Books
a division of Baker Book House Company
P.O. Box 6287, Grand Rapids, MI 49516-6287

Printed in the United States of America

Library of Congress Cataloging-in-Publication Data

Hecksher, Marilyn, 1925–
    Thank you, Holy Spirit : meditations from Genesis to Revelation / Marilyn Hecksher.
       p.   cm.
    Includes index.
    ISBN 0-8007-9294-7 (pbk.)
    1. Holy Spirit—Meditations. 2. Bible—Meditations. I. Title.
BT122 .H43 2001
242′.5—dc21
                                            2001028645

For current information about all releases from Baker Book House, visit our web site:
http://www.bakerbooks.com

CONTENTS

PART 4   THE HOLY SPIRIT IN THE CHURCH

PREFACE

*T*his study was born out of a need to know God, our Holy Spirit.

In two ongoing Bible studies I conducted, we agreed to start at the beginning of Scripture and learn about the Holy Spirit by acknowledging every reference to Him—what He does and what He is like. These references we called His *work* or *Person*. We studied them verse by verse, one at a time, using other Scriptures to clarify, magnify and edify.

To begin, we asked ourselves three questions:

1. What do I know about the Holy Spirit?
2. What is the condition of my own spirit now?
3. What is the most important thing in my life?

In answering the first question, we determined we were not as well acquainted with this Holy Spirit as we would like to be and did not recognize all His work on our behalf.

The answer to the second question was as varied as those in the room. Some were worried, fearful or anxious, depressed, even sorrowful. Others were peaceful, receptive, expectant, excited, joyful.

To the third question we agreed with the psalmist David when he cried out, "Take not thy holy spirit from me" (Psalm 51:11).

The answers to the questions told us the importance of getting to know the Holy Spirit better so that we might appreciate Him and welcome what He has been doing from the beginning.

We studied the Holy Spirit in the Old Testament, in Jesus' life, in Jesus' teachings (from the gospels) and in the Church (from the New Testament). We found ourselves continually saying, "Thank You, Holy Spirit, for what You have done."

This book is the result of that study and is presented in the hope that all might know Him.

INTRODUCTION

The eternal Spirit . . .
HEBREWS 9:14

The Holy Spirit is "eternal Spirit." His nature or Person is revealed as immortal. It is His permanence that warrants our study, for God has put eternity into our hearts.

The third Person of the Trinity, the Holy Spirit administrates the entire wealth of the Godhead. He is the executor of God's *will* and *testament.* He is the final *witness* to Jesus Christ.

Whatever God the Father initiates He does through the Holy Spirit. Whatever we do of eternal value we do through Him. Nothing and no one bypasses the Holy Spirit.

The Person and work of the Holy Spirit is one of the most profound revelations of the Bible. Through Him we receive a kind of knowledge we could not receive any other way. He holds the key to eternal life.

Just as it seemed good to Luke to write an orderly account to Theophilus "of all that Jesus began both to do and teach, until the day in which he was taken up" (Acts 1:1–2), so it seemed good to me to write an orderly account of the acts of the Holy Spirit from Genesis to Revelation, "that you may know the certainty of those things in which you were instructed" (Luke 1:4, NKJV).

On the Day of Pentecost, 120 believers gathered in the Upper Room to await the promise of the Father. Each of the 120 chapters in this book is a testament to what God made available to them—and to you.

Every chapter concludes with a short prayer. It is my desire that these words will become an expression of your heart, that you may also say, "Thank You, Holy Spirit."

To God be the glory, great things He has done.

PART ONE

THE HOLY SPIRIT
IN THE OLD TESTAMENT

1

MOVEMENT

The Spirit of God moved....
GENESIS 1:2

God, the Holy Spirit, is introduced to us in the third sentence of the Bible. There we read of His first work: *movement.* Although some may not consider this as "work," moving describes the Holy Spirit's active personal nature. The Holy Spirit moves to perform the functions of the Godhead, bringing about God's ultimate intention for time and eternity.

In the second verse of Genesis, Scripture records the beginning of time as we know it and the death of the earth. The earth had become an indistinguishable ruin. Without form. Empty. But the Spirit of God was there, hovering over the desolate chaos, brooding over the waste, "and darkness was upon the face of the deep. And the Spirit of God moved upon the face of the waters" (Genesis 1:2).

The Spirit of God moved over the dark vapors, waiting for a Voice, a command—ready to act to make the Word happen. Then came the instant:

"Light, be!"
"Firmament, be!"
"Earth, be!"
"Oceans, be!"
"Vegetation, be!"
"Sun, moon, stars, be!"
"Animals, fowls, fishes, creeping things, be!"
"Mankind, male and female: Be in the image of God!"

Movement. Change. Beauty. Provision. The Holy Spirit, the active agent of God's spoken Word, moved to birth light out of darkness, to renew order out of chaos, to resurrect the earth and to breathe God's life into molded clay. God saw the work and called it good.

It is awesome to contemplate the creative power of the Holy Spirit. Mankind dreams of capturing that creative energy and discovering all its secrets. How He moves we cannot fathom, but we see the evidence of His miraculous work. His ways are past finding out. Yet we are invited to know Him and experience Him in our own spirits.

What can we know about the Holy Spirit? The Holy Spirit is not resting. He is working. He is movement. He is action. He is divine energy. He is breath. He is life. He is spirit. He is God!

> By the word of the LORD the heavens were made, and all the host of them by the breath of His mouth. . . . He spoke, and it was done; He commanded, and it stood fast.
>
> Psalm 33:6, 9, NKJV

> O LORD, how manifold are Your works! In wisdom You have made them all. The earth is full of Your possessions. . . . You send forth Your Spirit, they are created; and You renew the face of the earth.
>
> Psalm 104:24, 30, NKJV

> "The Spirit of God has made me, and the breath of the Almighty gives me life."
>
> Job 33:4, NKJV

> "In Him we live and move and have our being. . . . 'For we are also His offspring.'"
>
> Acts 17:28, NKJV

How marvelous is our God! Our roots are in Him. His roots are in us. We are eternal beings whose destination is determined in time. And we also must *move:* toward eternal life or eternal death. Which direction shall it be?

Hovering Spirit,
move upon the chaos of my spirit, soul and body
to birth Your light out of the darkness.

2
STRIVING

My spirit shall not always strive with man.

GENESIS 6:3

hat was declared "good" in the beginning became evil—corrupt. Mankind grew so wicked he filled the earth with violence, and "every imagination of the thoughts of his heart was only evil continually" (Genesis 6:5).

The Lord reacted: "My Spirit must not forever be disgraced in man, wholly evil as he is. I will give him 120 years to mend his ways" (Genesis 6:3, TLB).

The work of the Holy Spirit in man is like a judge or umpire, ruling, contending with mankind, pleading the cause of the righteous against the ungodly. The Spirit of God strives within man to resist his rebellion, but not forever. Only while Noah prepared the ark would the Spirit labor on man's behalf, urging him to repent before it was too late.

It took Noah 120 years to build the ark. And the Spirit stopped striving. God saved only eight people out of that wickedness: Noah, his wife, their three sons and their wives.

God uses the times of Noah to illustrate to every generation that the Holy Spirit will not be patient forever. "For in the days before the flood, people were eating and drinking, marrying and giving in marriage, up to the day Noah entered the ark; and they knew nothing about what would happen until the flood came and took them all away. This is how it will be at the coming of the Son of Man" (Matthew 24:37–38, NIV).

If there is striving in your spirit, heed these words of encouragement: "Don't you realize how patient he is being with you? Or don't you care? Can't you see that he has been waiting all this time without punishing you, to give you time to turn from your sin? His kindness is meant to lead you to repentance" (Romans 2:4, TLB).

Repent! How?

Build an ark! Agree with the umpire as Noah did. "By faith Noah, being warned of God of things not seen as yet, moved with fear, prepared an ark to the saving of his house; by the which he condemned the world, and became heir of the righteousness which is by faith" (Hebrews 11:7).

Go ahead. Be afraid. Don't wait. Repent. Do it, now.

Patient Holy Spirit,
Thank You for striving with me. Teach me to number my days that I may apply my heart unto wisdom and save me and my house.

3

INDWELLING MAN

Can we find . . . a man in whom the Spirit of God is?
GENESIS 41:38

*Y*es, such a man was to be found. Joseph, whose jealous brothers sold him into slavery, served in the courts of Pharaoh when Pharaoh had his dreams. All the wise men and magicians of Egypt had failed to bring Pharaoh understanding of his "sevens" dreams. Seven fat and seven lean. "I cannot do it," Joseph replied to Pharaoh, "but God will give Pharaoh the answer he desires" (Genesis 41:16, NIV).

"The dreams of Pharaoh are one and the same. God has revealed to Pharaoh what he is about to do" (Genesis 41:25, NIV).

The whole course of Egypt's history began to unfold through the interpretation of Pharaoh's dreams. God revealed to Joseph that there would be seven years of abundance in Egypt when food could be stored up to be used in the seven years of famine that would immediately follow.

Indeed, the Spirit of God had moved in Joseph with divine understanding, and Pharaoh rejoiced to know. "Since God has made all this known to you [Joseph], there is no one so discerning and wise as you. You shall be in charge of my palace, and all my people are to submit to your orders. Only with respect to the throne will I be greater than you" (Genesis 41:39–40, NIV).

A man can sometimes recognize God's man by his spirit. Joseph himself bore witness to the truth that it was God in him who interpreted Pharaoh's dreams, whereby he not only saved Egypt and all the countries round about but also magnified Egypt above all the nations of the earth and preserved the Seed of Israel.

More than two hundred years later other men were found in whom the Spirit of God moved. The Lord, speaking to Moses, directed him to bring seventy of Israel's elders before the tent of meeting saying, "I will come down and talk with you there. I will take of the Spirit that is upon you and will put the same upon them" (Numbers 11:17, NKJV).

And so it was that when God's Spirit rested upon them they began to prophesy, sounding forth the praises of God and declaring His will.

The Book of Deuteronomy closes with the death of Moses, "whom the Lord knew face to face" (Deuteronomy 34:10), but not before Moses laid his hands upon Joshua, the son of Nun. Immediately, Joshua was filled with the Spirit of wisdom, and afterward he became the great military leader who conquered the Promised Land.

Yes, the personal nature of the Holy Spirit is *in* men.

Thank You, Spirit of God,
for sharing Yourself so intimately!

4

CRAFTSMANSHIP

Speak unto all that are wisehearted, whom I have filled with the spirit of wisdom.

EXODUS 28:3

*T*he function of the Holy Spirit revealed here is the Spirit of wisdom for work.

Moses had been with God forty days and forty nights receiving the pattern of a sanctuary on earth for God, so that He might live among the children of Israel.

His earthly dwelling place, called the Tabernacle, with its furniture, furnishings, curtains, utensils, anointing oil, incense and priestly garments, had never been seen before. Yet the instructions from God were to make everything *exactly* as it had been shown to Moses on the mountain.

How do you make something you have never seen before? Where do you learn the skills needed for the work? It is through the supernatural power of the Creator at work within you. God can be your wisdom, understanding and knowledge in all manner of workmanship. His qualifications are well documented. "God blessed (spoke good of) the seventh day, set it apart as His own, and hallowed it, because on it God rested from all His work which He had created and done" (Genesis 2:3, AMPLIFIED).

God, being the author of creative work, gave a high priority to craftsmanship when He instructed Moses: "See, I have called by name Bezaleel the son of Uri, the son of Hur, of the tribe of Judah. And I have filled him with the Spirit of God, in wisdom, in understanding, in knowledge, and in all manner of workmanship, to design artistic works, to work in gold, in silver, in bronze, in cutting jewels for setting, in carving wood, and to work in all manner of workmanship" (Exodus 31:2–5, NKJV).

Think of it! All manner of workmanship that God demanded was supplied. Bezaleel is the first man Scripture says was *filled* with the Spirit of God. This gave him supernatural knowledge of the skills necessary to produce the Tabernacle of the Most High God.

What a privilege it is to craft anything for God. He accepted this earthly dwelling of perfection and beauty, made by men and women, for Scripture says He lived among the curtains (1 Chronicles 17:1). This same God, who made the heavens and the earth out of nothing, moves upon men today by the same Spirit. He shares His wisdom, understanding and knowledge—*to work*—with His offspring. Like Father, like son. He even calls us by name. How blessed we all can be with His wise heart.

Thank You, Creative Spirit,
for Your supply of all we need, to do all You ask.

5
COMING UPON SINNERS

Balaam . . . saw Israel . . . and the spirit of God came upon him.

NUMBERS 24:2

Is God allowed to move by His spirit on whomever He pleases? Even upon a man like Balaam, a wise man from the East, a diviner, a sorcerer?

Is God allowed to move by His Spirit wherever and whenever He chooses?

If you are not sure that the answer is yes, you will need to adjust your thinking.

Balak, king of Moab, hired Balaam to curse the Israelites, those whom God had blessed by choosing them for His own. In panic, Balak pleaded with Balaam to come to him saying,

> "A vast horde of people has arrived from Egypt, and they cover the face of the earth and are headed toward me. . . . Please come and curse them for me, so that I can drive them out of my land; for I know what fantastic blessings fall on those whom you bless, and I also know that those whom you curse are doomed."
>
> Numbers 22:6, TLB

On the way to Moab, the Angel of the Lord frightened the donkey Balaam was riding, causing Balaam's foot to be crushed against a wall. When Balaam struck the donkey angrily, the Lord opened Balaam's eyes to see the Angel resisting him. The Angel said: "Behold, I have come out to stand against you, because your way is perverse before Me" (Numbers 22:32, NKJV).

No wonder Balaam was ready to obey the Spirit of God and speak only what God told him! He explained to Balak, "God is not a man, that He should lie, nor a son of man, that He should repent. Has He said, and will He not do? Or has He spoken, and will He not make it good? Behold, I have received a command to bless; He [God] has blessed, and I cannot reverse it. He has not observed iniquity in Jacob, nor has He seen wickedness in Israel. The Lord his God is with him, and the shout of a King is among them" (Numbers 23:19–21, NKJV).

In spite of this, Balaam went through his enchantments over and over again. He would draw breath to speak curses upon Israel, and out of his mouth would come only blessings. "There is no sorcery against Jacob, nor is there any divination against Israel. It now must be said of Jacob and of Israel, 'Oh, what God has done!'" (Numbers 23:23, NKJV).

What was wrong? Why could Balaam not curse Israel and claim the high rewards of divination from Balak?

Balaam finally stopped resorting to sorcery when he viewed Israel's encampment from a mountaintop. Seeing their tribes below in orderly array and the beauty of the tents of Israel, he became convinced that it pleased the Lord to bless Israel. The Spirit of the Lord came mightily upon him there, and he prophesied the joys awaiting Israel, as well as their future Savior. He exclaimed, "How lovely are your tents, O Jacob! Your dwellings, O Israel! . . . Blessed is he who blesses you, and cursed is he who curses you. . . . I see Him, but not now; I behold Him, but not near; a Star shall come out of Jacob; a Scepter shall rise out of Israel" (Numbers 24:5, 9, 17, NKJV).

The Spirit worked here by "coming upon" a man outside the tribes of Israel. God's Spirit of truth upon Balaam was stronger than Balaam's spirit. Yes, "Heaven and earth will pass away, but My words will by no means pass away" (Luke 21:33, NKJV).

Has God said He will bless, and will He not do it? Or has He spoken, and will He not make it good? He will! Ultimately, every knee bows and every tongue confesses that God is sovereign and merciful to those whom He has chosen. Could that be the reason why some fourteen hundred years later wise men from the East also came with gold, frankincense and myrrh to find the Star and worship Him who was born King of the Jews?

Spirit of God,
thank You for letting it be known as far as the east is from the west that
You reign over and bless Jacob's posterity forever.

6
ENABLING

The Spirit of the LORD came upon him.

JUDGES 3:10

After the death of Joshua, the history of Israel began to change. With no strong leadership, Israel fell into Balaam's trap, which was set to entice Israel to sin through compromise and intermarriage with the ungodly nations surrounding them, thus causing God to curse His chosen people (see Revelation 2:14).

Living among the nations that worshiped heathen gods, they began to eat meat sacrificed to idols and to commit fornication with the idolaters even though the Lord had forbidden it. "They sacrificed to demons, not to God, to gods they did not know, to new gods, new arrivals that your fathers did not fear" (Deuteronomy 32:17, NKJV).

When this happened Israel soon forgot God and did evil in His sight. That is, every man did what was right "in his own eyes." Today they would say, "I did it *my* way." As a result, God brought severe punishment upon them through their enemies until finally Israel cried out in repentance. The Lord would then have mercy upon Israel, raise up a deliverer—called a judge—and the land would have rest during their time. This repetition of disobedience, oppression, repentance and deliverance occurs throughout Scripture.

Israel's many "deliverers" were enabled to do *exploits* because the Spirit of the Lord came upon them mightily. *Exploit* means a bold, unusual act; a daring, heroic deed. For instance:

- The Spirit of the Lord came upon Othniel, and he went out to war against a Babylonian king who had kept Israel in bondage for years. Othniel won.
- The Spirit of the Lord came upon timid Gideon, and with three hundred men he delivered Israel from the host of the Midianites.
- The Spirit of the Lord came upon Jephthah, giving him victory over the Ammonites.

- The Spirit of the Lord came upon Samson, enabling him to destroy the Philistine oppressors. Samson's feats of superhuman strength are more exciting than any modern-day adventure story.
- The Spirit of the Lord came upon Saul, Israel's first king, and he began to prophesy.
- The Spirit of the Lord came upon Saul's men, whom he sent to kill David, and they all prophesied.
- The Spirit of the Lord came upon David when Samuel anointed this shepherd the second king of Israel. The Spirit rested upon David from that day forward. The giant Goliath was one of his conquests.

When the Holy Spirit comes upon men, a change is wrought. They are moved supernaturally in faith and works to accomplish the will of God. What more can be said? "It would take too long to recount the stories of the faith of Gideon and Barak and Samson and Jephthah and David and Samuel and all the other prophets. These people all trusted God and as a result won battles, overthrew kingdoms, ruled their people well, and received what God had promised them; they were kept from harm in a den of lions, and in a fiery furnace. Some, through their faith, escaped death by the sword. Some were made strong again after they had been weak or sick. Others were given great power in battle; they made whole armies turn and run away" (Hebrews 11:32–34, TLB).

What a great cloud of witnesses to encourage our faith to do exploits!

Spirit of the living God,
fall afresh upon me.

7
HYMNS OF PRAISE

"The Spirit of the LORD spoke by me, and His word was on my tongue."

2 SAMUEL 23:2, NKJV

*D*avid confessed that the Spirit of the Lord spoke words through him. In fact, he recognized the Godhead by name in a triple witness to the words he uttered. "The Spirit of the Lord spoke by me, and His word was on my tongue. The God of Israel said, the Rock of Israel spoke to me: 'He who rules over men must be just, ruling in the fear of God'" (2 Samuel 23:2–3, NKJV).

Notice the Trinity: the Father, God of Israel; the Son, the Rock of Israel; and the Holy Spirit.

David makes clear his divine inspiration and does not credit himself. As we meditate on what was spoken through David, we remember the mighty Psalms.

Psalms are praise hymns, spiritual songs accompanied by stringed instruments. And although it is not our purpose to dwell on them here, it does seem right to pause and reflect, for it would be impossible to worship and praise God without repeating much of what David spoke, wrote or put to music through the Spirit.

David built the Lord a house of praise. No wonder God loved him and gave this testimony concerning the sweet psalmist of Israel: "I have found David the son of Jesse, a man after My own heart, who will do all My will" (Acts 13:22, NKJV; see also 1 Samuel 13:14, NKJV; Psalm 89:20, NKJV).

As king of Israel, David appointed the first cantors as song leaders and formed choirs to offer praise to God. Their ancestry is so important to God it is recorded among the genealogies of the Levitical singers in 1 Chronicles 6:31–48.

One special chorus that the Lord spoke through David in Psalm 110:1 is repeated or referred to nine times in the New Testament. Since God would need to speak only once and it would be so, consider the implication of the Almighty repeating this theme time and time again: "The LORD said to my Lord, 'Sit at My right hand, till I make Your enemies Your footstool'" (Psalm 110:1, NKJV; Matthew 22:44, NKJV; Mark 12:36, NKJV; Luke 20:42–43, NKJV; Acts 2:34–35, NKJV; see also 1 Corinthians 15:25; Ephesians 1:20–22; Philippians 2:9–11; Hebrews 1:13; 10:12–13).

In this important verse it would seem that David penned for us the grand welcome into the throne room after Jesus' resurrection. As Jesus ascended in the cloud and was received into glory, His Father said, "Wait here until. . . ."

Thank You, Spirit of worship,
for uttering through David eternal praise songs to sing
while we wait "until."

8
SUPERNATURAL TRANSPORTATION

"The Spirit of the LORD will carry you to a place I do not know."
1 KINGS 18:12, NKJV

*O*ne of the Holy Spirit's greatest works is to transport people, to carry them away—literally. In the life of a superman named Elijah this was a frequent occurrence. So much so, in fact, that when Obadiah was asked to tell his boss Ahab that Elijah would see him, Obadiah was afraid Elijah would disappear again, and he would be in serious trouble. "It shall come to pass [Elijah], as soon as I am gone from you, that the Spirit of the LORD will carry you to a place I do not know; so when I go and tell Ahab, and he cannot find you, he will kill me" (1 Kings 18:12, NKJV).

Elijah promised to "be there" when Ahab went to meet him, and he was.

On another day, however, that would not be so. "The LORD was about to take up Elijah into heaven by a whirlwind . . ." (2 Kings 2:1, NKJV).

Elijah knew the day, and so did the other prophets Elijah had taught, including Elisha, who would not let Elijah out of his sight for fear he would miss the event. And "then it happened, as they continued on and talked, that suddenly a chariot of fire appeared with horses of fire, and separated the two of them; and Elijah went up by a whirlwind into heaven" (2 Kings 2:11, NKJV).

What an exciting glimpse we have here of the Spirit's power. It was the original spaceship for sure!

But is that the end of Elijah? No, we hear of him again on the mountain with Jesus about 930 years later. "Two men appeared and began talking with him—Moses and Elijah! They were splendid in appearance, glorious to see; and they were speaking of his death at Jerusalem, to be carried out in accordance with God's plan" (Luke 9:30–31, TLB).

In the New Testament, Scripture records another instance of supernatural transportation when Philip the evangelist was "caught away" by the Spirit of the Lord after he baptized the Ethiopian believer (Acts 8:39).

It was Enoch, however, who had the honor of being the first man in space. After 365 years on earth, "Enoch walked with God; and he was not, for God took him" (Genesis 5:24, NKJV).

The event was so spectacular that the Old Testament records it in Genesis and the New Testament records it in Hebrews. "Enoch was caught up and transferred to heaven, so that he did not have a glimpse of death; and he was not found, because God had translated him" (Hebrews 11:5, AMPLIFIED).

That's not all. The Bible promises yet another "catching up" when "the Lord Himself will descend from heaven with a shout . . . and the dead in Christ will rise first. Then we who are alive and remain shall be caught up together with them in the clouds to meet the Lord in the air" (1 Thessalonians 4:16–17, NKJV).

Uplifting Holy Spirit,
I'm glad You have already rehearsed and are ready for the shout!
Wean me from earth!

9

PROPHESYING

Then the spirit came upon Amasai . . . and he said. . . .

1 CHRONICLES 12:18

Then upon Jahaziel . . . came the Spirit of the LORD. . . . And he said. . . .

2 CHRONICLES 20:14—15

And the Spirit of God came upon Zechariah . . . and said unto them. . . .

2 CHRONICLES 24:20

Chronicles documents three witnesses to the Spirit coming upon individual men in the Old Testament. Each time, they prophesied the words of the Lord. Each time, it was an opportunity for the people to obey.

When the Spirit came upon Amasai, he convinced David of the strong loyalty of thirty men, who were then made captains of David's troops.

When the Spirit came upon Jahaziel, he spoke forth victory to those in Judah and Jerusalem, prophesying that they would not be defeated in battle because the battle was not theirs but God's. They needed only to stand still and see what the Lord would do. That "good news" resulted in worship and praise to God. When the Spirit of God came upon Zechariah he warned those in Judah and Jerusalem, but they would not listen. "Thus says God: 'Why do you transgress the commandments of the LORD, so that you cannot prosper? Because you have forsaken the LORD, He also has forsaken you'" (2 Chronicles 24:20, NKJV).

Zechariah was stoned to death in the courtyard of the Lord's Temple for speaking the word of the Lord to the people. No wonder, a thousand years later, their offspring knew what Jesus meant when He cried out, "O Jerusalem, Jerusalem, the one who kills the prophets and stones those who are sent to her! How often I wanted to gather your children together, as a hen gathers her chicks under her wings, but you were not willing! See! Your house is left to you desolate" (Matthew 23:37–38, NKJV).

Our houses are left void of God's help if we refuse the Spirit's word. All prophecy of the Godhead is the testimony of one Spirit. By whatever name He chooses to use, it is the same Spirit who has always operated to rescue mankind.

May we of this generation heed that Spirit of prophecy who warns us today so that it will not be said of us: "They were disobedient and rebelled against You, cast Your law behind their backs and killed Your prophets, who testified against them to turn them to Yourself" (Nehemiah 9:26, NKJV).

Longsuffering Spirit of God,
forgive us and let us not resist Your Spirit and shun the prophets You
still send to turn us to You.

10
OMNIPRESENCE

Whither shall I go from thy spirit?
PSALM 139:7

he personal nature of the Holy Spirit is brought into sharp focus with this question, posed by the psalmist David. We ponder the eternal Holy Spirit even as David did and ask ourselves, "Where can I go from Your Spirit? Or where can I flee from Your presence? If I ascend into heaven, You are there; if I make my bed in hell, behold, You are there. If I take the wings of the morning, and dwell in the uttermost parts of the sea, even there Your hand shall lead me, and Your right hand shall hold me. . . . Indeed, the darkness shall not hide [me] from You" (Psalm 139:7–10, 12, NKJV).

No, not even gross darkness can hide us from the Hound of Heaven because darkness and light are both alike to Him. The question still remains to haunt us, "So where *can* I go that the Spirit of God is not?" And God answers back: "Am I a God near at hand . . . and not a God afar off? Can anyone hide himself in secret places, so I shall not see him? . . . Do I not fill heaven and earth?" (Jeremiah 23:23–24, NKJV).

How about my thoughts? They are private, aren't they? My imaginations and fantasies are surely well hidden inside myself. No. The Word of God says, "You understand my thought afar off" (Psalm 139:2, NKJV).

The Holy Spirit, with His sharp sword, goes further than my thoughts, "piercing even to the division of soul and spirit, and of joints and marrow, and is a discerner of the thoughts and intents of the heart. . . . There is no creature hidden from His sight, but all things are naked and open to the eyes of Him to whom we must give account" (Hebrews 4:12–13, NKJV).

In short, there is no place to hide. There is no way to flee from the presence of the Holy Spirit. The Holy Spirit is the laser of the Lord. "The lamp of the LORD searches the spirit of a man; it searches out his inmost being" (Proverbs 20:27, NIV).

God is everywhere through the Holy Spirit. He fills the heavens and the earth. There is no place where God is not. The enormity of this truth warrants a big word: *omnipresent.* It means "present everywhere at the same time all the time."

How can that be? It can be because God is Spirit. It is His nature and purpose to fill *everything* with Himself.

How can I understand that? I can't. That is just the way God is, and He will not change even if I do not believe it, do not understand it or do not like it. He is the same yesterday, today and forever.

That truth is comforting. It is *good* that the Holy Spirit is omnipresent. As the psalmist reasoned after searching this out, no matter where I go, "even there your hand will guide me, your right hand will hold me fast. . . . For you created my inmost being; you knit me together in my mother's womb" (Psalm 139:10, 13, NIV).

Thank You, Holy Spirit,
for being with me right here, right now.

11
JUDGMENT AND BURNING

The spirit of judgment . . . the spirit of burning.
ISAIAH 4:4

*I*saiah depicts two aspects of the Holy Spirit's Person and work seldom addressed: judgment and burning. It is possible to say that the Holy Spirit *is* judgment (verdict) and the Holy Spirit *is* burning (fire). These two characteristics make possible the eradication of sin.

The Scriptures teach about a new age coming "wherein dwelleth righteousness" (2 Peter 3:13.) God's righteous requirements will abide in people who live on the earth as well as in heaven. God, through the presence of His Holy Spirit, will bring it to pass. Man tries to do it himself with good works, but fails. Only the zeal of God's judgment and burning can perform this.

Isaiah records how this righteousness comes and what the results are. "When the Lord has washed away the filth of the daughters of Zion, and purged the blood of Jerusalem from her midst, by the spirit of judgment and by the spirit of burning . . ." (Isaiah 4:4, NKJV); "it shall come to pass that he who is left in Zion and remains in Jerusalem will be called holy—everyone who is recorded among the living in Jerusalem" (Isaiah 4:3, NKJV).

Then God inspired Isaiah to declare what everyone will say: "'Come . . . let us go up the mountain of the Lord, to the Temple of the God of Israel; there he will teach us his laws, and we will obey them.' For in those days the world will be ruled from Jerusalem. The Lord will settle international disputes; all the nations will convert their weapons of war into implements of peace. Then at the last all wars will stop and all military training will end" (Isaiah 2:3–4, TLB).

Zechariah sees why Jerusalem needs to be holy: because Messiah will be there. "'Sing, Jerusalem, and rejoice! For I have come to live among you,' says the Lord" (Zechariah 2:10, TLB).

Zechariah answers another question: How long will it take to accomplish this transforming purification? Would you believe—one day? God spoke through His prophet, saying, "I will remove the sin of this land in a single day" (Zechariah 3:9, NIV).

It is true our God is a consuming fire and a just judge of sin. Shall not the Judge of the whole earth do right? Those who put themselves in opposition to Him can only face "a certain fearful expectation of judgment, and fiery indignation which will devour [them]" (Hebrews 10:27, NKJV).

But for those who welcome Him, this work of the Holy Spirit is grace, pure grace.

We need all Your works,
Spirit of judgment and burning.
Otherwise sin stays forever.

12

THE SEVENFOLD BLESSING

The spirit of the Lord . . . the spirit of wisdom and understanding,
the spirit of counsel and might, the spirit of knowledge and of the
fear of the Lord.

ISAIAH 11:2

*I*saiah the prophet makes clear a sevenfold reality of the Holy
Spirit's attributes. One would be enough for us to meditate
upon, but seven in a single verse of Scripture is the number of completeness not often found. Among many wondrous things, the Holy Spirit is:

1. The Spirit of the Lord
2. The Spirit of Wisdom
3. The Spirit of Understanding
4. The Spirit of Counsel
5. The Spirit of Might
6. The Spirit of Knowledge
7. The Spirit of the Fear of the Lord

The important question is: Who is the recipient of this fullness of the
Spirit? Scripture gives a clue. "The royal line of David will be cut off,
chopped down like a tree; but from the stump will grow a Shoot—yes, a
new Branch from the old root. And the Spirit of the Lord shall rest upon
him, the Spirit of wisdom, understanding, counsel and might; the Spirit of
knowledge and of the fear of the Lord" (Isaiah 11:1–2, TLB).

The man upon whom the Spirit would abide in all fullness would come
from the house of David, whose lineage is recorded in the first sentence of
the New Testament. Matthew identifies Him as "Jesus Christ, the son of
David, the son of Abraham" (Matthew 1:1).

There was no doubt about who Jesus was in His day. Common people
knew Him when they cried out, "Jesus, son of David, have mercy on me!"
After three years of Jesus' miracles, healings, teachings, casting out of
demons and raising the dead, the multitudes placed this son of David upon
a colt. As was customary in parades to honor princes and conquerors, they

spread their garments beneath His feet and cut down branches from the trees to pave the way for Him to ride through.

The crowds surged ahead and behind Him as the procession moved into Jerusalem, shouting, "'God bless King David's Son!' . . . 'God's Man is here!' . . . 'Bless him, Lord!' . . . 'Praise God in highest heaven!'" (Matthew 21:9, TLB).

The people that day fulfilled Zechariah's prophecy made 550 years before, which said, "Rejoice greatly, O my people! Shout with joy! For look—your King is coming! He is the Righteous One, the Victor! Yet he is lowly, riding on a donkey's colt!" (Zechariah 9:9, TLB).

There was no doubt about it. The King of glory had come. The Son of David had come to proclaim that He was the Son of God. Yeshua. Messiah. Immanuel. The Lord Jesus Christ—the Savior of the world, having "all the fullness of the Godhead bodily" (Colossians 2:9, NKJV).

Him, they crucified. But you cannot crucify the Holy Spirit. John sees Him alive in heavenly places directing the future world events. Yes, this mighty Lion from the tribe of Judah is the heir to David's throne, and He is not finished yet!

Sevenfold Spirit of God,
impart to me also the stature of the fullness of Christ,
which overcomes the world.

13

OMNISCIENCE

Who hath directed the Spirit of the Lord ...?
ISAIAH 40:13

*T*hrough the Holy Spirit, God knows everything; nothing is hidden from Him. The wisdom of God is so unsearchable there needed to be a word for it: *omniscience*. It means "knowing all things" and is reserved for the Godhead alone.

The word is not found in Scripture, but it is apparent in all that God does. For instance, Isaiah, when trying to fathom this omniscience, asked these pointed questions. "Who has directed the Spirit of the Lord, or as His counselor has taught Him? With whom did He take counsel, and who instructed Him and taught Him in the path of justice? Who taught Him knowledge, and showed Him the way of understanding?" (Isaiah 40:13–14, NKJV).

Clearly, no one has directed the Spirit of the Lord, nor known the mind of God. Through the Holy Spirit, God can do anything—everything. And there needed to be a word for that, too: *omnipotent*. It means God is "all powerful." This is the Spirit that moved upon the face of the deep in the beginning, putting the worlds into place. He is never faint or weary. Nothing is too hard for Him. He sits on the circle of the earth where "the heavens declare the glory of God; and the firmament shows His handiwork" (Psalm 19:1, NKJV).

Only a fool would say in his heart, "There is no God." Yes, what can be known about God has been shown to us. "For since the creation of the world His invisible attributes are clearly seen, being understood by the things that are made, even His eternal power and Godhead, so that they are without excuse" (Romans 1:20, NKJV).

Mankind has been without excuse since the foundation of the world. No one, seeing the glory of God in His creation, can deny God's existence.

What comfort there is in knowing our God reigns above all gods and laughs at the threats of men and angels against His Anointed One! This is the God who is *for* us and not against us; who is not willing that any should perish but that all should come to know Him. This is the God who seeks us out, who desires to open the windows of heaven and pour out blessings upon us. This is the God who longs to give us the Kingdom of heaven. Yes, this is the God who wants to share with us—*Himself!* But "he who comes to God must believe that He is, and that He is a rewarder of those who diligently seek Him" (Hebrews 11:6, NKJV).

What is so difficult about that?

Spirit of might and power,
the half has not been told me. You are full of wonder,
and You are mine!

14
PROFIT

*The Lord G*OD*, and his spirit, hath sent me. Thus saith the L*ORD*,*
*. . . I am the L*ORD *. . . which teacheth thee to profit.*

ISAIAH 48:16–17

oth the Lord God and His Spirit sent Isaiah to tell Israel about the work of the Holy Spirit. "Thus says the LORD, your Redeemer, the Holy One of Israel: 'I am the LORD your God, who teaches you to profit, who leads you by the way you should go'" (Isaiah 48:17, NKJV).

Using the authority of His name as their Redeemer, God promises He will teach the people to profit by sending His Spirit to lead them in the way they should go.

Profiting is the promise. The Spirit is the key. The people can be taught, and they can learn to profit, but only if they follow the Spirit's leading.

This was the same God who quieted Moses' complaints by saying He would be with his mouth and teach him what to say and do. As a result, the whole nation of Israel profited by getting out of bondage in Egypt in the most unusual way.

The Spirit knows how, when and why to lead us where we should go. He even guarantees the end result. What could possibly go wrong? Nothing, with God. His word is beneficial. "So shall My word be that goes forth from My mouth; it shall not return to Me void, but it shall accomplish what I please, and it shall prosper in the thing for which I sent it" (Isaiah 55:11, NKJV).

How wonderful to be taught God's word in this light! Spoken or written, every word He sends is expedient. It is how the Spirit leads us in the way that we should go. "All Scripture is given by inspiration of God, and is profitable for doctrine, for reproof, for correction, for instruction in righteousness, that the man of God may be complete, thoroughly equipped for every good work" (2 Timothy 3:16–17, NKJV).

It is the work of the Holy Spirit to perfect everything that concerns us. It is our work to let Him.

Thank You, Holy Spirit,
for teaching me to profit every step of the way.

15

LIFTING UP A STANDARD

When the enemy shall come in like a flood, the Spirit of the LORD shall lift up a standard against him.

ISAIAH 59:19

*T*his vital work of the Holy Spirit, expressed in scriptural terminology, is to lift up a standard—a banner, flag or ensign—to rally His people against the enemy.

What then is the standard? And what happens when it is lifted up? The Bible is full of clues.

One is given when Moses encountered the enemy, Amalek, in the wilderness. Aaron and Hur supported, or lifted up, Moses' hands while Moses lifted up the rod of God all day long. This action caused the defeat of the enemy. Moses even built an altar to commemorate the victory of Jehovah-Nissi, meaning "the Lord my Banner, my Ensign, my War-Flag" (see Exodus 17:8–16).

Another time, a plague of serpents killed many of the Israelites in the wilderness camp. God told Moses to lift up a serpent on a pole, and everyone who looked at it was healed (see Numbers 21:8–9).

Jesus predicted a recurrence of that scene when He reminded His followers of His mission: "As Moses lifted up the serpent in the wilderness, even so must the Son of Man be lifted up, that whoever believes in Him should not perish but have eternal life" (John 3:14–15, NKJV).

Jesus was the standard lifted up. Looking and believing upon Him would keep "whoever" from perishing.

These things have all happened in the past, but yet another standard is being lifted up today: the regathering of Israel into their land from the north, south, east and west. This is a banner God has set up to attract the attention of the nations. It is the fulfillment of the covenant with Abraham and preparation for the Messiah's Second Coming.

> And in that day there shall be a Root of Jesse, who shall stand as a banner to the people; for the Gentiles shall seek Him, and His resting place shall be glorious. It shall come to pass . . . that the Lord shall set His hand again the second time to recover the remnant of His people who are left. . . . He will set up a banner for the nations, and will assemble the outcasts of Israel,

and gather together the dispersed of Judah from the four corners of the earth.

Isaiah 11:10–12, NKJV

Who is the Standard whom the Holy Spirit lifts up to be the rallying point of all the nations? Messiah, the Branch from the Root of Jesse, David's father. To Him will the nations come and put their trust.

The Spirit of the Lord has always lifted Jesus up. So we today, like Moses, lift up holy hands in prayer and praise to Him without wrath or doubting so that the enemy will be overcome.

The Holy Spirit knows *how* to lift the Standard, *when* to rally the people and *where* to do it. He also knows the real enemy is not of flesh and blood: The coming of the "lawless one" or Antichrist, whose purpose it is to deceive the nations, "is according to the working of Satan, with all power, signs, and lying wonders" (2 Thessalonians 2:9, NKJV).

This enemy is so strong that unless the Holy Spirit opposed him for us we would believe his lies and perish with him. Now we know why the Son of God was lifted up: that He might destroy the works of the devil.

"There is no devil," you say?

Who told you that lie?

Thank You, Holy Spirit,
for lifting up Jesus. Praise You, Jesus, for destroying all the devil's works.

16

FULFILLING THE COVENANT

My spirit . . . and my words . . . shall not depart . . . for ever.
ISAIAH 59:21

*I*n Scripture, a covenant is the only way we relate to God. Without a covenant God does not communicate. It is His will, His word, His testament, His promise, His pledge, His agreement, His oath—His law. God is Spirit, and His Word is Spirit and truth. God cannot lie, nor will He alter the thing that goes out of His mouth. Everything He says, He will do.

Literally, the Old and New Testaments are the Old and New Covenants: God's eternal Word. Sometimes these covenants are *conditional,* depending upon man's acceptance and obedience. God says, "I will if you will." Other times they are *unconditional* and rely solely upon God's sovereign will.

Therefore, to appreciate this reference to the Holy Spirit, it is helpful to review the unconditional covenant God made with a special people He chose for Himself. Through Isaiah the prophet, God promised to give them a Redeemer, saying, "The Redeemer will come to Zion, and to those who turn from transgression in Jacob. . . . This is My covenant with them: My Spirit who is upon you, and My words which I have put in your mouth, shall not depart from your mouth, nor from the mouth of your descendants, nor from the mouth of your descendants' descendants . . . from this time and forevermore" (Isaiah 59:20–21, NKJV).

In other words, the "seed" of this promise would be in total agreement with Him. In addition to the promised Redeemer, the covenant affirmed God's Spirit and His Word remaining forever in the Redeemer's spiritual descendants.

Jeremiah throws more light on this covenant. Notice the word *new* as he prophesies: "The day will come, says the Lord, when I will make a new contract with the people of Israel and Judah. . . . I will inscribe my laws upon their hearts [rather than on tablets of stone], so that they shall want to honor me; then they shall truly be my people and I will be their God . . . everyone, both great and small, shall really know me then . . . and I will forgive and forget their sins" (Jeremiah 31:31, 33–34, TLB).

If you are not a Jew, perhaps you are thinking, *These promises are for Israel and Judah, not for me.* True. God gave His chosen people the covenants first. But this Old Testament covenant is repeated in the New Testament, where it includes *all* nations.

Speaking to the crowds on the Day of Pentecost, Peter, a Jew, explained to his listeners the new thing that had just occurred, and how it could happen to all of them. "[Jesus] being exalted to the right hand of God, and having received from the Father the promise of the Holy Spirit . . . poured out this which you now see and hear. . . . Repent . . . be baptized in the name of Jesus . . . and you shall receive the gift of the Holy Spirit. For the promise [of the Holy Spirit] is to you and to your children, and to all who are afar off, as many as the Lord our God will call" (Acts 2:33, 38–39, NKJV).

How did Peter know God was including the Gentiles in receiving the Holy Spirit? He was with the Gentiles in Cornelius' house when the Holy Spirit was poured out upon them (see Acts 10).

The Holy Spirit came to fulfill the New Covenant. He is the Person of the Godhead mentioned by name in the Old Testament. Yes, the Spirit, the Word and the Redeemer are in perfect agreement. The Godhead is willing.

Spirit of promise,
how grateful I am that the blessing of Abraham and his seed
remains forever.

17
ANOINTING

The Spirit of the Lord GOD is upon me; because the LORD hath anointed me. . . ."

ISAIAH 61:1

*A*nother way to word the above Scripture is: "Because the Lord has anointed me, the Spirit of the Lord is upon me." The Spirit *is* the anointing. The Spirit of the Lord upon you is called the *anointing* because God placed it there. The Word of God says exactly what it means.

Anointing is not a word commonly used in secular society, but it is used widely throughout Scripture. The dictionary defines *anoint* as "to put oil on, cover or rub with ointment, smear; to put oil on in a ceremony as a sign of consecration to office; to make sacred with oil."

To anoint, there must be something to anoint with. It must touch you, be applied and appropriated. In Scripture men use oil when anointing to represent the Holy Spirit. It is a symbol in the physical realm for what is happening in the spiritual realm.

In Scripture we find that everything belonging to the Lord is claimed by the Holy Spirit's presence upon it. Anointing sets it apart for God. Some examples are the Tabernacle and its furnishings; priests and their garments; offerings; and kings and prophets. All men, women and children who are willing to do God's will are anointed.

Men anoint with oil; God anoints with the Holy Spirit. Even so, God validates man's act of anointing in His name. For instance, when Jacob saw the ladder reaching from heaven to earth in a vision, and heard God confirm to him the same covenant of land, seed and blessings that He had given to his father, Isaac, and his grandfather, Abraham, he knew the place was holy. To act upon this fact, "Jacob rose early in the morning . . . took the stone that he had put at his head, set it up as a pillar, and poured oil on top of it" (Genesis 28:18, NKJV).

Years later, when Jacob was in another land, God reminded him of that anointing saying, "I am the God of Bethel, where you anointed the pillar and where you made a vow to Me" (Genesis 31:13, NKJV).

As a result, God commanded Jacob to return to the land of his fathers. When he obeyed, God changed Jacob's name to the name of the covenant land: *Israel.*

Do men still anoint with oil today? Absolutely. "Is anyone among you sick? Let him call for the elders of the church, and let them pray over him, anointing him with oil in the name of the Lord. And the prayer of faith will save the sick, and the Lord will raise him up. And if he has committed sins, he will be forgiven" (James 5:14–15, NKJV).

Notice the authority of the name of the Lord and the anointing by faith. It brings forth God's healing and His forgiveness of sins.

Does God still anoint today? Absolutely. Jesus fulfilled Isaiah's prophecy about the coming Messiah when He preached His first sermon in the synagogue at Nazareth. He told the people *why* the anointing was upon Him: "The Spirit of the LORD is upon Me, because He has anointed Me to preach the gospel to the poor; He has sent Me to heal the brokenhearted, to preach deliverance to the captives and recovery of sight to the blind, to set at liberty those who are oppressed; to proclaim the acceptable year of the LORD" (Luke 4:18–19, NKJV).

Yes, that was special for Jesus, you might be thinking. *But does God anoint ordinary people like me today?* Again, the answer is: absolutely! The apostle John wrote to the believers of his day to remind them: "You have an anointing from the Holy One, and all of you know the truth. . . . The anointing you received from him remains in you, and you do not need anyone to teach you. But as his anointing teaches you about all things and as that anointing is real, not counterfeit—just as it has taught you, remain in him" (1 John 2:20, 27, NIV).

The anointing of the Holy Spirit is vital, a matter of life or death. Nothing lives without it. Every truth we need is embedded in it. Unfortunately, not all want it.

Lucifer was anointed to be a covering cherub (see Ezekiel 28:14–15; Isaiah 14:12), but he refused to remain under the anointing. Therefore, God changed his name to Satan, the resister. Jesus said of him, "He was a murderer from the beginning and a hater of truth—there is not an iota of truth in him. When he lies, it is perfectly normal; for he is the father of liars" (John 8:44, TLB).

Satan's chief work is to "undo" the anointing. Pause and think of that! If the anointing of the Holy Spirit is not received, kept, appreciated, honored, respected, coveted, enjoyed, obeyed—but rather despised and rejected—God's wrath then abides upon that individual.

Holy Spirit,
Your anointing destroys every yoke, and I welcome it with gladness!

18

BEING VEXED

But they rebelled, and vexed his holy spirit.
ISAIAH 63:10

The Holy Spirit can be grieved because He too has personal attributes. Being spirit, He is sensitive to our spirits. He knows when we are not in agreement with Him. When our works and reactions oppose Him, He is grieved.

In this Scripture the rebellion of God's chosen people caused the Holy Spirit to be vexed. It provoked a devastating response: "But they rebelled and grieved His Holy Spirit; so He turned Himself against them as an enemy, and He fought against them" (Isaiah 63:10, NKJV).

They had started out right. What happened? God had spoken through Moses to Pharaoh, saying that "Israel is My son, My firstborn. So I say to you, let My son go that he may serve Me" (Exodus 4:22–23, NKJV).

God called Israel His son, and one of the first things a Father does in training a son is to remove him from the wrong environment. That is why God brought Israel out of Egypt (their house of bondage) into His Promised Land. God purposed to dwell with them there and be their God. They would be His people and serve Him. Israel agreed to this arrangement when they told Moses, "All the words which the LORD has said we will do" (Exodus 24:3, NKJV).

Israel was "brought up" by God, learning firsthand of His mighty signs and wonders. They saw their Father's faithfulness to do all He promised, giving Israel His inheritance in the land and overthrowing all their enemies. God even said of them: "'Surely they are My people, children who will not lie.' So He became their Savior. In all their affliction He was afflicted, and the Angel of His Presence saved them; in His love and in His pity He redeemed them; and He bore them and carried them all the days of old" (Isaiah 63:8–9, NKJV).

In spite of all this, Israel rebelled. Their actions did not agree with their words. They lied. "It was only with their words they followed him, not with their hearts; their hearts were far away. They did not keep their promises" (Psalm 78:36–37, TLB).

Rebellion! The Word of God says it is as bad as the sin of witchcraft. No wonder God turned Himself against Israel and fought against them.

Even so, ". . . [God] being full of compassion, forgave their iniquity, and did not destroy them. Yes, many a time He turned His anger away, and did not stir up all His wrath; for He remembered that they were but flesh" (Psalm 78:38–39, NKJV).

Why didn't God disown them? Because He is an "everlasting Father." And although Israel was a stubborn "son," God was determined to correct the people's rebellion and save them "for His name's sake, that He might make His mighty power known" (Psalm 106:8, NKJV).

The Spirit of God is justly vexed with our rebellion. But God's mighty power is demonstrated in turning rebellious sons of flesh into sons born of the Spirit who delight to do His will.

How God is accomplishing that fills the Old and New Testaments and continues in us today. It is the "promise of the Father."

Faithful Holy Spirit,
thank You for being vexed enough to resist our rebellion and save us.

19

DIRECTING

Whither the spirit was to go, they went. . . .
EZEKIEL 1:12

As we have already seen, "movement" was the Holy Spirit's first work in the re-creation of the earth. Now we find His work of movement in the heavens as well.

In Ezekiel 1:12, the Spirit of God is directing the movement of heavenly beings. "They" are the four living angelic beings, with the likeness of a man, called cherubim.

Through Ezekiel's vision, we can see into the invisible realm of the cherubim, who are being directed by the Holy Spirit. As we take a closer look, we notice that the Spirit moves the cherubim, who in turn move *something* (wheels) and *Someone* (God).

> The four wheels had rims and spokes, and the rims were filled with eyes around their edges. When the four living beings flew forward, the wheels moved forward with them. When they flew upwards, the wheels went up too. When the living beings stopped, the wheels stopped. For the spirit of the four living beings was in the wheels; so wherever their spirit went, the wheels and the living beings went there too.
>
> Ezekiel 1:18–21, TLB

Ezekiel not only saw things, he heard things. When the cherubim moved, ". . . their wings roared like waves against the shore, or like the voice of God, or like the shouting of a mighty army. When they stopped . . . there came a voice from the crystal sky above them" (Ezekiel 1:24–25, TLB).

Overwhelmed, Ezekiel realized he was having visions of the Most High God, who sits enthroned above the cherubim: "For high in the sky above them was what looked like a throne made of beautiful blue sapphire stones, and upon it sat someone who appeared to be a Man. From his waist up, he seemed to be all glowing bronze, dazzling like fire; and from his waist down he seemed to be entirely flame, and there was a glowing halo like a rainbow all around him" (Ezekiel 1:26–28, TLB).

When Ezekiel saw the glory of the Lord revealed, he was so shaken he fell face downward on the ground, as did Abram, Moses, Aaron, the children of Israel, Balaam, Balaam's donkey, Joshua, Manoah and his wife, Saul, Job, wise men from the East, Peter, James, John, Jairus, unclean spirits, the woman with the issue of blood, Zacharias, the leper, Mary (Lazarus' sister), Saul of Tarsus, the four beasts, the 24 elders, angels—and you and me.

I praise You, hovering Spirit.
Let me be shaken as Ezekiel was, in awe of Your glory.

20
REVIVING

The spirit entered into me . . . and set me upon my feet . . . [and]
spake unto me.

EZEKIEL 2:2

*E*zekiel, overwhelmed by the visions of God, fell face downward on the ground and needed to be revived by the Spirit. This unique work of the Holy Spirit, who entered into him and set him back upon his feet, was performed for a reason. God wanted to speak to him: "Son of man, I am sending you to the children of Israel, to a rebellious nation that has rebelled against Me; they and their fathers have transgressed against Me to this very day. For they are impudent and stubborn children. I am sending you to them, and you shall say to them, 'Thus says the Lord God'"(Ezekiel 2:3–4, NKJV).

The Spirit entered into Ezekiel a second time, and when Ezekiel saw the same visions of God's glory, he again fell prostrate. The work of the Spirit was the same: to revive and strengthen him: "Then the Spirit entered me and set me upon my feet, and spoke with me and said to me: 'Go . . .'" (Ezekiel 3:24, NKJV).

Note that the Holy Spirit *entered into* Ezekiel. The Old Testament records many incidents of the Holy Spirit being *in* men and not just *upon* them. They were filled with the Spirit—had the Spirit *in* and *within* them—always with the same result: to enable them to do what God asked.

Ezekiel records that he fell on his face six times. Many other prophets did, too. Often it was because God suddenly revealed His majesty. How good it is to remember this work of the Holy Spirit! He stoops to our weaknesses and lifts us up when we fall on our faces before the revelation of the Almighty. "Well, this never happened to me," you might say. No, but then you are not dead yet, either. Wait and see.

A similar event took place on the mountain of transfiguration, when a bright cloud overshadowed Peter, James and John, and a voice spoke out of that cloud. When the disciples heard it, "they fell on their faces and were greatly afraid. But Jesus came and touched them" (Matthew 17:6–7, NKJV).

On this occasion it was Jesus who revived them and told them to stand up and not be afraid. Years later, while exiled to the Isle of Patmos, John was in the Spirit on the Lord's day and having visions of the risen Christ. He recorded: "When I saw him, I fell at his feet as dead. And he laid his right hand upon me, saying . . . 'Fear not . . .'" (Revelation 1:17).

Fear not, little flock, for God says, "I am the same, yesterday, today and forever." When the Holy Spirit enters into a man or woman, He makes him or her eligible for duty. In every generation He provides Himself.

Thank You, Holy Spirit,
for setting me upon my feet, that I might "go upright."

21

VISIONS

The spirit lifted me up ... and brought me in the visions of God to Jerusalem.

EZEKIEL 8:3

Ezekiel and Daniel are both "vision" books written while Israel was held captive in Babylon. These prophets refer to the word 48 times. The difference is that Daniel, while on his bed, saw visions for the Gentiles, whereas Ezekiel was transported from place to place by the Spirit to see visions for the Jews.

Ezekiel expresses this action of the Holy Spirit in several ways: the Spirit "lifted me up," "took me away," "took me up" or "carried me out." All the references indicate the same thing. The Holy Spirit moved the prophet as He pleased so he could prophesy to the house of Israel.

"[The first time] the Spirit lifted me up and took me away . . . I went in bitterness, in the heat of my spirit; but the hand of the LORD was strong upon me," (Ezekiel 3:14, NKJV) Ezekiel confessed. His anger came from righteous indignation inspired by God against the sins committed by the people. In this vision, the Spirit transported Ezekiel to the exiles living in Tel Abib by the river Chebar. He sat among them for seven days, silent, overwhelmed by astonishment. At the end of this time, God spoke to him and commissioned him to be a "watchman" to the house of Israel. Ezekiel was told to speak God's words of warning to Israel to repent, whether they listened to him or not. If he did not watch and warn, Ezekiel would be held accountable for their sins—and die.

The second time Ezekiel saw visions of God he was taken by the hair of his head. He records: "The Spirit lifted me up between earth and heaven and in visions of God he took me to Jerusalem, to the entrance to the north gate of the inner court, where the idol that provokes to jealousy stood" (Ezekiel 8:3, NIV). The large idol Ezekiel saw was an image of a heathen god set up in God's place. He watched as seventy men from the house of Israel worshiped the abominable images they had painted on the walls, thick clouds of incense ascending from their censers.

The third time, "the Spirit lifted me up and brought me to the east gate of the LORD'S house, which faces eastward" (Ezekiel 11:1, NKJV). There

53

Ezekiel saw 25 of the most prominent men of Jerusalem, who were responsible for the wicked counsel being given to the people. God commanded Ezekiel to prophesy against them. When he obeyed, one of the men died.

Before Ezekiel left Jerusalem he witnessed, in a vision, the Shekinah glory of the Lord departing from the Holy of Holies, to the threshold of the Temple; from the threshold to above the cherubim; then to the door of the East Gate; moving out from the midst of the city to the Mount of Olives on the east side of Jerusalem. Yes: *Ichabod.* The glory of the Lord had departed from Israel.

After that, "the Spirit of God carried me back again to Babylon, to the Jews in exile there. And so ended the vision of my visit to Jerusalem. And I told the exiles everything the Lord had shown me" (Ezekiel 11:24–25, TLB).

In another miraculous vision, God showed Ezekiel the resurrection of the house of Israel from the graveyard of the nations where they have been buried since A.D. 70. He described it this way: "The power of the Lord was upon me and I was carried away by the Spirit of the Lord to a valley full of old, dry bones that were scattered everywhere across the ground" (Ezekiel 37:1, TLB).

God ordered Ezekiel to prophesy to the dry bones (the house of Israel) until the Spirit of the Lord comes into them and they live and stand upon their feet, a great army.

Ezekiel was told to "show the house to the house." The future of Israel was in his mouth. He was given the pattern of the new Temple to be built in the millennium, and he saw the glory of the Lord returning to it (see Ezekiel 43:5).

Visions and dreams are hard to differentiate. But through them the Lord gives pictures of His revelation knowledge to His people. The work of the Holy Spirit as a "vision porter" is not finished, nor has it passed away. Young men shall continue to see visions, and old men shall dream dreams until they have all been fulfilled.

Thank You for Your visions, omniscient Spirit,
so we can see what You see and not perish.

22
HEART TRANSPLANTS

I will put my spirit within you. . . .
EZEKIEL 36:27

he regenerating work of the Holy Spirit makes it possible for God to make a "New Covenant" with His people and keep it.

In other words: God said it, Jesus ratified it by shedding His blood and the Holy Spirit accomplishes it from within human hearts.

God made a promise to Israel to gather them out of all the countries where He had scattered them and bring them into their own land. There, He promised, "I will sprinkle clean water on you, and you shall be clean; I will cleanse you from all your filthiness and from all your idols. I will give you a new heart and put a new spirit within you; I will take the heart of stone out of your flesh and give you a heart of flesh" (Ezekiel 36:25–26, NKJV).

This divine surgery would result in a new birth, a new nation, a new race. This time there would be no serpent to interfere and no possibility of man's failure, for God would implant His own Spirit within them. This time would be different, for God said, "I will put My Spirit within you and cause you to walk in My statutes, and you will keep My judgments and do them" (Ezekiel 36:27, NKJV).

Both God and Israel would keep covenant. The Almighty did not need to say it more than once. Yet three times Ezekiel records this same work of the Spirit: "And I will give you the land of Israel. . . . Then I will give them one heart, and I will put a new spirit within them, and take the stony heart out of their flesh, and give them a heart of flesh, that they may walk in My statutes and keep My judgments and do them; and they shall be My people, and I will be their God" (Ezekiel 11:17, 19–20, NKJV).

God takes the initiative by scattering His people Israel, by drawing them back to Him and by raising them up at the last day; Ezekiel foresaw God's Spirit working within a whole nation. Now He works by His Spirit in individuals and the people of God live by faith. On that day the people of God will live by obedience, for God will be in His Holy Temple and all the earth will keep silence before Him.

We read in Habakkuk that this vision is yet for an appointed time. The Lord assures us, "Slowly, steadily, surely, the time approaches when the vision will be fulfilled. If it seems slow, do not despair, for these things will surely come to pass. Just be patient! They will not be overdue a single day!" (Habakkuk 2:3, TLB).

What takes so long? When shall these things be? The Lord says, "I am ready to hear Israel's prayers for these blessings, and to grant them their requests. Let them but ask and I will multiply them like the flocks that fill Jerusalem's streets at time of sacrifice. The ruined cities will be crowded once more, and everyone will know I am the Lord" (Ezekiel 36:37–38, TLB).

The Holy Spirit guarantees that which the Lord God has spoken. Let Israel but ask.

*Holy Spirit, give the prodigal son
the right prayer so he can come home again!*

23
POURED OUT

And it shall come to pass afterward, that I will pour out my spirit upon all flesh.

JOEL 2:28

The promise of the Father is to pour out His Spirit upon all flesh. Not just on chosen men and women, not just on religious professionals, but upon everyone—including animals.

Everyone will receive God's Holy Spirit in "that day." When that day comes, God says, "Your sons and daughters will prophesy, your old men will dream dreams, your young men will see visions. Even on my servants, both men and women, I will pour out my Spirit in those days" (Joel 2:28–29, NIV).

Peter referred to this Old Testament prophecy on the Day of Pentecost, saying, "this is that which was spoken by the prophet Joel" (Acts 2:16).

He then quoted word for word from Joel's prophecy.

When shall these things be? The timing of the promise is important. "The hour is coming, and now is," Jesus told His disciples in explaining spiritual matters (John 5:25, NKJV).

Before His resurrection, Jesus called the events of Pentecost "the promise of my Father" (Luke 24:49). It truly was. Peter called those same events the fulfillment of Joel's prophecy of the last days. It truly was. Is the prophecy finished? Did that which happened in Peter's day come to an end? No, Joel's prophecy of the last days began at Pentecost and now is and is coming in greater fullness in the age to come. Then we shall see the effects upon all flesh as prophesied.

> In that day the wolf and the lamb will lie down together, and the leopard and goats will be at peace. Calves and fat cattle will be safe among lions, and a little child shall lead them all. The cows will graze among bears; cubs and calves will lie down together, and lions will eat grass like the cows. Babies will crawl safely among poisonous snakes, and a little child who puts his hand in a nest of deadly adders will pull it out unharmed. Nothing will hurt or

destroy in all my holy mountain, for as the waters fill the sea, so shall the earth be full of the knowledge of the Lord.

Isaiah 11:6–9, TLB

When the Spirit of the Lord God is poured out upon all flesh, all flesh will become *spirit!*

> *Everlasting Holy Spirit,*
> *We love Your prophecies, Your dreams*
> *and Your visions.*
> *We love You!*

24

POWER TO PROPHESY

I am full of power by the spirit of the Lord. . . .
                                                    MICAH 3:8

he prophet Micah appreciated the work of the Holy Spirit in him to prophesy. That is why he could so boldly chastise the rulers of Israel in his day: "Truly I am full of power by the Spirit of the LORD, and of justice and might, to declare to Jacob his transgression and to Israel his sin. Now hear this . . ." (Micah 3:8–9, NKJV).

It is a fearful thing to speak truth when that truth is full of judgment and punishment for sin. It takes power from on high to resist men's lies and steadfastly declare the whole counsel of God. Therefore, God has empowered prophets in unbroken succession to instruct, warn and direct His people.

Micah contrasted the difference between the false prophets of his day who spoke lies (no power required) and himself who spoke truth (filled with power). They knew they were the ones "who abhor justice and pervert all equity, who build up Zion with bloodshed and Jerusalem with iniquity: her heads judge for a bribe, her priests teach for pay, and her prophets divine for money. Yet they lean on the LORD, and say, 'Is not the LORD among us? No harm can come upon us.' Therefore because of you Zion shall be plowed like a field, Jerusalem shall become heaps of ruins, and the mountain of the temple like the bare hills of the forest" (Micah 3:9–12, NKJV).

The power of the Spirit filled Micah's words. Every prophet of the Lord is so endowed. Even Jonah knew his prophesying would accomplish what God wanted, so he tried to run away and not speak it.

Paul spoke the same way about the work of the Holy Spirit in his day, saying, "My speech and my preaching were not with persuasive words of human wisdom, but in demonstration of the Spirit and of power, that your faith should not be in the wisdom of men but in the power of God" (1 Corinthians 2:4–5, NKJV).

To prophesy requires power from on high, and the opposite is also true. It takes power from God to *receive* prophecy and humble ourselves in repentance. "If My people who are called by My name will humble themselves, and pray and seek my face, and turn from their wicked ways, then I will hear from heaven, and will forgive their sin and heal their land" (2 Chronicles 7:14, NKJV).

We are responsible for the "if." The message is still the same. Selah!

Mighty Holy Spirit,
You are that Pentecostal power in every generation.
We are without excuse.

25

TEMPLE BUILDING

"Not by might, nor by power, but by my spirit,"saith the LORD.

ZECHARIAH 4:6

hat was it that could not be done by the might of armies or any earthly power? The rebuilding of God's Temple in Jerusalem after Israel's return from Babylonian captivity.

The books of Ezra and Nehemiah record the exiles' struggles traveling home and the tedious restoration of Jerusalem, its walls and gates. Primary in their thoughts, however, was the rebuilding of the house of God for worship. They had an altar and observed the sacrifices and offerings, but the foundation of the Temple was not laid until the second year after they returned. It took time to gather money, materials and men for such a great task.

When Zerubbabel and the rest of the workers began to lay the foundation, it brought forth a loud response in Jerusalem—of both joy and weeping. Joy from those who saw Temple construction begin for the first time, and weeping from the elders who remembered Solomon's Temple and compared its grandeur with Zerubbabel's "small thing." Zechariah comforted them with the word of the LORD: "Do not despise this small beginning, for the eyes of the Lord rejoice to see the work begin, to see the plumbline in the hand of Zerubbabel" (Zechariah 4:10, TLB).

Both God and the people rejoiced after that good beginning, but there the work stopped. For almost twenty years opposition by the devil's advocates hindered any building upon the foundation. That is why Zerubbabel needed to know about the help of the Holy Spirit. This was revealed to him in a vision of a golden candlestick with a bowl on top of it. The candlestick had seven lamps that were connected to seven pipes. Two olive trees poured oil into the bowl, which flowed through the pipes to light the lamps continuously. An angel spoke to Zerubbabel and interpreted this vision to prevent any misunderstanding:

> "This [addition of the bowl to the candlestick, causing it to yield a ceaseless supply of oil from the olive trees] is the word of the Lord to Zerubbabel, say-

ing, Not by might, nor by power, but by My Spirit [of Whom the oil is a symbol], says the Lord of hosts. For who are you, O great mountain [of human obstacles]? Before Zerubbabel . . . you shall become a plain."

Zechariah 4:6–7, AMPLIFIED

With the anointing coming through the Holy Spirit, not only would Zerubbabel finish the Temple but personally crown it with the headstone. But the glory would go to the Spirit of the Lord of hosts, who had a special interest in that Temple and would not allow the work to fail. The Holy Spirit guaranteed its success. "Zerubbabel laid the foundation of this Temple, and he will complete it . . . with mighty shouts of thanksgiving for God's mercy, declaring that all was done by grace alone" (Zechariah 4:9, 7, TLB).

And so Zerubbabel completed the Temple by the Spirit of grace alone. It was finished, dedicated with joy, used for worship many years—and is no more.

The Jews have no temple today. Yet we find here an unmistakable reference to another, more glorious Temple still to be built by a descendant of Zerubbabel's called the Branch. This Temple, built by Messiah, the Branch, at His Second Coming, shall last forever. The Temple will be new, but the Builder is the same.

Thank You, Spirit of grace,
for building a holy Temple, made without hands, eternal in the heavens.

26
GRACE AND SUPPLICATIONS

I will pour . . . the spirit of grace and of supplications.
ZECHARIAH 12:10

Zechariah reveals the spirit of grace and fervent prayer as two functions of the Holy Spirit desperately needed by the people of Jerusalem in a future day. Speaking for God, the prophet tells us why: "In that day . . . I will seek to destroy all the nations that come against Jerusalem. And I will pour upon the house of David, and upon the inhabitants of Jerusalem, the spirit of grace and of supplications: and they shall look upon me whom they have pierced, and they shall mourn for him, as one mourneth for his only son, and shall be in bitterness for him, as one that is in bitterness for his first-born" (Zechariah 12:9–10).

When the Holy Spirit moves upon the inhabitants of Jerusalem with supplications unequaled in history, the results will be "sorrow and mourning in Jerusalem. . . . All of Israel will weep in profound sorrow. The whole nation will be bowed down with universal grief—king, prophet, priest, and people. Each family will go into private mourning, husbands and wives apart, to face their sorrow alone" (Zechariah 12:11, 12–14, TLB).

As they individually recognize their Messiah they will in essence be repenting for generations of kinsmen who never acknowledged the King of glory. Then they will say, "Come, and let us return to the LORD; for He has torn, but He will heal us; He has stricken, but He will bind us up. After two days He will revive us; on the third day He will raise us up, that we may live in His sight" (Hosea 6:1–2, NKJV).

The Spirit of grace poured out will bring to pass that new heart and new mind necessary to enter into true worship in the millennium. After two full days of national mourning—on the *third* day—God will cleanse them from their sin. And so all Israel will be saved (Romans 11:26).

Yes, in that day Israel will look upon Him whom they have pierced and know Him, reminding us of Joseph's brothers, who in the privacy of his house *looked upon* their deliverer (see Genesis 45) and experienced the spirit of grace. And their ancestors *looked upon* the brass serpent Moses lifted up in the wilderness and experienced healing grace. Those who *looked upon*

Jesus lifted up at Golgotha entered into saving grace. Even doubting Thomas had to *look upon* those pierced hands before his confession of grace: "My Lord and my God!"

The order is important here. First godly grace, then godly sorrow, which leads to repentance. "I will be found by you" is the grace of God, who allows Himself to be found by penitent sinners in every generation. His grace is always poured out upon those who humbly cry to Him by faith. This is the way the Lord saves every captive of sin. Where sin abounds grace does much more abound.

Spirit of grace and supplications,
we need You. Come, that the King of glory
may come in for all to see—the Lord strong
and mighty, the Lord mighty in battle.

PART TWO

2
THE HOLY SPIRIT
IN JESUS' LIFE

27
CONCEIVING JESUS

Mary was . . . with child of the Holy [Spirit].
MATTHEW 1:18

*I*n the human realm, pregnancy and birthing are wondrous things. For instance:

The father is the source of life—*Initiation.*
The father must produce a living seed—*Viability.*
The seed must be received in the mother—*Conception.*
The sperm and ovum must become one—*Fertilization.*
The fetus must grow and mature—*Gestation.*
The baby must be brought forth—*Birth.*
The newborn must breathe—*Quickening.*

The birth of Jesus followed this pattern, for God used the womb of a virgin girl to birth His Son into the world. It began like this:

The Father's initiative. "For God so loved the world, that he gave his only begotten Son, that whosoever believeth in him should not perish, but have everlasting life" (John 3:16).
A viable seed. "In Him was life, and the life was the light of men" (John 1:4, NKJV).
Conception. "Behold, the virgin shall conceive and bear a Son, and shall call His name Immanuel" (Isaiah 7:14, NKJV). "Mary . . . you will conceive in your womb and bring forth a Son, and shall call His name JESUS" (Luke 1:30–31, NKJV).
Fertilization. "Mary . . . became pregnant by the Holy Spirit" (Matthew 1:18, TLB).
Gestation. "You made all the delicate, inner parts of my body, and knit them together in my mother's womb" (Psalm 139:13, TLB). "You were there while I was being formed in utter seclusion! You saw me before I was

born and scheduled each day of my life before I began to breathe" (Psalm 139:15–16, TLB).

Birth. "You are He who took Me out of the womb" (Psalm 22:9, NKJV). "When the fullness of the time had come, God sent forth His Son, born of a woman, born under the law" (Galatians 4:4, NKJV).

Quickening. "And the Word became flesh and dwelt among us, and we beheld His glory, the glory as of the only begotten of the Father, full of grace and truth" (John 1:14, NKJV).

The mystery of Christ sinking Himself into human flesh is beyond our understanding. Jesus was born *into* this world—not *from* it—by the Holy Spirit who conceived Him. He moved upon Mary to impregnate her so that the long-awaited messages of the prophets could be fulfilled. God with us: *Emmanuel!*

The Old Testament records the Holy Spirit's birthing of creation. The New Testament records the Holy Spirit's birthing of the omnipotent Creator Himself, who was willing to become the weakest thing in all the world: a baby.

How great the mystery of godliness! God: manifested in the flesh, vindicated by the Spirit, seen by angels, proclaimed among the heathen. The only-begotten Son of God becoming the Son of man so that the sons of men might become sons of God.

In His genes, our everlasting life.

Conceiving Holy Spirit,
my spirit rejoices with Mary's, for You are mighty and have done great
things. Holy, holy, holy is His name.

28

OVERSHADOWING PRESENCE

The Holy [Spirit] shall come upon thee, and . . . overshadow thee."

LUKE 1:35

The work of the Holy Spirit in overshadowing Mary tells us how she conceived the Son of God: "The Holy Spirit will come upon you, and the power of the Highest will overshadow you" (Luke 1:35, NKJV).

The word *overshadow* in Greek has a wider meaning of "superimposing" one object upon another by casting a shade upon it, or to envelop in a haze of brilliancy as a cloud. To get the fullest meaning of the word, *overshadow* here means "to flood with preternatural influence." Preternatural—meaning out of the ordinary course of nature; exceptional; unusual due to something supernatural such as incarnation, which is the embodiment of divine nature and human nature as one.

The same overshadowing form of the Holy Spirit that came upon Mary is referred to again in the transfiguration of Jesus. "While he [Peter] was still speaking, behold, a bright cloud overshadowed them; and suddenly a voice came out of the cloud, saying, 'This is My beloved Son, in whom I am well pleased. Hear Him!'" (Matthew 17:5, NKJV).

The Acts of the Apostles mentions another example of the supernatural presence of the Spirit of God. It is written that multitudes from the cities around Jerusalem brought the sick and those vexed with unclean spirits to Peter so that "at least the shadow of Peter passing by might fall on some of them . . . and they were all healed" (Acts 5:15–16, NKJV).

Scripture attributes the healing and deliverance to the shadowing presence of God's Spirit upon Peter.

This is the same hovering presence above the dark waters in the beginning that brought forth light. The same cloud that guided and protected the children of Israel by day and became a pillar of fire by night; never leaving them or forsaking them for forty long years in the wilderness. Indeed, the faithful, ever-present Holy Spirit was experienced by "all our fathers [who] were under the cloud . . . [and were] baptized into Moses in the cloud and in the sea" (1 Corinthians 10:1–2, NKJV).

Again, the overpowering brilliance of the Holy Spirit enveloped the Tabernacle when it was finished and later filled the Temple so the priests could not enter to minister (2 Chronicles 7:2).

Yes, the angel Gabriel promised Mary that she would be with child by the Holy Spirit—and she was. But there is another point here. In his announcement to Mary, Gabriel also said, "The baby born to you will be utterly holy—the Son of God" (Luke 1:35, TLB).

Without a doubt, the embodiment of Jesus is truly a *divine* conception. He is "holy, harmless, undefiled, separate from sinners, and made higher than the heavens . . . consecrated [perfected] for evermore" (Hebrews 7:26, 28).

"How shall these things be?" Mary asked Gabriel. The answer echoes back through the prophet Isaiah for us to ponder in our hearts today: *The Holy Spirit!* "Arise, shine; for your light has come! And the glory of the Lord is risen upon you. For behold, the darkness shall cover the earth, and deep darkness the people; but the LORD will arise over you, and His glory will be seen upon you" (Isaiah 60:1–2, NKJV).

Overshadowing Holy Spirit,
I welcome Your Shekinah glory that shines down on me. Birth me, too!

29

FORETELLING CHRIST

[He] was filled with the Holy [Spirit], and prophesied.

LUKE 1:67

God the Father made sure that those who surrounded the birth and life of His Son would know His identity and communicate it. To do this, the Holy Spirit filled them with supernatural revelation, which they spoke forth prophetically as the oracles of God.

Zacharias, the father of John the Baptist, was filled with the Holy Spirit when he named his son John in obedience to the angel's command. Immediately, God loosed his tongue to explain to the people that the Messiah was coming. "Praise the Lord, the God of Israel, for he has come to visit his people and has redeemed them. He is sending us a Mighty Savior from the royal line of his servant David, just as he promised through his holy prophets long ago" (Luke 1:68–70, TLB).

Elizabeth, the wife of Zacharias, in the fifth month of her pregnancy with John, also witnessed to Mary that she was bearing the Christ child. When Mary spoke to Elizabeth, "Elizabeth's child leaped within her and she was filled with the Holy Spirit. She gave a glad cry and exclaimed to Mary, 'You are favored by God above all other women, and your child is destined for God's mightiest praise. What an honor this is, that the mother of my Lord should visit me!'" (Luke 1:41–43, TLB).

Simeon, a man living in Jerusalem, was moved by the Holy Spirit to go to the Temple the day Mary and Joseph dedicated their baby, Jesus. It is written of Simeon that he "was a good man, very devout, filled with the Holy Spirit and constantly expecting the Messiah to come soon. For the Holy Spirit had revealed to him that he would not die until he had seen him—God's anointed King" (Luke 2:25–26, TLB).

As Simeon took the child in his arms, he praised God, saying, "Lord . . . now I can die content! For I have seen him as you promised me I would. I have seen the Savior you have given to the world. He is the Light that will shine upon the nations, and he will be the glory of your people Israel!" (Luke 2:29–32, TLB).

Anna is included in this list of eyewitnesses also. She represented the senior citizens of her time. Her custom was to stay at the Temple night and day, worshipping God in prayer and fasting. Upon hearing Simeon's prophecy to Mary and Joseph concerning Jesus, "she also began thanking God and telling everyone in Jerusalem who had been awaiting the coming of the Savior that the Messiah had finally arrived" (Luke 2:38, TLB).

Why was the coming of Jesus hedged about by the Holy Spirit with so many witnesses? So that the human race in every generation might know that Jesus Christ, God's Son, came in the flesh. Many false prophets, filled with the unholy spirit, continue to deny this truth. We are warned about them: "Many deceivers, who do not acknowledge Jesus Christ as coming in the flesh, have gone out into the world. Any such person is the deceiver and the antichrist" (2 John 7, NIV).

Praise God! No old wives' tales, cunningly devised fables or endless genealogies distorted by pride could make this historical fact of Jesus' birth only hearsay. The angels witnessed it, as well as wise men from the East, shepherds, the innkeeper, Herod, Caesar Augustus, scribes, Pharisees, Sadducees, chief priests, Pilate, centurions, Thomas, Peter, the other disciples and the common people who were touched by the Kingdom of heaven. They all *believed* Jesus came in a human body.

Yes, even the demons believe—and *tremble*.

Thank You, Holy Spirit,
for encompassing me about with so great a cloud of witnesses.
I believe that Jesus came—for me.

30

IDENTIFYING JESUS

The Holy Spirit descended ... upon Him.
LUKE 3:22, NKJV

*J*esus grew up in Nazareth, in His earthly father's house, as the son of a carpenter. Although little is known about His early years, this is written: "And the Child grew and became strong in spirit, filled with wisdom; and the grace of God was upon Him" (Luke 2:40, NKJV).

When Jesus was only twelve years old, His parents inadvertently left Him behind in Jerusalem. After searching three days for Him, they found Him in the Temple, sitting among the doctors of law, discussing deep questions with them and amazing everyone with His wise answers.

Jesus thought His parents would know where He was, so when they rebuked Him, He asked, "Why were you searching for me? . . . Didn't you know I had to be in my Father's house?" (Luke 2:49, NIV).

Being obedient to His parents, Jesus accompanied them back to Nazareth.

Eighteen years later, when Jesus was thirty, John baptized Him in the waters of the Jordan. All four gospel writers record the important event immediately afterward: "The Holy Spirit descended in bodily form like a dove upon Him, and a voice came from heaven which said, 'You are My beloved Son; in You I am well pleased'" (Luke 3:22, NKJV).

The heavens opened, and the Trinity came into full view. The Holy Spirit descended upon Jesus as God spoke in an audible voice saying, "This is My Son!" Jesus had acknowledged His Father, and His Father now acknowledged Him. Jesus heard the voice, John the Baptist heard the voice, the people there heard the voice, and so did Satan.

John the Baptist later explained what convinced him of Jesus' identity. "I didn't know he was the one . . . but at the time God sent me to baptize he told me, 'When you see the Holy Spirit descending and resting upon someone—he is the one you are looking for. He is the one who baptizes with the Holy Spirit.' I saw it happen to this man, and I therefore testify that he is the Son of God" (John 1:33–34, TLB).

The importance of this work of the Holy Spirit should not be overlooked. He both identified and ordained Jesus. John, having been sent by God to announce to Israel their Messiah, needed positive proof before he could fulfill his commission as a witness. The dove was the sign from heaven that John waited for. Then his work was done. The Holy Spirit was the anointing Jesus waited for. Then His work was just beginning.

No one could improve upon John's profoundly simple introduction of Jesus, inspired by the Holy Spirit at His baptism: "Behold! The Lamb of God who takes away the sin of the world! . . . This is He who baptizes with the Holy Spirit" (John 1:29, 33, NKJV).

Jesus the *Lamb;* Jesus the *Baptizer.* Do you know Him as both?

Lamb of God,
I am pleased to meet You. Be my Lamb! Be my Baptizer!

31

LEADING JESUS

Jesus being full of the Holy Ghost . . . was led by the Spirit [to be] tempted of the devil.

LUKE 4:1–2

onsider Jesus' preparation. Before being led by the Holy Spirit to encounter the devil, and prior to any public ministry, Jesus was fully equipped. He was baptized in water (to fulfill all righteousness for us), acknowledged by God as His Son and endued with the Holy Spirit's power.

Jesus' age was also part of the preparation. Note that His Father did not send Him forth until He was thirty years old, the minimum age requirement under the law for public service.

Jesus was ready, and in His first work He opposed the god of this world. To do this, the Holy Spirit led (more literally *drove*) Jesus into the wilderness where He was tempted of the devil.

Satan, originally named Lucifer, existed before the creation of the world. God created him an anointed covering cherub, perfect in wisdom and beauty until iniquity (lawlessness and violence) was found in him (Isaiah 14:12–17; Ezekiel 28:12–19).

When Lucifer did not fulfill the purposes for which God created him, God judged him and pronounced his doom: "You sinned; therefore I cast you as a profane thing out of the mountain of God; and I destroyed you, O covering cherub, from the midst of the fiery stones" (Ezekiel 28:16, NKJV). Note the origin of sin.

In the Garden of Eden the devil teased Eve with the first recorded question, suggesting that she doubt God's word. It was there that both Adam and Eve succumbed to his temptation by eating of the tree of the knowledge of good and evil. As a result everything that lived faced corruption and death. Satan usurped the realm of Adam's God-given authority and became the ruler of all those in rebellion against God. Adam and Eve forfeited their right to dominion in the earth and life in the Paradise of God.

No one in the history of the world had ever completely resisted the temptation of Satan. And now this same devil was tempting Jesus, who suffered great physical weakness from forty days in the wilderness without food.

Cunningly the devil began Jesus' temptation by suggesting twice that He doubt the truth of who He was, saying, "If you really are God's Son. . . ." The prince of this world made offers to entice Jesus' *body* with bread, His *spirit* with self-willed pride and His *soul* with lusting of the eyes to gain the whole world.

The devil's temptations have never changed. The temptations that the *first* Adam fell for are the same ones we all experience today, but the *last* Adam knew His tempter. "For all that is in the world—the lust of the flesh, the lust of the eyes, and the pride of life—is not of the Father but is of the world" (1 John 2:16, NKJV).

Jesus resisted the devil with the authority of God's Word, repeating: "It is written . . . it is written . . . it is written. . . ." It was as if Jesus said, "I will not obey you, Satan. God is My body's bread. God is My spirit's life. God is My soul's desire."

If Jesus had bowed to the tempter, even for a moment, He could not have been the Lamb of God introduced by John, the One who takes away the sin of the world. If Jesus had obeyed the devil, He would have given His approval to the knowledge of good and evil as the way to life.

Jesus, led forth by the Holy Spirit, was tempted of the devil for us. By overcoming Satan's wiles, He regained the authority over our common adversary and restored to man the life and purpose for which God created him. Indeed, "The reason the Son of God appeared was to destroy the devil's work" (1 John 3:8, NIV).

When the devil could not tempt Jesus to sin, nor find any way to accuse Him, he left Him temporarily. Then the Holy Spirit, who had led Jesus "out" into the wilderness to be tempted of the devil, led Jesus "into" Galilee, to change water into wine.

Thank You, Holy Spirit,
for leading Jesus in and out of the wilderness.
And thank You for leading me!

32
ANOINTING JESUS FOR MINISTRY

"The Spirit of the Lord is upon me, because he hath anointed me."

LUKE 4:18

ere Jesus acknowledges the Holy Spirit's work of anointing in His life, and He reveals the purpose of His anointing.

It happened like this. One Sabbath day, in the synagogue at Nazareth, Jesus stood up to read the scroll of Isaiah that was given to Him. Unrolling the scroll, He located the place where this was written: "The Spirit of the Lord is upon Me, because He has anointed Me to preach the gospel to the poor. He has sent Me to heal the brokenhearted, to preach deliverance to the captives and recovery of sight to the blind, to set at liberty those who are oppressed, to preach the acceptable year of the LORD" (Luke 4:18–19, NKJV; see Isaiah 61:1–2).

When Jesus finished reading, He gave the scroll to the attendant and sat down. The eyes of everyone in the synagogue fastened upon Him as they waited for Him to speak. What would He say? He was so different from the rabbis.

Jesus began to preach, saying, "Today this Scripture is fulfilled in your hearing" (Luke 4:21, NKJV).

Jesus meant *He* was the one the prophet Isaiah was referring to. The Gospel, or "good news," was for that day. In fact, Jesus Himself was the Good News. How fitting it was that He should announce in Nazareth, His hometown, the beginning of God's blessings for all who would come to Him!

At first, those present spoke well of Him and were amazed by the beautiful words He uttered. But as they reasoned among themselves, like men who do not understand the ways of God or the power of the Holy Spirit, their acceptance of this truth became short-lived. "'How can this be?' they asked. 'Isn't this Joseph's son?'" (Luke 4:22, TLB).

Insulted and angry enough to kill Him, they brought to pass the words of Jesus that "no prophet is accepted in his own country." As a result they limited the Holy One of Israel, and Scripture records their loss. "He did not do many mighty works there because of their unbelief" (Matthew 13:58, NKJV).

Throughout Jesus' earthly life and ministry the Holy Spirit's anointing remained upon Him despite people's unbelief. For it pleased the Father that all the fullness of the Godhead should abide in Him, without measure.

That day, when Jesus publicly admitted He was the One whom God had ordained by the anointing of the Holy Spirit, He accepted the work of His Father: the Lamb, who *takes away* sin; and the Baptizer, who *gives back* the Holy Spirit.

Blessed Holy Spirit,
thank You for Your fullness upon Jesus, which made Him different.
He was not ashamed of You.

33

CASTING OUT DEMONS

"I cast out devils by the Spirit of God. . . ."
MATTHEW 12:28

mpowered by God's Spirit, Jesus publicly cast out legions of demons. And as the religious leaders of His day saw the multitudes being loosed from demonic spirits, they were angry. They charged Jesus with casting out demons by Satan's power, but Jesus knew *how* He cast them out and boldly opposed them. "If Satan casts out Satan, he is divided against himself. How then will his kingdom stand? . . . But if I cast out demons by the Spirit of God, surely the kingdom of God has come upon you" (Matthew 12:26, 28, NKJV).

The issue here is the clash of two kingdoms that began with Jesus' anointing. The invisible war was out in the open between Satan's kingdom of this world and God's Kingdom of heaven. When Jesus cast out demons through the power of the Holy Spirit, the demons had to obey Him even though Satan was their prince. This war still continues today.

Jesus taught the reality of only two kingdoms. There is no third option. All those alive choose one or the other. Jesus established the dividing line: for or against. "Anyone who is not for me is against me; if he isn't helping me, he is hurting my cause" (Luke 11:23, TLB).

Jesus also taught the reality of only two fatherhoods. Indignant, the opposing Pharisees claimed God as their Father and accused Jesus of being a bastard and having a demon. Jesus said this in response to their charges: "If God were your Father, you would love Me, for I proceeded forth and came from God. . . . You are of your father the devil, and the desires of your father you want to do. He was a murderer from the beginning . . . he is a liar and the father of it" (John 8:42, 44, NKJV).

God the Father gave all authority in heaven, on earth and under the earth to Jesus. Even nature obeyed His voice. The demons knew the Kingdom of God had invaded their space even before the people understood. And when Jesus commanded them, out came the disobedient demon spirits with their manifestations of disease, depravity and death. Trembling in the presence of Jesus, for fear He had come to torment them "before their time," they begged Him, "Let us alone! What have we to do with You,

Jesus of Nazareth? Did You come to destroy us? [We] know who You are—the Holy One of God!" (Mark 1:24, NKJV).

Jesus shared the Kingdom of God with others. After casting out a legion of demons (perhaps six thousand) in the man from Gadara, He sent forth His own disciples to the lost sheep of the house of Israel, giving them "power and authority over all demons, and to cure diseases. He sent them to preach the kingdom of God and to heal the sick" (Luke 9:1–2, NKJV).

When the Twelve came back, they told Jesus of their success. And Jesus gave His authority to seventy more, sending them into all the cities He planned to visit. These seventy returned with great joy because the demons obeyed them too when they used Jesus' name. Jesus already knew that and said, "I saw Satan fall like lightning from heaven. Behold, I give you the authority to trample on serpents and scorpions, and over all the power of the enemy, and nothing shall by any means hurt you. Nevertheless do not rejoice in this, that the spirits are subject to you, but rather rejoice because your names are written in heaven" (Luke 10:18–20, NKJV).

Have you rejoiced in that fact? And have you, as the Lord's disciple, shared the Kingdom of God with others today? Evil spirits are subject to you too in the same mighty name of Jesus. Remember that when we do Jesus' works we show which kingdom we belong to and who is our Father. It also delights Jesus, our Brother. He was so happy with the 82 who triumphed over Satan's kingdom that Scripture says He praised God with the joy of the Holy Spirit: "I praise you, O Father, Lord of heaven and earth, for hiding these things from the intellectuals and worldly wise and for revealing them to those who are as trusting as little children. Yes, thank you, Father, for that is the way you wanted it" (Luke 10:21, TLB).

I praise God too Jesus,
and thank You for sharing Your Holy Spirit to do Your work.
I'm on Your team.

34

EMPOWERING CHRIST

God anointed Jesus of Nazareth with the Holy Spirit and with power.

ACTS 10:38, NKJV

*D*ivinely inspired, Peter summed up the entire earthly life of Jesus in one simple statement to the Gentiles in Cornelius' house. "Jesus of Nazareth was anointed by God with the Holy Spirit and with power, and he went about doing good and healing all who were possessed by demons, for God was with him" (Acts 10:38, TLB).

Notice the Trinity in agreement here. It was *God,* the Father, who anointed *Jesus* His Son with the *Holy Spirit* and power. God, Jesus and the Holy Spirit worked together; three in union as one.

Jesus openly healed all who were possessed by demons. He did not do these mighty works in secret. Yet in all of His works, He never called attention to Himself. He let the recipients of His goodness tell their own experiences. Then He gave credit to His heavenly Father. "The Son can do nothing by himself. He does only what he sees the Father doing, and in the same way" (John 5:19, TLB).

Yes, Jesus needed the Holy Spirit. He was the source of His earthly power in ministering deliverance and healing to the people. Even if the people did not believe what Jesus *said,* He wanted the works of His Father that He *did* to prove that He and His Father were one: "I and the Father are one. . . . Don't believe me unless I do miracles of God. But if I do, believe them even if you don't believe me. Then you will become convinced that the Father is in me, and I in the Father" (John 10:30, 37–38, TLB).

Jesus freely admitted that He and His Father were one, even though it was difficult for the people to understand. For this reason the Jews sought to kill Him. No one was ever this bold in making Himself equal with God.

We are not asked to explain the Godhead, but we are obligated to believe it. We must acknowledge this truth even though we cannot find the bottom. "The Father, the Word [Jesus], and the Holy Spirit . . . these three are one" (1 John 5:7, NKJV).

Each person who believes Jesus joins in fellowship with the Godhead and becomes one with the Father, Son and Holy Spirit. For instance: Add me, and these four are one. Add you, and these five are one. Add every believer in every generation and *all* are still one, by the power of Christ at work in us. Only in God is it possible to have such plural unity of one Spirit in inestimable myriads. This unity goes beyond our understanding, yet we need to get adjusted to God's arithmetic and the facts of the Spirit. For if Jesus was not one with the Father, we who are in Jesus can never be.

Jesus has already prayed for all the "additions" who believe His words and His works through our witness of Him. "I am . . . praying . . . for the future believers who will come to me because of the testimony of these. My prayer for all of them is that they will be of one heart and mind, just as you and I are, Father—that just as you are in me and I am in you, so they will be in us, and the world will believe you sent me" (John 17:20–21, TLB).

It is important for the whole world to believe that God sent Jesus and that they are one. It is a matter of life or death.

Holy Spirit,
You were obedient to the Father and anointed Jesus for our sakes. His mighty works convince me, and I believe, I believe, I believe!

35

PRESENCE AT CHRIST'S DEATH

Christ . . . through the eternal Spirit offered himself . . . to God.
HEBREWS 9:14

*W*ith the help of the eternal Holy Spirit, Jesus Christ, our Passover Lamb, offered Himself to God. Not to men. Not to Satan.

Consider His death from the divine standpoint. No one could *take* Jesus' life from Him. He would freely *give* it—laying it down for His friends. The choice was His. "No one can kill me without my consent—I lay down my life voluntarily. For I have the right and power to lay it down when I want to and also the right and power to take it again. For the Father has given me this right" (John 10:18, TLB).

After commanding His disciples to tell no one that He was the Messiah, Jesus "began to tell them about the terrible things he would suffer, and that he would be rejected by the elders and the Chief Priests and the other Jewish leaders—and be killed, and that he would rise again three days afterwards" (Mark 8:31, TLB).

Knowing why He had come into the world, Jesus determined to fulfill all the Scriptures concerning Him. He knew what was coming: "I came to send fire on the earth, and how I wish it were already kindled! But I have a baptism to be baptized with, and how distressed I am till it is accomplished!" (Luke 12:49–50, NKJV).

One week before His death, Jesus permitted Peter, James and John to see His divine nature. They beheld Jesus' glory as His appearance changed before their eyes on the mountain. "His face began to shine, and his clothes became dazzling white and blazed with light. Then two men appeared and began talking with him—Moses and Elijah! They were splendid in appearance, glorious to see; and they were speaking of his death at Jerusalem, to be carried out in accordance with God's plan" (Luke 9:29–31, TLB).

It was a breathtaking meeting: Jesus conferring with Moses and Elijah! God speaking! The Holy Spirit overshadowing! The disciples quaking!

After the disciples had glimpsed the Kingdom of God, Jesus commanded them to tell no one what they had seen or heard until *after* He had risen from the dead. For the timing of every detail of His life and death on earth was carefully planned in the Godhead. The *place* Jesus would die: Jerusalem. The *time* Jesus would die: Passover. The *way* Jesus would die: Hanging on a tree.

Indeed, the Scriptures cannot be broken. Jesus' death would be "according to the pattern" shown to many Old Testament prophets, even though they did not understand it at the time.

- Abraham saw His death when he offered up his only son Isaac on the same mountain where Moses and Elijah appeared to Jesus (see Genesis 22).
- Moses saw His death when he lifted up the serpent on the pole in the wilderness (see Numbers 21:8–9).
- Isaiah saw His death when he prophesied that "we did esteem him stricken, smitten of God, and afflicted . . . [for] the LORD hath laid on him the iniquity of us all" (Isaiah 53:4, 6).

Three days before His death, Jesus went from city to city and village to village doing good works. His destination: Jerusalem. For "it wouldn't do for a prophet of God to be killed except in Jerusalem!" (Luke 13:33, TLB).

Finally, the evening before Passover, as Jesus ate His last supper with His disciples, He initiated their birthright of bread and wine and announced His betrayer. "I must die just as was prophesied, but woe to the man by whom I am betrayed. Far better for that one if he had never been born" (Matthew 26:24, TLB).

After supper, outside in the Garden of Gethsemane, the hour arrived for Jesus to be handed over to His accusers. He asked Peter, James and John to pray with Him as He began to be filled with the horror of that dreadful hour. What if He could not make it to the cross? His spirit was willing but His soul was weak with grief and sorrow—to the point of death. So much so that He sweat great drops of blood. An angel intervened to strengthen Him as He "pleaded with God, praying with tears and agony of soul to the only one who would save him from [premature] death. And God heard his prayers because of his strong desire to obey God at all times. And even though Jesus was God's Son, he had to learn from experience what it was like to obey, when obeying meant suffering" (Hebrews 5:7–8, TLB).

When soldiers and officers from the chief priests and Pharisees drew near with swords and clubs to seize Him, Jesus' prayers had been answered. Revived, He reminded Peter, "Don't you realize that I could ask my Father for thousands of angels to protect us, and he would send them instantly? But if I did, how would the Scriptures be fulfilled that describe what is happening now?" (Matthew 26:53–54, TLB). "Shall I not drink from the cup the Father has given me?" (John 18:11, TLB).

Even Pilate could not prevent the events that were now set in motion, but he tried. Frustrated because Jesus would not answer his questions, Pilate threatened Him. "'You won't talk to me? . . . Don't you realize that I have the power to release you or to crucify you?' Then Jesus said, 'You would have no power at all over me unless it were given to you from above'" (John 19:10–11, TLB).

On the cross, that bleeding, suffering, dying form was an indistinguishable ruin. God-forsaken in outer darkness. Finished!

The eternal Spirit of God—satisfied.

Ah, yes, the ram caught in the thicket.
Eternal thanksgiving, Jehovah-Jireh, for
loving us enough to provide Yourself.

36

QUICKENING CHRIST FROM DEATH

Christ ... put to death in the flesh, but quickened by the Spirit ... preached.

1 PETER 3:18–19

As the Jews looked upon Him whom they had pierced, Jesus was taken down from the cross and laid in a sepulcher while they waited—wondering if the words of Jesus concerning His death would come to pass: "As Jonah was three days and three nights in the belly of the great fish, so will the Son of Man be three days and three nights in the heart of the earth" (Matthew 12:40, NKJV).

What happened to Jesus during those three days and three nights while His *body* lay embalmed in the borrowed tomb of Joseph of Arimathea? Ordinarily we would not ask such a question about a dead man. But then we would miss this work of the Holy Spirit: In the heart of the earth, Jesus was made alive and went about doing the work of His Father—*in hell!*

Jesus, having released His spirit into His Father's hands on the cross, died physically, and His soul descended into the terrors of hell. There He bore our sins away as the scapegoat to a place cut off from God (see Leviticus 16:22). His agony is described in Psalm 88.

Jesus tasted death for us in all three phases: body, soul and spirit. And when the wrath of God was fully satisfied, the Holy Spirit quickened Jesus' spirit. He was made alive in hell *before* He was resurrected from the dead. Jesus was "put to death in the body but made alive by the Spirit, through whom also he went and preached to the spirits in prison" (1 Peter 3:18–19, NIV).

Who were these spirits in prison? They were angels in Noah's time who rejected their God-assigned realm of authority in heavenly places and came down to earth and cohabited with the daughters of men. God never intended for angels to marry. Scripture tells us this fornication produced a monstrous race not ordained by Him. This is Noah's description of their rebellion: "Now a population explosion took place upon the earth. It was at this time that beings from the spirit world looked upon the beautiful earth women and took any they desired to be their wives. . . . When the evil beings from the spirit world were sexually involved with human women, their children became giants, of whom so many legends are told" (Genesis 6:1–2, 4, TLB).

This union of fallen angels and daughters of men was a satanic intervention in the human (earthly) race, intended to do away with the pure Adamic race created by God in His own image and likeness—*not* the image and likeness of angels. If Satan, himself an angelic being, could mar God's likeness in man and produce an impure race of giants *not* conceived by God, he would mutate and corrupt the woman's Seed who was destined to defeat him—God's Son, Jesus Christ.

Satan's plan failed, however, for God intervened with a mighty judgment to stop it. Now we know the purpose for all those seemingly endless genealogies in Scripture that chronicle the pure ancestry of Jesus Christ after the flood.

This sin of evil angels had corrupted all flesh upon the earth by Noah's time. God saw that the earth was filled with violence and that men's hearts were evil, so much so that it grieved Him that He had made man.

God's verdict: the destruction of all flesh by drowning—all except Noah, for he alone had found grace in the sight of the Lord. He walked with God and preached righteousness while he obediently prepared the ark of God to save his household.

You may remember the story. Seven days *before* the flood came, the Lord shut Noah, his family and the animals inside the ark. During that time, it is my belief that God's Spirit withdrew into the ark also. He no longer strived with men. For one last week (seven days) before the ark was borne heavenward by water, Satan's angelic spirits had free reign with the daughters of men. Then the fountains of the deep burst forth and the floodgates of the sky opened to inundate the whole earth. All flesh perished! Nor did God spare the angels, "but sent them to hell *[Tartarus]*, putting them into gloomy dungeons to be held for judgment" (2 Peter 2:4, NIV).

The Greek word for *hell* in this Scripture is *Tartarus*. According to the Greek lexicon, *Tartarus* is a place as far below hell as hell is below the surface of the earth. This prison is a special one for fallen angels from Adam to Noah who sinned before the flood. No human spirits or demons go to this prison.

What did Jesus preach to them? Most likely He announced, or proclaimed, the crucifixion and confirmed their just judgment. It was not an offer of a second chance. They now had a new Master who held the keys of death and hell. Yes, fallen angels are still loose today, but those remain bound. Their imprisonment in *Tartarus* is sure, for "the Lord knows how . . . to reserve the unjust under punishment for the day of judgment" (2 Peter 2:9, NKJV).

Scripture records that both men and angels have transgressed the sexual bounds God preordained for them. Homosexuality was the reason for the destruction of Sodom, Gomorrah and the surrounding cities by fire in the time of Lot (see Genesis 19). "And don't forget the cities of Sodom and Gomorrah and their neighboring towns, all full of lust of every kind including lust of men for other men. Those cities were destroyed by fire and continue to be a warning to us that there is a hell in which sinners are punished" (Jude 7, TLB).

Why give so much attention to these matters, which happened so long ago in Noah's day? It is for our sakes. Just as Noah preached righteousness to his generation, Jesus preached righteousness to His generation. Jesus used Noah's days as an example of unexpected destruction for the ungodly to look back upon with fear. He predicted that this pattern of behavior will be repeated at the close of this present age, when God again destroys the wicked. Heed the warnings of Jesus and be saved from eternal hell. Hear the word of the Lord.

> "[When I return] the world will be [as indifferent to the things of God] as the people were in Noah's day. They ate and drank and married—everything just as usual right up to the day when Noah went into the ark and the flood came and destroyed them all. And the world will be as it was in the days of Lot: people went about their daily business—eating and drinking, buying and selling, farming and building—until the morning Lot left Sodom. Then fire and brimstone rained down from heaven and destroyed them all. Yes, it will be 'business as usual' right up to the hour of my return."
>
> Luke 17:26–30, TLB

Those angelic spirits in prison know who Jesus is. They have seen Him and heard Him. And so have we, making sure this Scripture: "that at the name of Jesus every knee should bow, of those in heaven, and of those on earth, and of those under the earth, and that every tongue should confess that Jesus Christ is Lord, to the glory of God the Father" (Philippians 2:10–11, NKJV).

Quickening Holy Spirit, thank You
for being present with Jesus,
even when He made His bed in hell.

37
RESURRECTING JESUS

The Spirit . . . raised up Jesus from the dead.
ROMANS 8:11

*O*bedient in drinking the cup of death to its dregs, Jesus was vindicated by God in resurrection from the dead. For as Sunday morning dawned, the first day of the week, Joseph's borrowed tomb was *empty!*

- *Empty,* despite the fact that the chief priests and Pharisees had petitioned Pilate to secure the tomb by sealing it with a boulder and posting soldiers to guard against anyone spiriting Jesus' body away.
- *Empty,* because Jesus had finished the work of His Father, and hell and the grave could no longer hold Him.
- *Empty,* for the Holy Spirit had raised Him from the dead!

Death had lost its victory, and Paradise would be found in heaven.

Jesus had the honor of being the firstborn from the dead in an immortal body. Matthew's gospel records the events that happened in Jerusalem to others that followed Jesus in resurrection: "The graves were opened; and many bodies of the saints who had fallen asleep were raised; and coming out of the graves after His resurrection, they went into the holy city and appeared to many" (Matthew 27:52–53, NKJV).

Jesus showed Himself alive after His resurrection to many eyewitnesses. First to Mary Magdalene, then to Peter and the Eleven as they were eating. On one occasion more than five hundred people saw Him at the same time, as well as Thomas. Two men from Emmaus walked, talked and ate with Him—not realizing who He was until He broke bread with them. Jesus talked to them about how the writings of Moses, the prophets and the Psalms spoke about the things that had happened to Him, and He chided them for their unbelief.

In His resurrection body, Christ could appear and disappear. When this happened before ten of His disciples, they were frightened—supposing they had seen a spirit. But Jesus reassured them: "Behold My hands and My feet, that it is I Myself. Handle Me and see, for a spirit does not have flesh and bones as you see I have" (Luke 24:39, NKJV).

No, God had not left Jesus' soul in hell, nor allowed His Holy One to see corruption. Do we believe in His resurrection today two thousand years after the fact? Are the dead really raised? Paul's question to King Agrippa is for all of us to answer. "Why should it be thought incredible by you that God raises the dead?" (Acts 26:8, NKJV).

If it *is* incredible, how does that affect us? If Christ is not risen, then our faith is in vain. Who would believe a dead god could help them? In fact, if Christ is still dead and buried, that means we are yet in our sins and guilty as charged. What then was the point in Christ dying?

Yes, the resurrection of Jesus is credible. It was the turning point in history. The evidence remains in heaven, on earth and under the earth for all who want to know and believe. God says in His Word, "If you tell others with your own mouth that Jesus Christ is your Lord, and believe in your own heart that God has raised him from the dead, you will be saved" (Romans 10:9, TLB).

God raised Jesus from the dead by the power of the Holy Spirit and gave us the same promise: "If the Spirit of him who raised Jesus from the dead is living in you, he who raised Christ from the dead will also give life to your mortal bodies through his Spirit, who lives in you" (Romans 8:11, NIV).

Thank You, resurrecting Spirit,
for emptying the tomb so I can know Jesus and the power
of His resurrection.

38
DIVINE BREATH

"Receive ye the Holy [Spirit]."
JOHN 20:22

*H*fter His resurrection, Jesus remained on earth only forty days. At the end of that time His little band of disciples, who depended upon Him for everything, saw Him in the flesh no more. Ten days beyond that, when the Jews celebrated the feast of Pentecost, Jesus would be gone.

The things Jesus did for them, however, would not be gone. On the same day Jesus rose from the dead, He lost no time in taking care of the last of His Father's business: His disciples.

Jesus found them that evening hiding behind locked doors in Jerusalem, afraid for their lives. Suddenly appearing in their midst, Jesus spoke peace to their frightened hearts. And when He showed them His hands and side, the disciples were glad to see their resurrected Lord. "As the Father has sent me, I am sending you," (John 20:21, NIV) spoke the Master.

When He had said this Jesus did a very significant thing. He personally breathed on each one of the disciples, saying, "Receive (admit) the Holy Spirit!" (John 20:22, AMPLIFIED).

Quickened by this inbreathed breath of the Holy Spirit from Jesus, the disciples were reborn, freed from Adam's curse. Jesus had imparted to them His own resurrection life. "The first man Adam was made a living soul; [but] the last Adam [Jesus] was made a quickening spirit. . . . The first man is of the earth, earthy: the second man is the Lord from heaven. . . . As we have borne the image of the earthy, we shall also bear the image of the heavenly" (1 Corinthians 15:45, 47, 49). Jesus, the last Adam, sealed off man's evil inheritance on the cross and came forth from the grave, the first begotten from the dead, to share His life with His disciples.

As His Father had sent Him, now He was sending them. What Jesus had begun to do and teach, the disciples would be equipped to do and teach. The power and authority given to Jesus in heaven and earth were now their keys to the Kingdom of heaven. Jesus trusted them to open and close doors, bind and loose, in His name. His work was now their work, including the forgiveness of sins. Freely they had received forgiveness; freely they were to give forgiveness. "[Now having received the Holy Spirit, and being led and directed by Him] (Jesus said), if you forgive the sins of any one, they are forgiven; if you retain the sins of any one, they are retained" (John 20:23, AMPLIFIED).

At last the disciples were ready to be sent forth. Well, almost ready. One thing remained before they would be fully prepared to leave Jerusalem and go into all the world with the "good news." Jesus had finished His work as the Lamb but not as the Baptizer.

> *Breathe on me, Breath of God,*
> *Fill me with life anew,*
> *That I may love what Thou dost love,*
> *and do what Thou wouldst do.*
> *Edwin Hatch, 1878*

39
CONTINUING DIRECTIONS

Through the Holy Spirit [Jesus] had given commandments to the apostles.

ACTS 1:2, NKJV

*D*uring the forty days between Jesus' resurrection and ascension, He began to wean His disciples. Jesus, purposely, was not with them all the time as before. Going back to their former occupations, the Eleven soon ran into trouble and needed the Master. At the Sea of Galilee, Jesus appeared to His disciples, who had fished all night and caught nothing. He spoke "Peace" to them and bade them throw their net out on the right side of the boat. When they obeyed their net immediately filled with fish. No doubt they remembered their first meeting with Him three years earlier when the same thing happened. On that occasion, Jesus had prophesied they would become fishers of men! Soon they would know what that meant.

Even though Jesus appeared to the disciples in a resurrection body, He cooked breakfast for them and ate with them. He talked freely about things to come, discussing their personal lives, the Kingdom of God and signs that would follow their ministry. Jesus banished forever any doubt that He was the same Jesus they had known before His resurrection, and that He was indeed alive.

Jesus promised the disciples He would be with them always, even to the end of the world. How could that be when He already was no longer earthbound and could appear and disappear at will? Luke captures for us the reason why: "In my former book, Theophilus, I wrote about all that Jesus began both to do and to teach until the day he was taken up to heaven, after giving instructions through the Holy Spirit to the apostles he had chosen" (Acts 1:1–2, NIV).

Yes, Jesus would continue to be with them through the Holy Spirit, who would convey His directions to them. In this way they could go and teach all nations what Jesus had commanded them, baptizing them in the name of the Father, the Son and the Holy Spirit. And Luke, having written about the acts of Jesus, could now concentrate on writing about the acts of the apostles sent in Jesus' name.

Isaiah saw this post-resurrection work of the Holy Spirit when he wrote, "My Holy Spirit shall not leave them, and they shall want the good and hate the wrong—they and their children and their children's children forever" (Isaiah 59:21, TLB).

The last time the disciples saw Jesus, they walked with Him to the Mount of Olives. Jesus reminded them not to depart from Jerusalem—until He sent "the Promise of My Father upon you . . . [and] you are endued with power from on high" (Luke 24:49, NKJV).

While they looked at Him, Jesus lifted up His hands and blessed them, clouds receiving Him out of their sight.

Jesus was gone. The Holy Spirit was gone. The questions remained. Why was it good for them for Jesus to go away? What would happen to them without the Master? What was the "Promise of the Father" Jesus spoke about? How long would they have to wait in Jerusalem to find out?

Meanwhile, Pentecost was only ten days away.

Where are You, Jesus? Why did You go?
When will You come again? We miss You so.
Whom do we look for? "Another"—no name,
The Ghost of infinity? The object of shame?
Lord, quiet our hearts—without any dread,
To honor His coming and do all You've said.

3

THE HOLY SPIRIT
IN JESUS' TEACHING

40

NEW BIRTH

"Except a man be born of water and of the Spirit, he cannot enter into the kingdom of God."

JOHN 3:5

Jesus was a Teacher, the only teacher God ever sent from heaven. The only Teacher who could correctly instruct anyone about the Holy Spirit, the Kingdom of God and how we may live there.

Nicodemus, a teacher in Israel, recognized His wisdom. Convinced by the miracles Jesus did that God had sent Him as a Chief Rabbi, Nicodemus came to Him for private tutoring.

In three short sentences, Jesus taught Nicodemus about the first miracle of all: being born again of the Spirit. "You must be born again" (John 3:7, NKJV). "Unless one is born again, he cannot see the kingdom of God" (John 3:3, NKJV). "Unless one is born of water and the Spirit, he cannot enter the kingdom of God" (John 3:5, NKJV).

The Teacher made being born again of water and the Spirit more important than keeping the Law. A second birth was vital in order to *see* and *enter* God's Kingdom of heaven legitimately. And even though Nicodemus was a good man—a Pharisee who observed the traditions of his fathers, kept the Law, did good works and probably was very sincere—his own works could not qualify him for the Kingdom of heaven. He *must* be born again.

Amazed by this new teaching, Nicodemus wanted to know more. Being a religious Jew, he probably would not have entertained the thought of reincarnation, but he did ask Jesus the crucial question for all of us. "How can I be born again? Must I re-enter my mother's womb?"

Nicodemus thought in human terms. Jesus taught in spiritual terms. "Do not marvel that I said to you, 'You must be born again' (John 3:7, NKJV). "That which is born of the flesh is flesh, and that which is born of the Spirit is spirit" (John 3:6, NKJV).

Jesus taught Nicodemus the difference between the birth of the flesh and the birth of the Spirit. Men produce human life on earth, but the Holy Spirit reproduces a new life from heaven. A physical birth limits you to the earth. A spiritual birth gives you access to heaven. Human life is the birth of a mortal soul, but Spirit life is the birth of an immortal spirit.

Nicodemus knew he was not born the second time. Perhaps he thought, "This sounds good. I want to be born again, but how?" It was as if Jesus read his mind and said, "Through Me, Nicodemus, through Me. All you need to do is believe Me and receive Me. I will do it." As God foretold through the prophet Ezekiel, "I will sprinkle clean water on you, and you shall be clean; I will cleanse you from all your filthiness and from all your idols. I will give you a new heart and put a new spirit within you. . . . I will put My Spirit within you" (Ezekiel 36:25–27, NKJV).

New life in the Spirit happens the moment we believe and receive Christ. Jesus is the source of it and the way to the Father in heaven. Some might try to steal past Him through a way of their own, but the way is carefully guarded. Jesus spoke of the Kingdom of God as a sheepfold and Himself, the door. "He who does not enter the sheepfold by the door, but climbs up some other way, the same is a thief and a robber. . . . I am the door. If anyone enters by Me, he will be saved, and will go in and out and find pasture" (John 10:1, 9, NKJV).

Can we know for sure that we have been born again of the Spirit if we meet the conditions? Yes, we can. God would not lie. He has said in His Word that "everyone who believes—adheres to, trusts in, and relies [on the fact]—that Jesus is the Christ, the Messiah, is a born-again child of God" (1 John 5:1, AMPLIFIED).

A born-again child of God. An unfamiliar term, you say? A strange way to explain a change of life? What better way to teach this miracle? No one can improve upon the Chief Rabbi's teaching. Jesus made eternal life wonderfully simple with only one sentence. You must be born again of water and the Spirit.

Father of spirits,
birth me that I might live.
Wash me and I shall be
whiter than snow.

41
REPRODUCING HIS SPIRIT

"That which is born of the Spirit is spirit."

JOHN 3:6

*N*icodemus, well-versed in the teachings of Moses, was somewhat prepared for Jesus' teachings. He already knew that on the third day of creation God had set in motion a law of nature by which the earth and all its inhabitants were naturally reproduced. Moses had written: "God said, 'Let the earth bring forth grass, the herb that yields seed, and the fruit tree that yields fruit according to its kind, whose seed is in itself, on the earth'; and it was so" (Genesis 1:11, NKJV).

The seed in the original creation required no lengthy process of evolution. Because the seed is *in itself,* everything in creation easily reproduced after its own kind.

The same process occurred in human reproduction. *Homo sapiens* reproduced other *homo sapiens* because that seed was in them. This is God's physical law of reproduction.

Now Jesus was teaching Nicodemus a similar spiritual law. Using a spiritual language Nicodemus had never heard before, Jesus said, "That which is born of the Spirit is spirit" (John 3:6, NKJV).

Whoever heard of the Holy Spirit reproducing spirit? Although it had happened many times before, no one had the authority to express it in words as Jesus did.

Continuing the lesson, Jesus compared the Holy Spirit's nature (seed) to that of the wind. "Just as you can hear the wind but can't tell where it comes from or where it will go next, so it is with the Spirit. We do not know on whom he will next bestow this life from heaven" (John 3:8, TLB).

The wind is a good analogy. The reproductive work of the Holy Spirit, like wind, is unpredictable, unseen and unsearchable. The miracle is, His birthing does not have to be understood or deserved to be believed and received.

The Holy Spirit unites God's Word with our faith to reproduce His Spirit. Once the union is consummated, just as the natural man hears the wind, the born-again man hears the Spirit. It may be the still small voice of the Spirit as Elijah heard (see 1 Kings 19:12) or the sound of a mighty rushing wind such as on the Day of Pentecost (see Acts 2:2). Or it may be heard secretly in our womb of faith and learned slowly as young Samuel experienced it (see 1 Samuel 3:7), or even a doubting conversion as happened to Thomas (see John 20:27–28).

But for every spirit born again there is a sure testimony to this miracle of believing grace. It happens in the twinkling of an eye and lasts forever. Why? Because God loves us. He wants us to be like Him—in Spirit and in Truth.

O mighty Wind of the Spirit,
blow upon me. Create in
me a clean heart and renew
a right spirit within me.

42
WORSHIP

"Worship the Father in spirit and in truth."
JOHN 4:23–24

orship became the subject of an impromptu teaching Jesus gave to a poor Samaritan woman at Jacob's well.

Perceiving Jesus to be a prophet, she asked Him a religious question. "Where should men worship?"

Jesus responded by taking the emphasis off the *place* of worship and putting it on *whom* to worship and *why*. He answered her, "True worshipers . . . worship the Father in spirit and truth; for the Father is seeking such to worship Him" (John 4:23, NKJV).

The Samaritans practiced false worship, for they really did not know *whom* they were worshiping as the Jews did. Nor did they understand *how* to worship the Father with the Holy Spirit's help. They did not realize the *place* of worship was not restricted to Jerusalem or a particular mountain shrine in Samaria, but was in their hearts.

The topic of true worship gave Jesus the opportunity to teach the Samaritan woman about the Holy Spirit. "God is Spirit, and we must have his [the Holy Spirit's] help to worship as we should. The Father wants this kind of worship from us" (John 4:23–24, TLB).

Spiritual worship is different from ritual worship. Jesus made this point when He discerned the hearts of the religious leaders of His day, calling their traditional worship hypocritical: "Well did Isaiah prophesy about you, saying: 'These people draw near to Me with their mouth, and honor Me with their lips, but their heart is far from Me. And in vain they worship Me, teaching as doctrines the commandments of men'" (Matthew 15:7–9, NKJV).

Jesus dealt kindly with the adulterous woman as He explained the change coming in the way all people would worship God. They would truly honor God because true worship is not about man-made rituals and prayers, learned by repetition, but worshiping God Jesus' way. For if we do not worship God, who is Spirit, with the Holy Spirit *in* our spirits, then we do not worship God at all.

Yes, another work of the Holy Spirit—true worship—is made possible through the work of Jesus. Paul confirmed this later in a letter to the church at Philippi, saying, "We [Christians] are the true circumcision, who worship God in spirit and by the Spirit of God, and exult and glory and pride ourselves in Jesus Christ, and put no confidence or dependence [on what we are] in the flesh" (Philippians 3:3, AMPLIFIED).

In Greek, the word *worship* means "to kiss the hand toward." It reminds me of a special friend who frequently kisses her hand and raises it toward heaven while blessing God—and me.

It is interesting to note that Jesus taught Nicodemus how to enter God's Kingdom of heaven: in spirit. He taught the Samaritan woman the purpose of being there: to worship God in spirit and in truth. These vital truths were not spoken to the twelve disciples or the chief priests, but to two unlikely people chosen by Jesus. Each of them had private lessons on the Holy Spirit that changed their lives forever.

Holy Spirit,
I welcome Your help to
worship my Father
in spirit and in truth.

43

MAKING US ALIVE

"It is the Spirit that quickeneth. . . ."
JOHN 6:63

*I*n this Scripture, Jesus bears witness to the work of the Holy Spirit by telling the people how they may receive eternal life. "It is the Spirit who gives life; the flesh profits nothing. The words that I speak to you are spirit, and they are life" (John 6:63, NKJV).

In other words, eternal life is in the *words* Jesus speaks. The Word is alive. The Word is Spirit. The Word and the Spirit agree. So it can be said that it is the Spirit who quickens the Word, which makes us alive. The Spirit *is in* and cannot be separated from the Word we receive from Jesus.

The Greek word for *quickened* means "to revitalize, make alive, impart life." The word *quickened* is not used much today, but it is found in the familiar Apostles' Creed: "[T]he third day He [Jesus] rose from the dead; He ascended into heaven, and sitteth at the right hand of God the Father Almighty; from thence He shall come to judge the quick [those alive] and the dead."

While teaching in the synagogue at Capernaum, Jesus spoke boldly to the people about spiritual things. He said if they would come to Him, they would never hunger or thirst again. Many found these truths shocking and difficult to understand. Perhaps we all do at first. Yet every time we hear what Jesus said, we make a decision to accept it or reject it; to swallow it or spit it out. At that point, faith is either *quickened* or *quenched.* We believe and receive what we do not know for sure yet—by faith—or continue "waiting" to believe while existing in a state of doubt, sin and death. "For whatsoever is not of faith is sin" (Romans 14:23).

The conditions Jesus laid down for being quickened by the Spirit were unheard of. He said, "With all the earnestness I possess I tell you this: Unless you eat the flesh of the Messiah and drink his blood, you cannot have eternal life within you. But anyone who does eat my flesh and drink my blood has eternal life, and I will raise him at the Last Day" (John 6:53–54, TLB).

How was this possible? Even if they could literally eat His flesh and drink His blood, it would not save their souls. Jesus was talking about receiving supernaturally the benefits of the sacrifice of His body and blood.

Since there is life (spirit) in the very words He spoke, they could be eaten (ingested). Eaten by the mind, the will and the heart—digested by faith. The words could be believed and implanted inside where they would spring up into eternal life.

Jesus is the true Bread from heaven. This bread (His body) was broken for us to receive just as Jesus broke the five loaves to feed five thousand people. And His blood poured out on the cross was the blood of the New Covenant, instead of the blood of bulls and goats.

Jesus knew this would offend His followers, and many of them did turn away. However, the Twelve who stayed understood more fully when they gathered in the Upper Room, two years later, for their last supper together. It was then that Jesus took bread and wine, blessed it and gave it to His disciples to eat, saying, "Take, eat; this is My body. . . . Drink . . . for this is My blood of the new covenant, which is shed for many for the remission of sins" (Matthew 26:26–28, NKJV).

This is how they could eat His flesh and drink His blood. They did it. And so can we, because of the intricate work of the Godhead displayed here. The Father draws us to the Son; the Son provides His life; and the Holy Spirit imparts it to us.

We come to Your table and thankfully dine,
O Lord, for Your food and drink make us
alive with Your Spirit.

44

FLOWING IN ME

Rivers of living water . . . This spake he of the Spirit.

JOHN 7:38–39

*T*he Jews considered the Samaritans outcasts, outside the house of Israel. They also considered women to be inferior to men in religious matters. Yet Jesus chose a *Samaritan woman* to whom to reveal His true identity as the Messiah and to introduce the Holy Spirit.

Meeting the woman at Jacob's well, where she habitually came to draw water, Jesus opened the conversation by asking her for a drink of water. Knowing that the Jews refused to use utensils the Samaritans used, she wondered how she could give Him a drink. Jesus continued the conversation by avoiding the problem and discussing the *water*. He said, "If you only knew what a wonderful gift God has for you, and who I am, you would ask me for some living water!" (John 4:10, TLB).

Water? She probably thought of H_2O, but Jesus was speaking of *living* water—found only in the spiritual realm.

She asked if His water really was better than the water in Jacob's well and where He would get this living water.

Again, Jesus pressed hard on her *need* for the water He could give her. With His water she would never be thirsty again nor ever run out of water. Jesus explained, "The water I give . . . becomes a perpetual spring within [you], watering [you] forever with eternal life" (John 4:14, TLB).

If what this man said were true, it would be much easier for her, the woman thought. She wanted water so she would not have to come so far, so often, and work so hard to draw it.

Finally convinced, she accepted Jesus' offer. No longer needing her water pot, she left it beside the well and hurried back to the village to share the good news with everyone. For Jesus had told her plainly, "I am the Messiah!" (John 4:26, TLB).

What Jesus told the Samaritan woman at the well, He shouted to the hostile Jewish crowds in Jerusalem six months before His death. At the climax of the Feast of Tabernacles in the Temple courtyard, Jesus extended the "water" invitation to everyone.

"If anyone is thirsty, let him come to me and drink. For the Scriptures declare that rivers of living water shall flow from the inmost being of anyone who believes in me" (John 7:37–38, TLB).

Spiritual language again. Translation: "living water"—eternal life, flowing perpetually inside the believer. By living water, "[Jesus] was speaking of the Holy Spirit, who would be given to everyone believing in him; but the Spirit had not yet been given, because Jesus had not yet returned to his glory in heaven" (John 7:39, TLB).

The clues are all through the Scriptures.

- Moses wrote of the Tree of Life in the midst of the Garden (Genesis 2:9).
- Jeremiah wrote of the Fountain of Life (Jeremiah 2:13).
- Ezekiel wrote of the River of Life (Ezekiel 47).
- Joel wrote of the pouring out of the Spirit of Life upon all flesh (Joel 2:28–29).
- Zechariah wrote of living waters flowing out from Jerusalem (Zechariah 14:8).
- Peter preached the *pouring out* of the Spirit at Pentecost (Acts 2:17–18).
- John wrote of a pure river of Water of Life, clear as crystal, proceeding from the throne of God and of the Lamb. He also wrote of a Tree of Life in the New Jerusalem (Revelation 22:1–2).

For every believer this refreshing stream of God, the Holy Spirit, is a limitless resource. This message is so important that Scripture begins and ends with the Water of Life.

Scripture paints a dismal portrait of those who come but refuse to drink. They are forever dry. Like "clouds without water, carried about by the winds; late autumn trees without fruit, twice dead, pulled up by the roots; raging waves of the sea, foaming up their own shame; wandering stars for whom is reserved the blackness of darkness forever" (Jude 12–13, NKJV).

Everyone who is thirsty, come to the fountain of living water and drink. And into and out of your innermost being will flow the Spirit of life.

Fairest Lord Jesus,
I'm thirsty. Give me living
Water, and I'll thirst no more.
Spring up, O well, inside of me!

45
RESPONDING TO MY INVITATION

"Your heavenly Father give[s] the Holy Spirit to them that ask him."
LUKE 11:13

Jesus taught His disciples the Kingdom principle of *asking*. We ask our earthly parents for our temporal needs—the physical, earthly things of this world. In like manner, Jesus taught us to ask our heavenly Father for spiritual needs—forgiveness, mercy, righteousness, holiness—things in the Kingdom of God.

Spiritual needs require God's divine intervention and cannot be provided through human means or effort. Jesus taught the truth this way: "If a son asks for bread from any father among you, will he give him a stone? Or if he asks for a fish, will he give him a serpent instead of a fish? Or if he asks for an egg, will he offer him a scorpion? If you then, being evil, know how to give good gifts to your children, how much more will your heavenly Father give the Holy Spirit to those who ask him?" (Luke 11:11–13, NKJV).

Our heavenly Father provides the best gifts, ones that do not perish with the using. But consider this teaching of Jesus: He told us to ask the Father for the Holy Spirit. He even agreed He would join us in asking the Father for us. "I will pray the Father, and He will give you . . . the Holy Spirit, whom the Father will send in My name" (John 14:16, 26, NKJV). Have you asked your heavenly Father for the Holy Spirit?

The Holy Spirit is a sweet, gentle Spirit. He will not come where He is not welcome. He waits to be invited. It is our work, our privilege, to ask for Him. The Holy Spirit's work is to come when the Father sends Him.

Heavenly Father,
I ask You for the Holy Spirit. Be it
unto me according to Your Word.

46
COMFORTING ME

"The Comforter . . . the Holy [Spirit] . . ."

As Jesus prepared to leave the earth, He began to reveal to His disciples more about the personal nature and work of the Holy Spirit.

Today, we have the benefit of an amplified meaning of the one whom Jesus said would come in His place. Seven characteristic works of the Divine Comforter are implied in this text. Jesus said, "I will ask the Father, and He will give you another Comforter (Counselor, Helper, Intercessor, Advocate, Strengthener, and Standby), that He may remain with you forever" (John 14:16, AMPLIFIED).

The Greek word for *comforter* is *parakletos,* which means one called alongside for help or counsel. Jesus promised that whatever "help" we may need, the Holy Spirit is able to supply.

"My God shall supply all your need according to His riches in glory by Christ Jesus" (Philippians 4:19, NKJV).

The Holy Spirit is a Person. Often He is divested of His personal characteristics because we think of a spirit as a mystical, abstract identity. But Jesus describes the Holy Spirit as another member of the Godhead, just like Himself and the Father. That is why Jesus could tell His disciples, "I will not abandon you or leave you as orphans in the storm—I will come to you. In just a little while I will be gone from the world, but I will still be present with you" (John 14:18–19, TLB).

Jesus Himself would be with them always in the Person of the Holy Spirit. When He said He would not leave them orphans, Jesus meant He would be their Helper in heaven, and the Holy Spirit would be their Helper, or Comforter, on earth.

The disciples did not grasp the importance of Christ's going—let alone the Comforter's coming. They became confused and sorrowful. Again, Jesus comforted them. "I tell you the truth. It is to your advantage that I go away; for if I do not go away, the Helper [Comforter] will not come to you; but if I depart, I will send Him to you" (John 16:7, NKJV).

The Holy Spirit *could not come* until Jesus returned to His Father in heaven. The Spirit would remain with Jesus until Jesus and His Father released Him to comfort the Church on earth.

This comforting work of the Holy Spirit is made possible because of the finished work of Jesus Christ, God's Lamb and Baptizer. Now we can forever say, "Blessed be the God and Father of our Lord Jesus Christ, the Father of mercies and God of all comfort, who comforts us in all our tribulation, that we may be able to comfort those who are in any trouble, with the comfort with which we ourselves are comforted by God" (2 Corinthians 1:3–5, NKJV).

God of all comfort,
thank You for not only speaking comfort
to me, but for being comfort
to me always.

47
TESTIFYING THROUGH ME

"The Holy [Spirit] shall teach you . . . what ye ought to say."
LUKE 12:12

*J*esus knew how badly the disciples would be treated after He was gone. They would be hated of all nations for His name's sake. Persecuted. Martyred. Like sheep in the midst of wolves, their lives would be in constant danger from those who knew not the Father, nor His precious Son.

Having loved His disciples to the very end, Jesus now comforted them. To prepare them for things to come, He told them of another work of the Holy Spirit: Instant teaching. Instant testimonies. Instant help. Jesus said, "When they bring you to the synagogues and magistrates and authorities, do not worry about how or what you should answer, or what you should say. For the Holy Spirit will teach you in that very hour what you ought to say" (Luke 12:11–12, NKJV). He added, "It will turn out for you as an occasion for testimony. Therefore settle it in your hearts not to meditate beforehand on what you will answer; for I will give you a mouth and wisdom which all your adversaries will not be able to contradict or resist" (Luke 21:13–15, NKJV).

Jesus was emphatic. No anxiety. No premeditation. No human reasoning necessary in advance, "for it is not you who speak, but the Holy Spirit" (Mark 13:11, NKJV).

The council of the Godhead would enter into these crises. Everything the believers needed would be provided as they spoke to convict the hearers.

Peter and John found this promise to be true after Pentecost. The Sanhedrin had them arrested for healing the lame man and preaching the resurrection of Christ. They were brought before the council of Jewish leaders, who questioned their authority to heal. Then Peter, being filled with the Holy Spirit, gave his first testimony crediting the power and authority of Jesus Christ. He declared: "Let it be known to you all, and to all the people of Israel, that by the name of Jesus Christ of Nazareth, whom you crucified, whom God raised from the dead, by Him this man stands here before you whole" (Acts 4:10, NKJV).

When the council saw the boldness of Peter and John and heard them speak, they realized what Jesus had done for them. It was such a threat to their own authority that they warned them never to speak or teach in the name of Jesus again.

But the apostles obeyed God rather than men. Their instructions from Jesus had been to carry the Gospel to the uttermost parts of the earth.

The instant testimonies given by the Holy Spirit were not limited to just the apostles. Stephen, one of the first deacons, delivered a powerful rebuke to the religious leaders of his day. It is worth reading Acts 7 to understand the power of the Holy Spirit at work spontaneously. Stephen was so eloquent when he testified to the hostile Sanhedrin that his face shone like the face of an angel.

Holy Spirit,
have I ever thanked You for being with my mouth and
teaching me what to say? You give me
the words to speak in the hour I need them.

48
TEACHING ME

"The Holy [Spirit] . . . shall teach you all things."
JOHN 14:26

Jesus told the disciples the Holy Spirit would not only teach them *what* to say in the time of trouble, but He would continue to teach them *all* things. Like Jesus, the Holy Spirit is a Teacher.

Three *omnia* words describe the Holy Spirit's qualifications. He is omniscient, omnipresent and omnipotent. He knows *all* things, He is present everywhere at the same time (*all* present) and He has *all* power. Nothing is hidden from Him.

Scripture declares that "the Spirit searches all things, even the deep things of God. . . . No one knows the thoughts of God except the Spirit of God" (1 Corinthians 2:10–11, NIV). "Nothing in all creation is hidden from God's sight. Everything is uncovered and laid bare before the eyes of him to whom we must give account" (Hebrews 4:13, NIV).

Since there was not enough time in three and a half years for Jesus to teach those unlearned fishermen all they needed to know and understand about the kingdom of God, the Holy Spirit would be their private tutor.

Jesus explained that the whole Godhead was involved in their education. All those drawn by God come to Jesus and are taught by the Holy Spirit. "No one can come to Me unless the Father who sent Me draws him. . . . It is written in the prophets, 'And they shall all be taught by God.' Therefore everyone who has heard and learned from the Father comes to me" (John 6:44–45, NKJV).

Praise God, the Scripture cannot be broken! Are you one of those taught by God?

Welcome, holy Teacher.
I want to learn.
Make me teachable.

49

REMINDING ME

"The Holy [Spirit] . . . shall . . . bring all things to your remembrance."

JOHN 14:26

*J*esus promised the disciples that the Holy Spirit would remind them of everything He had said. This was essential for the early Church, which did not have the advantage of the written Word of God. But this work of the Holy Spirit was by no means limited to those days. Even with the many versions of Scriptures available today, printed in most languages, we continue to rely upon the Holy Spirit as our "remembrancer." He is the one who communicates the right word at the right time.

The struggles of the Israelites under Moses in the Old Testament remind us of how difficult it was to remember all God said. Moses warned the people over and over again to listen closely and obey each command so as not to forget God's word. But it was work to rehearse God's words all day long—to bind them upon their heads, to tie them on their fingers, to write them on the doorposts of their houses, to teach them diligently to their children whenever they sat in their house, or walked by the way, or laid down at night, or rose up in the morning.

Psalm 119 is the longest and most emphatic plea for remembering the whole counsel of God. Only two verses of the 176 (122 and 132) do not contain some reminder of God's law, His truth and faithfulness. The psalmist vows to remember and keep God's word, but with so much to remember, who of us would not forget something?

Jesus did not forget. He was always careful to remember what His Father told Him. He said, "I did not speak of my own accord, but the Father who sent me commanded me what to say and how to say it. I know that his command leads to eternal life. So whatever I say is just what the Father has told me to say" (John 12:49–50, NIV).

Now Jesus would enable the disciples to speak His words as the Holy Spirit "re-minded" them. The "Helper . . . whom the Father will send in My name . . . [will] bring to your remembrance all things that I said to you. . . . My peace I give to you. . . . Let not your heart be troubled, neither let it be afraid" (John 14:26–27, NKJV).

No wonder Jesus could leave them in peace. Prompted by the Holy Spirit, the disciples would recall everything Jesus said while He was with them. The Holy Spirit would be their personal *Remembrancer.*

When Jesus was no longer with them, Peter illustrated this work of the Holy Spirit. While preaching in the house of Cornelius, a Gentile, the Holy Spirit interrupted Peter with the same supernatural utterances from the Gentile hearers that Peter experienced in the Upper Room at Pentecost. To explain the meaning of all this, Peter "remembered what the Lord had said: 'John baptized with water, but you will be baptized with the Holy Spirit'" (Acts 11:16, NIV).

How important the Holy Spirit is to our memory! We would be forgetful without Him. Without His work we would be ineffectual witnesses, under continual condemnation and still in our sins. We would commit the same sin the children of Israel did by forgetting God.

The last command Jesus gave to His disciples before His death was to remember—remember His death until He comes.

If we do not remember His death, we forget our life.

If we do not remember His death, we forget our righteousness.

If we do not remember His death, we forget our hope of His coming.

If we do not remember His death, we have no covenant.

Spiritual memory is holy privilege, inspired and renewed moment by moment by the Holy Spirit to remind us of the living word hidden in our hearts.

Thank You, Holy Remembrancer,
for not allowing me to forget Your
wonderful words of life!

50
EVANGELISM

"He [the Holy Spirit] shall testify of me."
JOHN 15:26

*J*esus could not possibly bear witness to everything He wanted His disciples to know about Him in the short period of time He spent with them on earth. They could hardly deal with all that He had already said and done. "I still have many things to say to you [Jesus said], but you cannot bear [grasp] them now" (John 16:12, NKJV).

This was another reason Jesus sent the Holy Spirit, so the disciples could testify of what they had seen, heard and knew. Reassuring them, Jesus said, "The Holy Spirit . . . will tell you all about me. And you also must tell everyone about me, because you have been with me from the beginning" (John 15:26–27, TLB).

"He shall testify of me," Jesus said of the Holy Spirit, and cautioned the disciples to be wary of others, who would testify of themselves. He warned them, "If anyone tells you, 'The Messiah has arrived at such and such a place, or has appeared here or there,' don't believe it. For false Christs shall arise, and false prophets, and will do wonderful miracles, so that if it were possible, even God's chosen ones would be deceived. See, I have warned you" (Matthew 24:23–25, TLB).

Testifying of Jesus is a distinctive work of the Holy Spirit, which He is well qualified to do, for He has always been with Jesus. When Jesus spoke the Word, the Holy Spirit did the work. The Holy Spirit conceived Jesus. The Holy Spirit prepared a body for Him to dwell among us. Jesus was born of the Spirit, led by the Spirit, empowered by the Spirit, sustained by the Spirit, resurrected by the Spirit and escorted into glory by the Spirit.

Since the Holy Spirit continues to proclaim Jesus to us, our joy and fellowship with Him remains alive. We are eager to share it with others. John clearly stated this when he wrote the reason for his evangelizing: "We are telling you about what we ourselves have actually seen and heard, so that you may share the fellowship and the joys we have with the Father and with Jesus Christ his Son" (1 John 1:3, TLB).

Because of the witness of the Holy Spirit, we have the same reality of Jesus as those who walked with Him upon the earth. We know Him not in the flesh, but in the Spirit. That is why Jesus could say, "Be sure of this— that I am with you always, even to the end of the world" (Matthew 28:20, TLB).

Thank You, Chief Evangelist,
for continuing to bear witness to Jesus,
whom, having not seen, I love.

51

CONVICTING THE WORLD

"And when he [the Holy Spirit] is come, he will reprove the world of sin, and of righteousness, and of judgment."

JOHN 16:8

*U*p to this point, all of Jesus' teachings to the disciples about the Holy Spirit dealt with His comforting work on behalf of believers. This work was different, however. It was intended for those who had not yet believed in Jesus—those whom Jesus called "the world."

Jesus said when the Holy Spirit came, He would convict (reprove, convince) the world of three things: sin, righteousness and judgment—"of sin, because they do not believe in Me; of righteousness, because I go to My Father and you see Me no more; of judgment, because the ruler of this world is judged" (John 16:9–11, NKJV).

Jesus' coming into the world made possible a sin not possible before: the sin of denying Him as God's Son and Savior of the world.

What is the world's sin? In a word: *unbelief.* Jesus summed it up this way: "If I had not come and spoken to them, they would not be guilty of sin. Now, however, they have no excuse for their sin. He who hates me hates my Father as well. If I had not done among them what no one else did, they would not be guilty of sin. But now they have seen these miracles, and yet they have hated both me and my Father. But this is to fulfill what is written in their Law: 'They hated me without reason'" (John 15:22–25, NIV).

Jesus asked those of His day, "Whom do you say that I am?" Today, the Holy Spirit still asks us the same question. It is no longer a "sin" question but a "Son" question. The Holy Spirit makes sure everyone knows the difference.

The work of the Holy Spirit is to convince the world of Jesus' righteousness. The world had judged Jesus guilty of sin and put Him to death. They hated Him without a cause, but a holy God vindicated the Son He sent by receiving Him back—not guilty and alive. His grave is not found in the world today.

How do we know that all our sins, as well as the sins of the whole world, were not left upon Jesus when He died on the cross? How can we be sure that after Jesus rose from the dead and ascended into heaven, He was considered righteous by God and exalted to His right hand? A witness was sent from heaven to tell us: the Holy Spirit. Peter answered the Sadducees, who denied the resurrection, this way: "The God of our fathers raised up Jesus whom you murdered by hanging on a tree. Him God has exalted to His right hand to be Prince and Savior, to give repentance to Israel and forgiveness of sins. And we are His witnesses to these things, and so also is the Holy Spirit whom God has given to those who obey Him" (Acts 5:30–32, NKJV).

For those who believe Jesus, forgiveness is a fact of history as well as a conviction of the Holy Spirit. His witnesses today are *in* the world but not *of* the world.

Another work of the Holy Spirit is to convince the world of Satan's judgment. The Scriptures tell us the prince of this world is already judged. This is not a *future* judgment but a *past* judgment. Satan has been judged and the sentence written in the Book.

When was Satan judged?

1. In the beginning when God passed judgment on him.
   "I will put enmity between you and the woman, and between your seed and her Seed [Christ]; He shall bruise your head, and you shall bruise His heel" (Genesis 3:15, NKJV).
2. On the cross when Jesus defeated him.
   "He became flesh and blood too by being born in human form; for only as a human being could he die and in dying break the power of the devil who had the power of death" (Hebrews 2:14, TLB).
3. In the future by an angel who will
   "cast him into the bottomless pit, and shut him up, and set a seal on him, so that he should deceive the nations no more till the thousand years were finished" (Revelation 20:3, NKJV).
4. God's last judgment when fire comes down from heaven.
   "The devil, who deceived them, was cast into the lake of fire and brimstone where the beast and the false prophet are. And they will be tormented day and night forever and ever" (Revelation 20:10, NKJV).

Although Satan's final destination is still future, the Holy Spirit works to convince the world that he has already been judged and his doom is sure, lest they be deceived. Satan, the god of this world, does not want anyone to know he is a loser, for then he would forfeit his control.

Just as God was in Christ reconciling the world to Himself, so is He at work through the Holy Spirit reconciling the world to Himself.

Faithful Holy Spirit, sent from heaven,
don't take no for an answer.
The world needs Your undeniable conviction.

52
GUIDING US TO TRUTH

"When he, the Spirit of truth, is come, he will guide you into all truth."

JOHN 16:13

*A*ll truth has one source: the Godhead. Truth is a living entity, a Person. The Person is Jesus Christ, who came to earth "full of grace and full of truth."

An exchange of divine Persons was coming. Jesus was going away, but His truth would remain. The Holy Spirit would be Jesus' agent and the personal representative of the Godhead on earth. His work would channel truth into earthen vessels.

In describing the Holy Spirit to His disciples, three times Jesus called the Holy Spirit the Spirit of truth, saying, "I will ask the Father, and he will give you another Counselor to be with you forever—the Spirit of truth" (John 14:16–17, NIV). He promised His disciples that "when the Helper comes . . . the Spirit of truth . . . He will testify of Me" (John 15:26, NKJV). And "when . . . the Spirit of Truth (the truth-giving Spirit) comes, He will guide you into all the truth—the whole, full truth" (John 16:13, AMPLIFIED).

Yes, the changeover would be easy, for the "Spirit of truth" would be with the disciples to counsel them and show them the way into *all* truth.

"What exactly is truth?" Pilate had asked Jesus. And although Jesus never told him, He did tell His disciples. How many people would define truth as Jesus did when He prayed about His disciples to the Father? "Sanctify them—purify, consecrate, separate them for Yourself, make them—holy by the Truth. Your Word is Truth" (John 17:17, AMPLIFIED).

What is truth? God's Word. And Jesus is the Word. The Holy Spirit is the Spirit of Jesus, the Word of truth. He is the one behind the Word, who inspires the Word of truth, breathes forth the Word of truth and rightly divides the Word of truth to the hearers.

The Holy Spirit is the conveyor through whom truth flows into all believers. Holy men and women of God still communicate the same truths in the same way from the same Spirit: written and spoken and dramatized for all to read, hear and understand. Why? So that God might have a people made holy by the truth for His inheritance.

Jesus made Himself holy with truth so that He might make us holy by the same truth. But not everyone is eligible for this privilege. He limited the truth with an "if" by declaring, "If ye continue in my word, then are ye my disciples indeed; and ye shall know the truth, and the truth shall make you free" (John 8:31–32).

The Spirit of truth is God's last offer to receive the love of the truth. Refusing to believe the Holy Spirit is to make God a liar. The Holy Spirit cannot be bypassed without suffering the consequences. There is no neutral ground. No purgatory.

The world does not have liberating truth, for Jesus is not of this world. Neither is God's truth found in the knowledge of good and evil in the world. The Spirit of truth cannot be bought with money, as Simon the sorcerer discovered (Acts 8:18–24). To have truth, you must have Him. That is what Jesus meant when He told His followers that "the Holy Spirit [is] the Spirit who leads into all truth. The world . . . cannot receive him, for it isn't looking for him and doesn't recognize him. But you do, for he lives with you now and some day shall be in you" (John 14:17, TLB).

The importance of this work of the Holy Spirit cannot be overemphasized. It all boils down to two awesome facts: no Holy Spirit, no truth. No truth, the devil wins.

Guide me, O Thou Truth-giving Spirit,
—pilgrim through this barren land.

53
REVEALING THINGS TO COME

"And he [the Holy Spirit] will shew you things to come."
JOHN 16:13

Much of the Holy Spirit's work in guiding us into all truth deals with showing us "things to come." Jesus had already begun this ministry with the men from Galilee whom He called His friends. He said, "You are my friends if you obey me. I no longer call you slaves, for a master doesn't confide in his slaves; now you are my friends, proved by the fact that I have told you everything the Father told me" (John 15:14–15, TLB).

To be God's friend and know "things to come" demands an obedient relationship with Him. Abraham was the first friend of God listed in the Bible. Because Abraham obeyed God, the Father shared with him His future plans for the destruction of Sodom and Gomorrah.

Moses, too, obeyed God. He had the distinction of being a friend of God with whom the Almighty spoke face to face (see Exodus 33:11). God showed Moses His glory, which we have yet to see.

Joseph, filled with the Spirit of God, revealed to Pharaoh what his dreams signified for the next fourteen years. He saved a whole generation from famine and preserved the seed of Israel.

Daniel, greatly loved by God, interpreted King Nebuchadnezzar's dreams and predicted the whole course of world history in advance. It is still unfolding today.

Jesus' ministry was filled with the knowledge of things to come. Especially when He taught about what the kingdom of heaven was like and what would happen after He was gone. For example, He said not one stone of the Temple would be left standing upon another.

The conclusion is clearly stated by the psalmist. "Friendship with God is reserved for those who reverence him. With them alone he shares the secrets of his promises" (Psalm 25:14, TLB).

While it is true that secret things belong to the Lord, nevertheless "those things which are revealed belong to us and to our children forever" (Deuteronomy 29:29, NKJV).

How else could mere men see, hear or know the things God has planned for those who love Him, if not for this work of the Holy Spirit? It would be impossible if God had not "sent his Spirit to tell us. . . . his Spirit searches out and shows us all of God's deepest secrets" (1 Corinthians 2:10, TLB).

How privileged we are to know the deep things of God. No guesswork. No psychic friends necessary. No disappointments. No broken promises. We can know the destiny of God's friends and His enemies, for the Holy Spirit "will be passing on . . . what he has heard. He will tell you about the future" (John 16:13, TLB).

The apostle Paul used two favorite phrases when he introduced "things to come" to his brethren: "Behold, I show you a mystery" and "I would not have you ignorant." Yet even with these many revelations, some choose to remain ignorant of God's future plans and the Second Coming of the Messiah.

Peter recorded that "in the last days there will come scoffers who will do every wrong they can think of, and laugh at the truth. This will be their line of argument: 'So Jesus promised to come back, did he? Then where is he? He'll never come! Why, as far back as anyone can remember everything has remained exactly as it was since the first day of creation'" (2 Peter 3:3–4, TLB).

These scoffers ignore the fact that God destroyed the world in judgment before—and at His Second Coming He will do it again. How can we be sure of this? Read the Revelation of Jesus Christ. Blessed are they who read, hear and heed those things that are written there, for the time is at hand!

Spirit of revelation,
thank You for Your friendship
and for showing me things to come,
especially Jesus.

54

GLORIFYING JESUS

"He [the Holy Spirit] shall glorify me. . . ."
JOHN 16:14

The Holy Spirit is the source of divine revelation about Jesus, for who would better know the Christ? All Jesus *is*, all Jesus *has* and all Jesus *does* the Spirit delights to share with us.

Jesus explained how the Holy Spirit would do this: "He [the Holy Spirit] shall praise me and bring me great honor by showing you my glory. All the Father's glory is mine; this is what I mean when I say that he will show you my glory" (John 16:14–15, TLB). In other words, the Holy Spirit glorifies Jesus by showing us the riches of the Godhead. Knowing Christ's perfection of beauty results in true worship and praise as we glorify His holy name.

An example of this occurred in King Solomon's day. The Queen of Sheba, overwhelmed with curiosity about the glory of Solomon's kingdom, determined to know for herself about his fame. She traveled to Jerusalem to seek his wisdom. And when she began to fully comprehend Solomon's earthly glory, she confessed to the king, "I didn't believe it until I came [and saw your glory], but now I have seen it for myself! And really! The half had not been told me! Your wisdom and prosperity are far greater than anything I've ever heard of! Your people are happy and your palace aides are content—but how could it be otherwise, for they stand here day after day listening to your wisdom" (1 Kings 10:7–8, TLB).

Solomon was generous. He shared with the queen some of his glory. He "gave to the queen of Sheba all she wanted, whatever she asked, besides his gifts to her from his royal bounty" (1 Kings 10:13, AMPLIFIED).

She returned to her own country richer and wiser. But note that Solomon did not give the queen *all* he had.

In contrast, Jesus came to earth full of His Father's glory and offered it all to us, as well as Himself. Everything He is and everything He has is ours. How can this be? This is a secret, "kept . . . for centuries and generations past, but now at last it has pleased him to tell it to those who love him and live for him . . . the secret: *that Christ in your hearts is your only hope of glory*" (Colossians 1:26–27, TLB).

Yes, one greater than Solomon has come. How else could we have waited expectantly down through the ages without this "hope of glory" in our midst—without that revelation of Jesus Christ high and lifted up? That hope of glory in us purifies us. It anchors our soul to the Father behind the veil. Our every need is supplied from His riches in glory. We are strengthened with might in the inner man as the knowledge of His glory keeps changing us so "we can be mirrors that brightly reflect the glory of the Lord. And as the Spirit of the Lord works within us, we become more and more like him" (2 Corinthians 3:18, TLB).

To know the glorified Christ is to have a foretaste of glory divine. Only God's Holy Spirit reveals Jesus as Lord, exalted to the right hand of the Father. God forbid that we should refuse this mighty work of the Spirit, "for it is impossible for those who were once enlightened, and have tasted the heavenly gift, and have become partakers of the Holy Spirit, and have tasted the good word of God and the powers of the age to come, if they fall away, to renew them again to repentance" (Hebrews 6:4–5, NKJV).

Have I ever thanked You
for glorifying Jesus, Holy Spirit?
The things of earth do grow strangely dim
in the light of His glory and grace.

55
WARNING AGAINST BLASPHEMY

"Blasphemy against the Holy [Spirit] shall not be forgiven."
MATTHEW 12:31

According to Scripture, there is only one unpardonable sin: blaspheming the Holy Spirit. How is that done? Jesus explained it when He warned the scribes and Pharisees they were moving in that direction. When they could not deny that Jesus had cast out demons, they said He was demon-possessed. "His trouble is that he's possessed by Satan, king of demons. That's why demons obey him. . . . He did his miracles by Satan's power [instead of acknowledging it was by the Holy Spirit's power]" (Mark 3:22, 30, TLB).

We blaspheme the Holy Spirit by saying His work is done by Satan. When the Pharisees accused Jesus of using Satan's power to cast out demons they not only denied Christ's authority but discredited the Holy Spirit through whom Jesus had cast them out. In other words, they made the unholy spirit more powerful than the Holy Spirit and called the Spirit of God in Jesus demonic.

Because Jesus had not yet finished His work on earth as the Son of God, some people doubted His word or even blasphemed Him. But He willingly forgave them on the cross and asked His Father to forgive them also, saying, "Father, forgive these people . . . for they don't know what they are doing" (Luke 23:34, TLB).

Today, we *do* know what we are doing. We have the opportunity to correct our unbelief and mistakes. Jesus prayed for us and sent the Holy Spirit from heaven. The historical facts are in, and the Holy Spirit came to verify the work of Jesus a second time. We have double proof of His deity; there will not be another.

Since slandering the Holy Spirit is a spoken sin of intentional malice, Jesus warns that this sin is eternal, saying that "speaking against the Holy Spirit shall never be forgiven, either in this world or in the world to come" (Matthew 12:32, TLB).

The serpent would subtly question, "Has God really said there is an unpardonable sin?" To which the Word of God emphatically replies, yes,

125

there is "that one fatal sin . . . which ends in death and if he has done that, there is no use praying for him" (1 John 5:16, TLB).

The good news is God is not willing that we should perish and has done something about it.

Bless You, Spirit of God.
You keep me from falling and are able
to present me faultless before
the throne of grace.

56
POWER

"Baptized with the Holy [Spirit] . . . ye shall receive power."

ACTS 1:5, 8

Jesus' last teaching to the disciples was about the coming of the Holy Spirit and how it would transform their lives. He promised, "I will send the Holy Spirit upon you, just as my Father promised. . . . Stay here in the city until the Holy Spirit comes and fills you with power from heaven" (Luke 24:49, TLB).

Jesus called the Holy Spirit "the promise of my Father" and stated that His purpose in coming was to *fill* them with "power from heaven." On resurrection evening, Jesus gave them a foretaste of the Holy Spirit when they received His holy breath. But as the Baptizer, Jesus had not immersed them with the Holy Spirit and fire yet, for it was not the right time.

Jesus reminded the disciples there were two baptisms—the first one with John the Baptist and the other yet to come. "John baptized you with water . . . but you shall be baptized with the Holy Spirit in just a few days" (Acts 1:5, TLB). And "when the Holy Spirit has come upon you, you will receive power to testify about me with great effect . . . about my death and resurrection" (Acts 1:8, TLB).

After He spoke these things, Jesus rose into the sky and disappeared into a cloud, leaving the disciples staring after Him. It happened so suddenly that two angels appeared to tell them to go home. Returning to Jerusalem from the Mount of Olives, the disciples waited in the Upper Room as Jesus had instructed them. They continued to worship and pray there for several days. Meanwhile, their numbers increased to 120 people. They also took care of some unfinished business: Judas had committed suicide, and they needed someone to take his place, one who had witnessed Jesus' baptism by John and His death, burial and resurrection. Peter reminded them, "King David's prediction of this appears in the Book of Psalms. . . . 'Let his home become desolate with no one living in it . . . and . . . let his work be given to someone else to do'" (Acts 1:20, TLB).

Nine long days had passed since Jesus left them.
Tomorrow—Pentecost Sunday!

O Father,
how we praise You for Your promise
of joy, which comes in the morning!

4

THE HOLY SPIRIT
IN THE CHURCH

57

PENTECOST

And they were all filled with the Holy [Spirit], and began to speak with other tongues, as the Spirit gave them utterance.

ACTS 2:4

*P*entecost! Nine o'clock Sunday morning.

Suddenly, everything was different. A loud noise from heaven and a roaring, rushing windstorm invaded the house where the believers waited in Jerusalem. And something that looked like flames or tongues of fire came to rest upon their heads. At the same time they all began to speak noisily, uttering languages they did not know.

What had happened to them? The Father's promise had arrived. Jesus the Baptizer—baptized! The Holy Spirit came in such power they knew their time of waiting was over.

Scripture records the earthly events like this: They "were all filled—diffused throughout their souls—with the Holy Spirit and began to speak in other (different, foreign) languages, as the Spirit kept giving them clear and loud expression in each tongue in appropriate words" (Acts 2:4, AMPLIFIED).

Two things happened simultaneously. They spoke; He uttered. The Holy Spirit used their mouths to speak in unknown tongues. This was something unique, absolutely unheard of before. They did not speak in tongues to obtain the Holy Spirit, they spoke in tongues because they received the Holy Spirit.

"Utterance" in the Greek language means to declare, say, speak forth, enunciate plainly, to say much in a few words full of meaning. Yes, this new language came by the Holy Spirit, but what in the world were those uneducated Galileans saying that was so important?

The multitudes of foreigners gathered in Jerusalem to celebrate the Feast of Pentecost made this observation: "We all hear them speaking in our own native tongues [and telling of] the mighty works of God!" (Acts 2:11, AMPLIFIED).

Still, they wondered how this could be. Perhaps they were drunk. This Peter refuted, saying, "Ye men of Judaea, and all ye that dwell at Jerusalem, be this known unto you, and hearken to my words: For these are not drunken, as ye suppose, seeing it is but the third hour of the day. But this is that which was spoken by the prophet Joel; and it shall come to pass in the last days, saith God, I will pour out of my Spirit upon all flesh" (Acts 2:14–17).

Pentecost was the ordained time for them to receive the gift of the Holy Spirit. The out-poured Spirit had come. And His coming ushered into being the "last days."

The holy breath Jesus breathed *into* the disciples on resurrection Sunday evening now came *out* of them. The Spirit, as rivers of living water, flowed from their innermost beings just as Jesus had said: "Whoever believes in me, as the Scripture has said, streams of living water will flow from within him" (John 7:38, NIV).

Peter told the crowds what happened to Jesus "in heavenly places" in order to make this day possible. "God has raised this Jesus to life, and we are all witnesses of the fact. Exalted to the right hand of God, he has received from the Father the promised Holy Spirit and has poured out what you now see and hear" (Acts 2:32–33, NIV).

All three Persons of the Godhead are represented in this out-pouring. God the Father, along with the glorified Son, released the Holy Spirit from heaven, who came and filled the waiting 120 believers. Now they could pass it on. They could baptize in the name of the Father, the Son and the Holy Spirit as Jesus had commanded them to do.

What did it all mean? It meant:

- the resurrected Christ was now glorified, and the disciples never again wondered where Jesus was.
- that God had accepted the blood of the covenant, made with Jesus' blood, and a New Covenant of Spirit was in effect.
- the Spirit of God was a gift to all generations born of the Spirit by receiving Jesus.
- the Holy Spirit now resided on earth to make ready the Body of Christ— taken from every race, kindred, tribe and nation.
- the tongue of the natural man, set on fire by hell, was replaced by the tongue of the spiritual man, set on fire from heaven.
- a reversal of the confusion of tongues at the tower of Babel (see Genesis 11:9), with the spiritual tongue of the redeemed in Jerusalem.

- the disciples were now *apostles.*
- the Holy Spirit had an earthly temple.

We are still discovering the fullness of the Holy Spirit's work on our behalf as the power of His presence manifests through vessels of clay.

Under the old covenant, the priests celebrated the Feast of Pentecost by waving before the Lord two loaves baked with leaven, made from the firstfruits of the newly ripened wheat (see Leviticus 23:15–22).

When something is ripe, it is fully developed. It is ready to be used. It is in season. This account in the Old Testament agrees with the second chapter of Acts. Those filled that day with the Holy Spirit were fully ripe—mature. The harvest of three thousand souls waved before the Lord became the firstfruit of a new creation empowered by the Holy Spirit. These living creatures came to be called the *Church,* the Body of Christ.

Holy Spirit,
I greet You and welcome
Your power to utter the
wonderful works of God
to the children of men.

58
BOLDNESS

*They were all filled with the Holy [Spirit], and they spake the word
of God with boldness.*

ACTS 4:31

he coming of the Holy Spirit to fill the disciples made an
immediate difference in their lives. Only a few weeks
before Pentecost, they were doubting, questioning, denying their Master and running for their lives. After Pentecost, they were just the opposite: believing, knowledgeable, bold in their
witness of the Messiah's resurrection and unafraid.

The change showed up first in Peter as he preached his first sermon and
answered the questions of the multitudes concerning the strange happen-
ings in Jerusalem. He laid the blame on that generation for crucifying the
Messiah. He told them what they must do to get right with God, saying,
"Repent, and be baptized every one of you in the name of Jesus Christ for
the remission of sins, and ye shall receive the gift of the Holy [Spirit]. For
the promise is unto you, and to your children, and to all that are afar off,
even as many as the Lord our God shall call" (Acts 2:38–39).

Three thousand people received Peter's exhortation gladly, and they
were baptized the same day.

A holy fear came upon everyone, as the apostles performed many signs
and wonders. Peter and John spoke healing to a lame man in the name of
Jesus, and the man rose up and walked.

The miracle gave Peter another opportunity to admonish the people as
he reminded them again that they had asked for a murderer to be released
and Jesus killed. This time Peter said, "Now, brothers, I know that you
acted in ignorance, as did your leaders. But this is how God fulfilled what
he had foretold through all the prophets, saying that his Christ would suffer. Repent, then, and turn to God, so that your sins may be wiped out,
that times of refreshing may come from the Lord" (Acts 3:17–19, NIV).

The people received Peter's preaching, but, as with Jesus, the religious
leaders grew angry. They particularly hated the apostles confirming that
Jesus had risen from the dead. Therefore, to stop the multiplying of the

Church, the Sanhedrin jailed Peter and John. Even so, the number of believers grew to five thousand.

When Peter and John were brought before the council of Jewish leaders in Jerusalem, they questioned who had given them the authority to heal the lame man. Once more, Peter, filled with the Holy Spirit, boldly told the truth concerning Jesus' death saying, "Let me clearly state to you and to all the people of Israel that it was done in the name and power of Jesus from Nazareth, the Messiah, the man you crucified—but God raised back to life again. It is by his authority that this man stands here healed!" (Acts 4:10, TLB).

The Holy Spirit was not only teaching Peter and John *what* to say (Luke 12:12), but *how* to say it. Hearing the apostles' authority and seeing the evidence of the lame man's healing, the council members did not know what to do with them. They warned them, however, to speak no more or teach in the name of Jesus. And after further threatening, they let them go.

Reporting back to the disciples, Peter and John told them all that had happened. They prayed together for boldness as they remembered what David had prophesied of their day: "Why do the nations conspire and the people plot in vain? The kings of the earth take their stand and the rulers gather together against the Lord and against his Anointed One" (Acts 4:25–26, NIV; Psalm 2:1–2, NIV).

Persecution was on the way for them just as it had been for Jesus. And they knew it. But the power of the Holy Spirit at work in them gave them boldness to withstand the enemies of the Gospel. Supernatural boldness— to speak and do the work assigned to the Church. And who is "the Church"? As many as the Lord our God shall call.

And so it has been recorded to encourage us, that "when they had prayed, the place in which they were assembled was shaken; and they were all filled with the Holy Spirit, and they continued to speak the Word of God with freedom and boldness and courage" (Acts 4:31, AMPLIFIED).

Holy Spirit,
thank You for Your boldness to do
the greater works, in Jesus' name.

59

DEMANDING TRUTH

"Why hath Satan filled thine heart to lie to the Holy [Spirit], and . . . tempt the Spirit of the Lord?"

ACTS 5:3, 9

After Pentecost, the Church held everything in common. The believers shared with one another by selling their possessions and giving the money to the apostles. The apostles, in turn, gave to everyone as he had need.

That is, until Ananias and Sapphira sold some property and privately agreed to keep back a portion of the money for themselves. When Ananias brought the money to Peter, the apostle rebuked him, saying, "Why hath Satan filled thine heart to lie to the Holy [Spirit], and to keep back part of the price of the land? . . . Why hast thou conceived this thing in thine heart? thou hast not lied unto men, but unto God" (Acts 5:3–4).

As Ananias heard these words, he died; the young men present buried him. Fear came upon all who learned what had transpired.

Soon Sapphira came in, not knowing what had happened to her husband. Peter questioned her also. "Tell me whether ye sold the land for so much? And she said, Yea, for so much. Then Peter said unto her, How is it that ye have agreed together to tempt the Spirit of the Lord? behold, the feet of them which have buried thy husband are at the door, and shall carry thee out" (Acts 5:8–9).

Sapphira died immediately and was buried beside her husband. Great terror spread throughout the whole church.

The warning given to Ananias and Sapphira are reminiscent of what happened in the Garden of Eden. Just as Satan tempted the first man and woman with wisdom, he tempted those in the first Church with wealth.

Is lying to the Holy Spirit the chief sin of believers today? Men might lie to other men. But it is not possible to lie to the Holy Spirit, even though Satan tempts us to try. The Holy Spirit is the Spirit of truth (John 16:13). He is omniscient. He is able to discern our motives. The psalmist speaks about the situation this way: "They say, 'The Lord does not see; the God of Jacob pays no heed.' Take heed, you senseless ones among the people;

you fools, when will you become wise? Does he who implanted the ear not hear? Does he who formed the eye not see? Does he who disciplines nations not punish? Does he who teaches man lack knowledge? The LORD knows the thoughts of man; he knows that they are futile" (Psalm 94:7–11, NIV).

Thus, the record of Ananias and Sapphira in Acts 5 tells us several things about our relationship to the Holy Spirit. It gives insight into His personal nature as truth and how we, at times, sin by trying to deceive Him. When we lie to men, we also lie to the Holy Spirit. We test the Spirit of the Lord.

This is a work for which *we* are held accountable.

O, Holy Spirit,
Satan would lead us into temptation.
Deliver us from this evil one.

60

SPIRITING US AWAY

The Spirit of the Lord caught away Philip. . . .
ACTS 8:39

s the number of believers who shared everything in common multiplied, an administration problem arose. It concerned the daily task of distributing food. The apostles called a meeting of the assembly to deal with the situation, and they stated their case. "We should spend our time preaching, not administering a feeding program" (Acts 6:2, TLB).

They agreed to select seven men to care for this matter who met the following requirements: They were to be wise, full of the Holy Spirit and well thought of by everyone.

Of the seven deacons selected by the apostles, Philip and Stephen are remembered the most. Philip is the only evangelist mentioned by name in Scripture, and Stephen was the first martyr to die for his faith in Jesus.

A great anointing fell on the deacons as well as the apostles. It is recorded that Stephen did spectacular miracles among the people by the power of the Holy Spirit. This angered the Jewish leaders who used lying witnesses to convict him. And because they could not resist the Spirit by whom Stephen spoke the truth about them, he was stoned by an angry mob who laid their clothes at the feet of Saul: the next persecutor of the Church.

This erupting persecution in Jerusalem served a dual purpose. It scattered the believers throughout the regions of Judea and Samaria, and it scattered the Gospel.

Philip fled to Samaria where he preached the Good News about Jesus. As he spoke, revival broke out there. Evil spirits were cast out of people, and many who were paralyzed and lame got healed miraculously. This brought much joy to the whole city, resulting in the baptism in water of many who believed in Jesus.

The angel of the Lord directed Philip to go south from Samaria to the desert of Gaza. There he met the treasurer of Ethiopia, a eunuch of great authority under Queen Candace, and explained to him a Scripture that he could not understand. Philip assured him that the passage he was reading from Isaiah referred to Jesus, who had already come. Immediately, believing that Jesus Christ was God's Son—the lamb led to the slaughter—he asked Philip to baptize him. "And when they were come up out of the water, the Spirit of the Lord caught away Philip, that the eunuch saw him no more: and he went on his way rejoicing. But Philip was found at Azotus" (Acts 8:39–40). Thus, Philip spread the Gospel through Africa.

The Holy Spirit in Scripture is often called the Spirit of the Lord. His work in suddenly "catching away" Philip to Azotus thirty miles to the north is the same work of supernatural transport experienced by Elijah in the Old Testament (see 2 Kings 2).

Paul also described a similar experience when he wrote, "I know a man in Christ who fourteen years ago was caught up to the third heaven . . . to paradise" (2 Corinthians 12:2, 4, NIV).

Being "caught up" or transported by the power of the Holy Spirit is perhaps unknown to many today. Yet to the Christian, this is our blessed hope in the near future. "For the Lord himself will come down from heaven, with a loud command, with the voice of the archangel and with the trumpet call of God, and the dead in Christ will rise first. After that, we who are still alive and are left will be caught up together with them in the clouds to meet the Lord in the air. And so we will be with the Lord forever" (1 Thessalonians 4:16–17, NIV).

Yes, God, the Holy Spirit, is the same yesterday, today and forever. The old song of Fanny Crosby still rings true. "When clothed in His brightness, transported I rise to meet Him in clouds of the sky, His perfect salvation, His wonderful love, I'll shout with the millions on high."

Spirit of the Lord,
I'm shouting already!
I know You will come to snatch us away.
We encourage ourselves with
these promises, until You do.

61

FALLING UPON US

The Holy [Spirit] fell on all.
ACTS 10:44

*A*mong the last instructions given the apostles by Jesus was the command to preach the Gospel to *all* nations. Until this time, the Gospel had been *of* the Jews, *by* the Jews and *for* the Jews. All nations now included Gentiles.

Peter was the first to break this tradition, even though initially he did not understand what he was doing.

In a vision, repeated three times, God instructed Peter not to call unclean or common what the Lord had cleansed. As Peter "was puzzling over the vision, the Holy Spirit said to him, 'Three men have come to see you. Go down and meet them and go with them. All is well, I have sent them'" (Acts 10:19–20, TLB).

Peter did as he was told and arrived at the house of Cornelius. Greeting him, Peter said, "You know it is against the Jewish laws for me to come into a Gentile home like this. But God has shown me in a vision that I should never think of anyone as inferior. So I came as soon as I was sent for. Now tell me what you want" (Acts 10:28, TLB).

Cornelius assured Peter that all those present in his house were waiting to hear what the Lord had to tell them. As Peter began to preach Christ to them, "the Holy Spirit fell upon all those listening! The Jews who came with Peter were amazed that the gift of the Holy Spirit would be given to Gentiles too! But there could be no doubt about it, for they heard them speaking in tongues and praising God" (Acts 10:44–47, TLB).

Peter then baptized Cornelius and his household with water in the name of the Lord. Why not; they had already been baptized with the Holy Spirit.

Notice Scripture's use of the terms *fell upon, come upon* and *baptize* to denote the Holy Spirit's presence. These appropriately describe the ever-present actions of the Holy Spirit, which still may be associated with a divine utterance in other tongues or prophesying.

When the news of the Gentiles' baptism reached the brothers in Judea, Peter had more explaining to do. They were already upset with him because he visited the Gentiles and had eaten with them. Such a thing was not allowed. So Peter defended himself. "The Holy Spirit told me to go with them and not to worry about their being Gentiles!" (Acts 11:12, TLB). And when "I began telling them the Good News . . . the Holy Spirit fell on them, just as he fell on us at the beginning! Then I thought of the Lord's words when he said, 'Yes, John baptized with water, but you shall be baptized with the Holy Spirit.' And since it was God who gave these Gentiles the same gift he gave us when we believed on the Lord Jesus Christ, who was I to argue?" (Acts 11:15–17, TLB).

Why argue? God had granted repentance to the Gentiles without even asking their permission. He had given them the gift of the Holy Spirit too, just as He did the Jews at Pentecost.

God was no respecter of persons. With this action, He had declared the Gentiles kosher. Nothing would stop the Holy Spirit. Faith in Jesus Christ was enough.

God had visited the Gentiles as He had promised: "to take out of them a people for his name" (Acts 15:14).

You didn't forget the rest of us, Father.
Holy Spirit, You fall upon
everyone who takes Jesus' name.

62
ORDAINING

They . . . sent forth by the Holy [Spirit]. . . .

ACTS 13:4

*T*he Holy Spirit ordained Saul, the chief persecutor of the Church, to be the chief apostle to the Church.

The story of Saul's persecution and hatred for the disciples of the Lord is well known historically. So is his conversion to Christ.

While on the road to Damascus, Jesus revealed Himself personally to Saul and asked him this haunting question: "'Saul, Saul, why do you persecute me?' 'Who are you, Lord?' Saul asked. 'I am Jesus, whom you are persecuting,' he replied" (Acts 9:4–5, NIV).

Through this divine encounter, Saul was converted, baptized and filled with the Holy Spirit. He was ready to be used.

He began to speak out boldly in the synagogues of Damascus that Christ was indeed the Messiah. And so Saul, himself, became such an enemy of established Jewry that they sought to kill him. He literally had to run for his life.

Back in Jerusalem, Saul attempted to associate himself with the disciples there, but they did not trust him either. They were afraid of him, having heard how he terrorized the saints in Jerusalem.

Barnabas came to Saul's rescue by speaking well of him. Barnabas was the one who sold his goods and laid them at the apostles' feet in Jerusalem. Scripture records that Barnabas "was a good man, and full of the Holy [Spirit] and of faith" (Acts 11:24).

Saul made Antioch his headquarters, however, being more accepted there. It had become the center of Gentile Christianity. So much so that the disciples were first named "Christians" there.

Having been a Christian for more than twelve years, Saul (whose name was changed to Paul) became a leader in the Antioch church. One day at a meeting of certain prophets and teachers in the local church, "they were worshiping the Lord and fasting, [when] the Holy Spirit said, 'Set apart for me Barnabas and Saul for the work to which I have called them'" (Acts 13:2, NIV).

The Holy Spirit had spoken in the first person as God. He had chosen the people, the time, the work and the destination. The Church is not run by the cunning of men, nor by Satan and his hosts, but by the power and authority of God, the Holy Spirit.

When He spoke, the leaders obeyed. And after a time of prayer and fasting, they placed their hands on Paul and Barnabas and sent them off. "The two of them, sent on their way by the Holy Spirit, went down to Seleucia and sailed from there to Cyprus" (Acts 13:4, NIV).

The first missionaries were thus ordained. The work for which Paul and Barnabas had been prepared and called was the work of establishing churches. They were ordained and sent forth as apostles by the Holy Spirit. In the Greek language, the word *apostolos* literally means "one sent forth."

In later years, Paul confirmed it was the Holy Spirit who called him. He reminded the elders of the church at Ephesus of his apostolic work and exhorted them: "I didn't shrink from declaring all God's message to you. And now beware! Be sure that you feed and shepherd God's flock—his church, purchased with his blood—for the Holy Spirit is holding you responsible as overseers" (Acts 20:27–28, TLB).

Did not Jesus tell Peter after He had chosen him that He would build His Church, and the gates of hell would not prevail against it (Matthew 16:18)? Jesus left, but He sent another, the Holy Spirit. And just as Jesus chose and sent forth His apostles, so the Holy Spirit chooses and sends forth His apostles.

No wonder the gates of hell still quake,
Holy Spirit. They know, too, that You are in
command of the Church.

63

MAKING DECISIONS

It seemed good to the Holy [Spirit], and to us.

ACTS 15:28

The Holy Spirit ordained the men to enlarge the Church, and together with them, established the rules by which it should be governed.

Many things were different after Pentecost. Converts were no longer limited to the house of Israel, and multiple questions arose as a result.

Should the Gentiles become Jews under the Law? Were the new converts required to embrace old traditions and circumcision? How were they to be saved? By keeping the Law, or by keeping Jesus? In short, would this "new wine" fit into the "old wineskins"? Who would make such life-changing decisions?

As dissention arose between the Judaizers and the apostles over the new believers, a meeting was held in Jerusalem to consider the matter. Peter summarized for those present what the pattern had been since Pentecost. "Brothers, you all know that God chose me from among you long ago to preach the Good News to the Gentiles, so that they also could believe. God, who knows men's hearts, confirmed the fact that he accepts Gentiles by giving them the Holy Spirit, just as he gave him to us. He made no distinction between them and us, for he cleansed their lives through faith, just as he did ours. And now are you going to correct God by burdening the Gentiles with a yoke that neither we nor our fathers were able to bear? Don't you believe that all are saved the same way, by the free gift of the Lord Jesus?" (Acts 15:7–11, TLB).

When Peter finished speaking, Paul and Barnabas gave their agreement. They testified that the same things were happening to the Gentiles through their ministry.

There was no further discussion. The council all acknowledged that God had included the Gentiles in His plan of salvation by receiving Jesus. James spoke forth the decision. "And so my judgment is that we should not insist that the Gentiles who turn to God must obey our Jewish laws, except that we should write to them to refrain from eating meat sacrificed to idols, from all fornication, and also from eating unbled meat of strangled animals. For these things have been preached against in Jewish synagogues in every city on every Sabbath for many generations" (Acts 15:19–21, TLB).

This judgment pleased the whole assembly. Therefore, they sent word of their decision in writing to the Gentile believers in Antioch, Syria and Cilica. The letter read in part, "It seemed good to the Holy Spirit and to us to lay no greater burden of Jewish laws on you than to abstain from eating food offered to idols and from unbled meat of strangled animals, and, of course, from fornication. If you do this, it is enough" (Acts 15:27–29, TLB).

"It seemed good to the Holy Spirit and to us," they said. All those present recognized the participation of the Holy Spirit in settling the argument.

So as the apostles journeyed through the towns and cities, they delivered the new "grace-laws" with instructions to keep them.

What seemed good to the Holy Spirit and to the first Church is still effectual today. In the midst of the Church, the Holy Spirit presides!

Lord,
do we hear what the
Spirit is saying to the Church today?
Forgive us our trespasses.

64

FORBIDDING US

[They] were forbidden of the Holy [Spirit] to preach the word in Asia.

ACTS 16:6

he Holy Spirit not only sent forth the apostles but at times *refused* to send them forth. The Holy Spirit was definitely involved in the route they followed to evangelize the nations.

On Paul's second missionary journey, he thought they were going to Asia. But God stopped them—not once, but twice. Scripture records that "they traveled through Phrygia and Galatia, because the Holy Spirit had told them not to go into the Turkish province of Asia at that time. Then going along the borders of Mysia they headed north for the province of Bithynia, but again the Spirit of Jesus said no" (Acts 16:6–7, TLB).

They knew where *not* to go; but where *should* they go? To erase all doubt, Paul was given a vision. He "saw a man over in Macedonia, Greece, pleading with him, 'Come over here and help us'" (Acts 16:9, TLB).

Immediately Paul and his companions left Troas for Macedonia in Europe, certain that God was sending them there.

Macedonia was both a Greek kingdom and a Roman province. Because of this journey the Gospel was planted in Europe.

Familiar places like Philippi, Thessalonica, Berea, Athens, and Corinth were included in Paul's second missionary journey.

Familiar people like Silas, Timothy and Luke accompanied him there.

In every place they visited, their message stirred up much strife and hatred. This kept them constantly on the move and worked to spread the Gospel even more quickly.

Jesus had instructed His disciples when He was with them, "When they persecute you in this city, flee ye into another: for verily I say unto you, Ye shall not have gone over the cities of Israel, till the Son of man be come" (Matthew 10:23).

The Spirit of Jesus was with them. He had come to the lost sheep of the house of Israel, but they had refused Him. Now, whosoever would, could come: Jew or Greek, bond or free, male or female. "For now we are all children of God through faith in Jesus Christ, and we who have been baptized into union with Christ are enveloped by him. We are no longer Jews or Greeks or slaves or free men or even merely men or women, but we are all the same—we are Christians; we are one in Christ Jesus" (Galatians 3:26–28, TLB).

We are a people called out for His name. "The church (assembly) of the First-born who are registered [as citizens] in heaven" (Hebrews 12:23, AMPLIFIED).

Registered in heaven, our roots go back to Jesus and the acts of the apostles. Yes, the Holy Spirit still works to make sure we are in the right place at the right time.

Thank You, Spirit of Jesus,
for saying yes and saying no.

65

USING OUR MOUTHS

The Holy [Spirit] came on them; and they spake with tongues, and prophesied.

ACTS 19:6

*I*t took more time for the news of the Gospel to reach believers in the first century. For example, Apollos, a Jew born at Alexandria in Egypt, was an excellent teacher, well versed in the Old Testament Scriptures. He had become a disciple of John the Baptist and taught concerning the Messiah to come. Although fervent in spirit, he taught only what John the Baptist had taught. That was all he knew.

When Apollos journeyed to Ephesus to preach John's baptism for repentance, Priscilla and her husband, Aquila, heard him speak. After that, they took him aside and explained to him what had happened in the life of Jesus since the death of John.

Apollos revised his teaching and moved on to Corinth. There he publicly debated with the Jews, proving from the Scriptures that *Jesus* was the Christ. The Messiah they had been waiting for had already come.

Meanwhile, Paul went to Ephesus and updated the disciples there. He asked them pointedly, "Did you receive the Holy Spirit when you believed?" (Acts 19:2, NIV).

They answered no. They admitted they had not even as much as *heard* of the Holy Spirit.

"Then what baptism were you baptized with?" inquired Paul.

"The baptism of John," they replied.

Paul explained to them that John's baptism was a baptism of repentance; repentance for their past sins under the law. It demonstrated a willingness to turn from sin and to receive God's forgiveness. But those receiving John's baptism must then go on to believe in Jesus and receive the gift of the Holy Spirit. "On hearing this, they were baptized into the name of the Lord Jesus. When Paul placed his hands upon them, the Holy Spirit came on them, and they spoke in tongues and prophesied" (Acts 19:5–6, NIV).

Notice the complete teaching of Paul: Repentance unto God, believing in Jesus and receiving the Holy Spirit. Or, as Jesus had instructed, baptiz-

147

ing them in the name of the Father, the Son and the Holy Spirit (Matthew 28:19, NIV). Each Person of the Godhead is acknowledged and honored.

Jesus had instructed the disciples before He died that they were to *ask* the Father for the Holy Spirit. "If you . . . know how to give good gifts to your children, how much more will your Father in heaven give the Holy Spirit to those who ask him!" (Luke 11:13, NIV).

> *We praise You, Father, Son and*
> *Holy Spirit, for Your full name—*
> *and for being ours when we ask.*

66
REVEALING HIS WILL

The Holy [Spirit] witnesseth. . . .
ACTS 20:23

s prophesied by Jesus, the Holy Spirit would show us "things to come."

Paul received this work of the Holy Spirit when he determined to go to Jerusalem at the end of his third missionary journey.

The Holy Spirit's witnessing came to Paul through different people in every city, but they all warned him of the same danger.

In Tyre, the disciples "said to Paul through the Spirit, that he should not go up to Jerusalem" (Acts 21:4).

In Caesarea, Agabus the prophet took Paul's belt, tied his own hands and feet with it and said, "The Holy Spirit says, 'In this way the Jews of Jerusalem will bind the owner of this belt and will hand him over to the Gentiles'" (Acts 21:11, NIV).

Even Luke pleaded with Paul not to go. But Paul, himself having been shown by the Holy Spirit that trouble awaited him in Jerusalem, still determined to go.

Paul's boldness in the Spirit was evident as he answered those who begged him to change his mind. He declared, "Now I am going to Jerusalem, drawn there irresistibly by the Holy Spirit, not knowing what awaits me, except that the Holy Spirit has told me in city after city that jail and suffering lie ahead. But life is worth nothing unless I use it for doing the work assigned me by the Lord Jesus—the work of telling others the Good News about God's mighty kindness and love" (Acts 20:22–24, TLB).

Paul's reasons for going to Jerusalem seemed to be many. He wanted to take money, gathered from the Gentile churches in Greece and Asia Minor, to be distributed to the needy saints there. It was no small amount, since he had spent over a year collecting it.

He wanted to meet with the elders, especially James, the head of the church. There was much to tell them about the Gentile Christians, and he wanted to encourage the bond of love between the Jew and Gentile believers.

Paul also wanted to make a vow in the Temple, to prove he kept the Jewish laws. He hoped to put an end to the rumor that he taught Gentiles they could be Christians without regard for the Law.

The work of the Holy Spirit in witnessing to Paul's future enabled the saints to know how to pray for him. It was through his imprisonment, later on in Jerusalem, that Paul appealed to Caesar. He was escorted to Rome, where he had planned to go next.

Showing us things to come is not intended to make us fear the future. Rather, it is so we will know the will of God and not be tempted to trust in "lying vanities." What are lying vanities? Vain idols. Speaking through Isaiah, God had said, "I have declared things to come to you of old; before they came to pass I announced them to you, so that you could not say, My idol has done them . . . and my molten image have commanded them" (Isaiah 48:5, AMPLIFIED).

For the same reason, Jesus foretold His own betrayal to His disciples. "I am telling you now before it happens, so that when it does happen you will believe that I am He" (John 13:19, NIV).

Our hearts are not troubled,
O Lord, for You do not
keep us ignorant.

67
HOLINESS

According to the spirit of holiness . . .
ROMANS 1:4

A name in Scripture is indicative of a nature. This is especially apparent in the original Hebrew and Greek texts where the names of the Godhead reveal the characteristics of God the Father, God the Son and God the Holy Spirit.

The "spirit of holiness" is a name rightly given to the Holy Spirit, because He Himself is holy. His essence, His being, His nature—is holy.

Holiness is a Person. It is the Lord our God. In fact, "There is none holy as the LORD" (1 Samuel 2:2).

Moses first declared God's holiness when he spoke for God to the people saying, "I am the LORD your God: ye shall therefore sanctify yourselves, and ye shall be holy; for I am holy" (Leviticus 11:44).

A holy God demands holy people. The children of Israel were to *make themselves holy* (sanctify themselves); for they were the people of God. Yet they failed to do so.

David was the first to ask the Holy Spirit for help. He cried out from the depths of his soul, realizing his unholiness. "Hide thy face from my sins, and blot out all mine iniquities. Create in me a clean heart, O God; and renew a right spirit within me. Cast me not away from thy presence; and take not thy holy spirit from me" (Psalm 51:9–11).

If the Holy Spirit were taken from David, how could he possibly become holy? If his iniquities were not forgiven, how could he have a clean heart? And how can we? Surely every Christian worth his salt covets holiness, this awesome image and likeness of the Godhead.

Making us holy is the work of the Spirit of Holiness. He imparts to us the very nature of God, Himself. Us, meaning the elect of God. Scripture reminds us that we "were chosen and foreknown by God the Father and consecrated (sanctified, made holy) by the Spirit to be obedient to Jesus Christ, the Messiah, and to be sprinkled with [His] blood" (1 Peter 1:2, AMPLIFIED).

Praise God, David's cry and our cry were heard. Through David's greater son, a right spirit has been renewed within us and all our iniquities blotted out. Jesus grafted us, like a rib, into His side and shared His own divine nature—His Holy Spirit. "According as his divine power hath given unto us all things that pertain unto life and godliness, through the knowledge of him that hath called us to glory and virtue: whereby are given unto us exceeding great and precious promises: that by these ye might be partakers of the divine nature, having escaped the corruption that is in the world through lust" (2 Peter 1:3–4).

And so, through God's grace, we have the spirit of Christ, who was the seed of David according to the flesh. This Christ was "declared to be the Son of God with power, according to the spirit of holiness, by the resurrection from the dead" (Romans 1:4).

How vast is that power of holiness that raised Jesus from the dead. God declared Him Holy. Holiness—can raise the dead!

Yes, there is power in everything that is holy. So much so that the power of sin is swallowed up by the power of holiness. Holiness is the power of an endless life without which no man shall see God.

As saints of the Most High God,
we worship You, O Lord, in the beauty of holiness.
Grant that we might be still more holy.

68
LOVE

The love of God is shed abroad in our hearts by the Holy [Spirit].
ROMANS 5:5

*T*he very first work done by the Holy Spirit was this flooding of our hearts with God's love. God's perfect love has always been there, for God *is* eternal love. But our hearts were not always able to receive Him. So before the Holy Spirit could do His work, our hearts had to be fixed "with the precious blood of Christ, as of a lamb without blemish and without spot: who . . . was foreordained (to die) before the foundation of the world" (1 Peter 1:19–20).

Jesus cleansed our hearts by His atoning death to receive God's gift of love; not because we deserved it, but because God willed it. Only then could the Holy Spirit fill our hearts with God's holy love.

God's love is the strongest thing in the universe. His love within us overcomes anything, even death. Scripture confirms it is stronger than death and without price. "Love is strong as death. . . . Many waters cannot quench the flame of love, neither can the floods drown it. If a man tried to buy it with everything he owned, he couldn't do it" (Song of Solomon 8:6–7, TLB).

Jesus proved *love* was stronger than *death* by rising from the dead. Death could not hold Him, nor will it hold us. And so the love of God constrains us, holds us together; it controls, urges and impels us. "For when we were yet without strength, in due time Christ died for the ungodly. For scarcely for a righteous man will one die; yet peradventure for a good man some would even dare to die. But God commendeth his love towards us, in that while we were yet sinners, Christ died for us" (Romans 5:6–8).

The Holy Spirit is the agent of the Godhead who pours out the love of God into these vessels of clay, making us vessels of the Spirit. Therefore, we really do not need to pray for love.

After we have been baptized in the Holy Spirit the flood begins, and we need only to draw on the love God has provided. "And so we know and rely on the love God has for us. God is love. Whoever lives in love lives in God, and God in him" (1 John 4:16, NIV).

It was this very love that Paul asked the Roman Christians to use on him. "For the Lord Jesus Christ's sake, and because of your love for me—given to you by the Holy Spirit—pray much with me for my work" (Romans 15:30, TLB).

Precious Holy Spirit,
they will know we are Christians by God's
love, which You continually pour.

69

NO CONDEMNATION

There is . . . no condemnation to them . . . who walk . . . after the Spirit.

ROMANS 8:1

The Holy Spirit is spoken of nineteen times in Romans 8. This concentration of His work and Person emphasizes how the Holy Spirit helps the sons of men become sons of God. "There is therefore now no condemnation to them which are in Christ Jesus, who walk not after the flesh, but after the Spirit" (Romans 8:1).

"No condemnation" seems too good to be true, because we all were born condemned to die. Scripture states our past condition: "Once you were under God's curse, doomed forever for your sins. You went along with the crowd and were just like all the others, full of sin, obeying Satan, the mighty prince of the power of the air, who is at work right now in the hearts of those who are against the Lord. All of us used to be just as they are, our lives expressing the evil within us, doing every wicked thing that our passions or our evil thoughts might lead us into. We started out bad, being born with evil natures, and were under God's anger just like everyone else" (Ephesians 2:1–4, TLB).

This kind of nature, inherited from Adam, is called the natural man and is written about in Scripture as the flesh. No one in that condition could ever please God, the flesh being corrupt. That is why everyone needs a new beginning, a new birth of the spiritual man. Not a rebirth of flesh and blood from man, but a new birth of Spirit from God. This God provided in Jesus two thousand years ago when Jesus died to give us His Spirit. And now, "ye are not in the flesh, but in the Spirit, if . . . the Spirit of God dwell in you. Now, if any man have not the Spirit of Christ, he is none of his" (Romans 8:9).

Two names of the Holy Spirit are mentioned here. He is called the Spirit of God, and the Spirit of Christ. These names give credence to Him as a Person of the Godhead and prove the three are one Spirit.

God considers Christians born of the Spirit as being *in Christ.* Jesus told His disciples they would understand this better after the Holy Spirit was birthed in them. "On that day [Pentecost] you will realize that I am in my Father, and you are in me, and I am in you" (John 14:20, NIV).

Because we were born of God, there is therefore now no condemnation. The old "law of sin and death" over us has been broken and we are free to live by the new "law of the Spirit of life." We can *choose* to walk in the power of the Spirit and not in the flesh. For while we still live in this earthly body, we live with two natures opposing each other. The flesh and the spirit. That is why Paul concluded, "This I say then, Walk in the Spirit, and ye shall not fulfill the lust of the flesh. For the flesh lusteth against the Spirit and the Spirit against the flesh: and these are contrary the one to the other: so that ye cannot do the things that ye would" (Galatians 5:16–17).

Cannot means cannot. We cannot walk in the flesh and please God. We cannot walk in the flesh and do the things of the Spirit. Nor can we walk in the flesh and the Spirit at the same time. Therefore, the flesh must die so that the Spirit can live. Our responsibility is to put it to death; to not give it breath, so it cannot speak. To not give it life, so it cannot act.

Yes, we have been set free from the condemnation and power of sin, but not from the presence of sin. Sin is still in the world, the flesh and the devil. Thus, when we do fail to walk in the Spirit there is a provision made by God for us. Repentance. "If we confess our sins, he is faithful and just to forgive us our sins, and to cleanse us from all unrighteousness" (1 John 1:9).

Our sins are not condemning anymore. They are forgiven and forgotten by God's grace. The big question is how to walk in the Spirit all the time. The simple answer is: by faith. Those who are without condemnation (the justified) live by faith. This faith is supplied as a fruit of walking in the Spirit (Galatians 5:22), and as a gift administered by the Holy Spirit (1 Corinthians 12:9). We live now by the same faith Jesus lived by because God is our Father, too, and He loves us. He is not against us; He is for us. And so our faith in Him makes us "confident of this very thing, that he which hath begun a good work in you will perform it until the day of Jesus Christ" (Philippians 1:6).

The work of the Holy Spirit makes no condemnation ours. He guides us into this truth, so that we have life and peace *now*. It is not "pie in the sky by and by," but a present reality made possible by Jesus Christ and administered to every generation by the working of the Holy Spirit within.

Why is all of this so important? Do not miss the point. We live and walk in the Spirit of Christ in order to bring forth good fruit. Fruit is the scriptural name for the good works God foreordained that we should produce. To do that, we must live in Christ: "Abide in me, and I in you. As the branch cannot bear fruit of itself, except it abide in the vine; no more can ye, except ye abide in me. I am the vine, ye are the branches: He that abideth in me and I in him, the same bringeth forth much fruit: for without me ye can do nothing" (John 15:4–5).

Holy Spirit,
we would stay
in Christ, walking with You.

70

LIFE

The Spirit of life . . .
ROMANS 8:2

The Holy Spirit is life: the Spirit of life. Life is His Person; it is His very being, His nature. So much so that He is the source of all life, and without Him there is only death.

These spiritual truths about the Spirit of life can only be known through the Word of God. We have no other reference to consult about the eternal life of the Godhead. Our natural minds just cannot comprehend life without beginning or ending. We only understand these things by faith in God's Word.

Scripture tells of an unusual man named Melchizedek who illustrates this life. He was the king of Salem and priest of the Most High God, to whom Abraham paid tithes. It is recorded of this king that he was "without father or mother, without genealogy, without beginning of days, or end of life, like the Son of God" (Hebrews 7:3, NIV).

Melchizedek is like the Son of God whom John wrote about, whose life always was and can never be extinguished. "In him was Life; and the life was the light of men" (John 1:4).

Life and light are in the Godhead. Light and life are synonymous in Scripture. Jesus admitted He was the light of life, as well as the way, the truth and the life. He spoke these words about Himself: "I am the light of the world: he that followeth me shall not walk in darkness, but shall have the light of life" (John 8:12).

How do we follow Jesus when He is at the right hand of the Father on high? We follow Jesus through His Spirit. The Holy Spirit is the reason Jesus could promise *life* to all those who would believe in Him.

The Spirit of life enters believers when they are born again and comes in greater fullness as they yield to the filling of the Spirit of life. It is the same life the Godhead has—without beginning or ending.

However, it is not just the duration of this endless life that awes us, but the essence of it as well. This abundant life bestowed at Pentecost influenced and empowered those who received it *immediately*. It was not necessary for them to die to receive it. Paul wrote about the benefits of the Spirit of life: "The law of the Spirit of life in Christ Jesus hath made me free from the law of sin and death . . . that the righteousness of the law might be fulfilled in us, who walk not after the flesh, but after the Spirit" (Romans 8:2, 4).

Thus, the new law of the Spirit of life is a stronger law than the old law of sin and death. The Spirit of Life, which we now have from Christ Jesus, not only sets us free from death but empowers us to set our minds upon, and do, the things of God's Kingdom.

The divine work of the Holy Spirit is to lead us in these paths of love and righteousness—for His name's sake. "'Love the Lord your God with all your heart, soul, and mind.' This is the first and greatest commandment. The second most important is similar: 'Love your neighbor as much as you love yourself.' All the other commandments and all the demands of the prophets stem from these two laws and are fulfilled if you obey them. Keep only these and you will find that you are obeying all the others" (Matthew 22:37–40, TLB).

When we walk in the Spirit of life, we obey the righteous requirements of the law of love commanded by Jesus.

The results of this way of life bring peace—that special peace from God that passes all understanding because it keeps our hearts and minds fixed on Him.

Spirit of life:
It is and shall be so.
Amen and amen!

71
QUICKENING US

He shall "quicken your mortal bodies by his Spirit."
ROMANS 8:11

Resurrection life is the work of the Holy Spirit. Not only have our *spirits* been quickened (born again) by the Holy Spirit, but our *bodies* shall also be quickened after we die. We shall be made alive physically, after death, by the same mighty power that raised Jesus from the dead. Scripture assures us that "if the Spirit of him who raised Jesus from the dead is living in you, he who raised Christ from the dead will also give life to your mortal bodies through his Spirit who lives in you" (Romans 8:11, NIV).

These mortal bodies in which we live are destined for death because of sin, but the born-again spirit inside is alive because of righteousness. No matter how we try to prevent it, sooner or later death comes to everyone and the Scriptures are proven true: "It is appointed unto men once to die, but after this the judgment" (Hebrews 9:27).

Death is a fact of life. There is hidden meaning in that statement, for we must die before we can live. Paul uses the illustration of a garden to explain how our resurrection body will differ from our earthly body. He says, "When you put a seed into the ground it doesn't grow into a plant unless it 'dies' first. And when the green shoot comes up out of the seed, it is very different from the seed you first planted. . . . In the same way, our earthly bodies which die and decay are different from the bodies we shall have when we come back to life again, for they will never die" (1 Corinthians 15:36–37, 42, TLB).

The mortal body the Holy Spirit quickens will be imperishable, glorious and powerful. When our spirit leaves this body of clay, we are clothed with a body not made with hands—an eternal house.

This mortal body is not our permanent dwelling place, nor is this earth our permanent home. Even our earthly father Abraham was convinced of this although he lived centuries before Christ. It is written of him, "by faith he made his home in the promised land like a stranger in a foreign country; he lived in tents, as did Isaac and Jacob, who were heirs with him of the same promise. For he was looking forward to the city with foundations, whose architect and builder is God" (Hebrews 11:9–10, NIV).

Their destiny was a city built by God in the heavens. To get there, they needed new bodies, resurrection bodies like Jesus'.

The Feast of Tabernacles is celebrated every year by living in tents. It is like God telling us, "I give you a tent (perishable body) to remind you it is not My permanent dwelling place or yours. I have prepared a place for you where I am, which is permanent and cannot be moved. It has eternal foundations in the heavens and is glorious in beauty, for this city was built by me."

The anticipation of this fact does something for us. Those who believe in Christ's resurrection from the dead have faith for their own resurrections. This hope continually purifies the recipient. Yes, "our citizenship is in heaven. And we eagerly await a Savior from there, the Lord Jesus Christ, who, by the power that enables him to bring everything under his control, will transform our lowly bodies so they will be like his glorious body" (Philippians 3:20–21, NIV).

Praise God, this body is exchangeable. Our total salvation from death—spirit, soul and body—will be complete with the redemption of our bodies. We shall be just *like* Him, for we shall see Him as He really is.

Blessed Holy Spirit,
You did it before,
and You can do it again.
Hurry us up!

72

LEADING US

Led by the Spirit of God . . .
ROMANS 8:14

The work of the Holy Spirit in this lifetime is to lead us to our destination in God.

To be led by the Spirit of God is a privilege. For the Christian it is not optional, it is mandatory. It is presumptuous to assume we know the way, the truth and the life, without being led by God. Therefore, in addition to the written Word of God—the Bible—and the living word of God—Jesus—we also have an internal witness of God: the Holy Spirit.

In the beginning, the way to the Tree of Life in the Garden of Eden was blocked after Adam sinned. "Thus God expelled him, and placed mighty angels at the east of the garden of Eden, with a flaming sword to guard the entrance to the Tree of Life" (Genesis 3:24, TLB).

Since then, the way of life has not been available to the natural man. Only the Holy Spirit knows where and how to lead us into paths of righteousness for His name's sake, and it is His responsibility to do so. "For we are his workmanship, created in Christ Jesus unto good works, which God hath before ordained that we should walk in them" (Ephesians 2:10).

The Holy Spirit, residing within the believer, is able to communicate God's will to each one individually. Through revelation knowledge, we are inspired and enabled to fulfill the purpose for which we were created.

Every child of God should learn to be sensitive to the Holy Spirit and know His voice. We must cultivate a personal relationship and dependence upon Him, even as Jesus did. Jesus, with that gentle, lamb nature, allowed the dove to rest and remain upon Him. We are responsible to still our fleshly nature and know that He is God. If we do not, we quench (smother) His divine presence.

Our attitude and prayer should be as the psalmist David: "Help me to do your will, for you are my God. Lead me in good paths for your Spirit is good" (Psalm 143:10, TLB).

There is no end to the goodness and mercy we experience as we follow the leading of the Spirit. Romans chapter 8 lists some of them. There is life and peace. We are not under the law, but under grace. We do not fulfill the lusts of our flesh. We are righteous. We please God. We mature. And Paul writes that "as many as are led by the Spirit of God, they are the sons of God" (Romans 8:14).

He leadeth me: O blessed thought!
O words with heavenly comfort fraught!
Whate'er I do, where'er I be,
Still 'tis God's [Spirit] that leadeth me.

Joseph H. Gilmore, 1862

73

BEARING WITNESS

The Spirit . . . beareth witness with our spirit.
ROMANS 8:16

The Holy Spirit "bears witness" with our spirits that God has made us sons by adoption. To testify to this, the Holy Spirit is rightly called "the Spirit of adoption." His name describes the nature of His work: the inward conviction that we belong to God.

The Spirit of adoption urges us to call God *Father!* And every time we speak this name it reminds us that we are sons of the Most High God, accepted in the beloved. Therefore, "we should behave like God's very own children, adopted into the . . . family and calling to him, 'Father, Father'" (Romans 8:15, TLB).

Using God's personal name of "Father" was not possible under the Old Covenant. Until Christ came we were subject to all the rituals of the Law, "for we thought they could save us. But when the right time came, the time God decided on, he sent his Son . . . to buy freedom for us who were slaves to the law so that he could adopt us as his very own sons" (Galatians 4:3–5, TLB).

Our adoption was legally paid for with Christ's own blood. He confirmed this immediately after His resurrection by telling Mary to "go to my brethren, and say unto them, I ascend unto my Father, and your Father; and to my God, and your God" (John 20:17).

These powerful words show the change in relationship we share with Jesus, our brother. God is now *our* God and *our* Father, too. Therefore, we have additional benefits. We are heirs of God and joint-heirs with Jesus Christ in two aspects: His glory and His suffering. And "since we are his children, we will share his treasures—for all God gives to his Son Jesus is now ours too. But if we are to share his glory, we must also share his suffering" (Romans 8:17, TLB).

Suffering touches everything and everyone. The word *suffering* denotes the hardships and afflictions we experience as the result of Adam's transgression. The corruption of sin, sickness, decay and death even affect nature, and it longs to be freed from the curse of thorns and thistles. As the writer of Ecclesiastes wisely observed, "all is vanity and vexation of the spirit." Thus, "we know that the whole creation has been groaning as in pains of childbirth right up to the present time. Not only so, but we ourselves, who have the firstfruits of the Spirit, groan inwardly as we wait for our adoption as sons, the redemption of our bodies" (Romans 8:22–23, NIV).

As we wait for these bodies from heaven we are privileged to be parented by God. He takes the responsibility for our upbringing by conforming us to His likeness through obedience to His will, even though it means suffering. Jesus learned obedience this way, and if we do not allow God to train us we are not true sons. We are fatherless, illegitimate. For this reason the Father corrects all His sons and daughters, instructing us to be holy as He is. Listen to our Father's encouragement: "My son, do not make light of the Lord's discipline, and do not lose heart when he rebukes you, because the Lord disciplines those he loves, and he punishes everyone he accepts as a son" (Hebrews 12:5–6, NIV).

God purposed from the beginning to bring many sons to glory for He is an eternal Father. "His unchanging plan has always been to adopt us into his own family by sending Jesus Christ to die for us. And he did this because he wanted to!" (Ephesians 1:5, TLB).

My God and Father,
thank You for
Your Spirit of adoption who reassures me
till Jesus comes.

74
HELPING OUR INFIRMITIES

The Spirit also helpeth our infirmities. . . .
ROMANS 8:26

*I*n the same way the Holy Spirit bears witness with our spirit to give us hope of His *future* help, He likewise helps our infirmities *now*. That is, He helps us in the general weakness of our spiritual life in its present state. "So too the (Holy) Spirit comes to our aid and bears us up in our weakness" (Romans 8:26, AMPLIFIED).

The Greek word describing the help the Holy Spirit gives is very explicit. It means "to lift up again (by taking the other end), to heave with us in lifting a burden, to work together with."

Infirmities (weaknesses) come from three major sources: the world, the flesh and the devil. They take the form of trials, temptations, diseases, ignorance, foolishness, sins, sorrows, lack of faith and persecutions—to name a few. Every Christian knows that our spirit is willing to do the will of God, but our flesh is weak (see Matthew 26:41; Mark 14:38). Therefore, we need the ministry of the Holy Spirit to help us overcome our weaknesses.

What are our weaknesses? Adultery. Anger. Confusion. Dissensions. Doubting. Drugs. Drunkenness. Envyings. Factions. Fightings. Fleshly mind (imaginations). Fornication. Gossip. Hatred. Heresies. Homosexuality. Idolatry. Immorality. Impure thoughts. Jealousies. Lasciviousness (eagerness for lustful pleasure). Murders. Orgies. Perversion. Philosophies (humanism). Sedition (complaints, criticisms). Selfish ambition. Strife. Talebearing. Traditions of men. Uncleanness. Vain deceits (pride). Witchcraft. Worldliness. Worshipping of angels. Wrath—and every evil work.

The Word tells us that "we by the help of the Holy Spirit are counting on Christ's death to clear away our sins and make us right with God" (Galatians 5:5, TLB). "For we naturally love to do evil things that are just the opposite from the things that the Holy Spirit tells us to do; and the good things we want to do when the Spirit has his way with us are just the opposite of our natural desires. . . . When you are guided by the Holy Spirit you need no longer force yourself to obey" (Galatians 5:17–18, TLB).

It is so encouraging to know God is our refuge and strength. Our help does come from the Lord. And when we are told to work out our own salvation with fear and trembling, it is not in our own strength, "for it is God Who is all the while effectually at work in you—energizing and creating in you the power and desire—both to will and to work for His good pleasure and satisfaction and delight" (Philippians 2:13, AMPLIFIED).

God, the Holy Spirit, works in us to will *and* to do what God wants us to do. He helps us act according to what our spirit knows is right. The Holy Spirit will not do it all, however. We must do our part. It is a joint effort. We cannot do anything without the Holy Spirit and He will not do it without us, weak as we are.

But therein is our real strength. At the point when we recognize our weakness and allow the Holy Spirit to help us, God's grace takes over.

Paul understood the reason for infirmities in our physical bodies because he had one. His was due to the abundance of revelations given to him by the Lord. Three times he asked the Lord to deliver him from this "messenger of Satan" as he called it. And although we really do not know exactly what it was, his testimony supports the work of the Holy Spirit on our behalf: "Now I am glad to boast about how weak I am; I am glad to be a living demonstration of Christ's power, instead of showing off my own power and abilities. Since I know it is all for Christ's good, I am quite happy about 'the thorn,' and about insults and hardships, persecutions and difficulties; for when I am weak, then I am strong—the less I have, the more I depend on him" (2 Corinthians 12:9–10, TLB).

Paul was not rejoicing in Satan's attack upon his body but in the Spirit's coming alongside to help him. He realized God's grace was more apparent when he was weak than when he tried to do it himself. He praised God all the more as he saw proof, time after time, of God's power released through his weaknesses—in whatever form they came.

We all need the help of the Holy Spirit. Yes, this Comforter is still present to aid us. No wonder Peter gave this resounding admonition to encourage us: "Let him have all your worries and cares, for he is always thinking about you and watching everything that concerns you. Be careful—watch out for attacks from Satan, your great enemy. . . . After you have suffered a little while, our God . . . personally will come and pick you up, and set you firmly in place, and make you stronger than ever. To him be all power over all things, forever and ever. Amen" (1 Peter 5:7–11, TLB).

What a fellowship, Holy Spirit,
what a joy divine, leaning on
the everlasting arms.

75

INTERCESSION

The Spirit . . . maketh intercession for us.
ROMANS 8:26

For the Christian, prayer is the most important thing to be learned. Prayer: that intimate, privileged communication between the Father and His child, made possible only through the intercession of Jesus and the Holy Spirit.

We need the help of the Holy Spirit in praying because we do not know *what* or *how* to pray as we should. Our knowledge is incomplete, for living by faith and not by sight is like seeing through a dark glass. Scripture tells us, "we know not what we should pray for as we ought: but the Spirit itself maketh intercession for us with groanings which cannot be uttered" (Romans 8:26).

The Holy Spirit Himself prays to the Father for us. Will we ever comprehend the value of it this side of eternity? For this is where we are so weak. This is where most of our doubts flourish. What is the will of God? If I only knew. I pray and pray, but the heavens seem like brass. Is it because I pray amiss? It must be. How can I know the mind of my Father in heaven? How can I know what prayers He will answer? I hate these vain repetitions, yet what more can I say?

Our solution is in knowing that the Holy Spirit does more than *help* us pray, He actually prays *for* us. He groans when we pray, with such emotion it cannot be expressed in mere words. And because He understands our inner longings better than we do, He represents us to the Father in perfect agreement with God's purposes for our individual lives. All things work together for good because the "*what* to pray for" and the "*how* to pray" are accomplished by the work of the Holy Spirit. The "Father who knows all hearts knows, of course, what the Spirit is saying as he pleads for us in harmony with God's own will" (Romans 8:27, TLB).

The Holy Spirit is our advocate here on earth, pleading our case, and Jesus Christ is our advocate in heaven. This High Priest, seated at the right hand of God the Father, has been interceding for the saints for two thousand years. He "is able . . . to save them to the uttermost that come unto God by him, seeing he ever liveth to make intercession for them" (Hebrews 7:25).

If we really want to pray effectually, we will yield to the Holy Spirit within and follow His leading. "Praying always with all prayer and supplication in the Spirit, and watching thereunto with all perseverance and supplication for all saints" (Ephesians 6:18).

In this blessed union there are no failures, and God is able to will and to do—in us—of His good pleasure.

Sweet Spirit of prayer,
most gladly will
I pray with You.

76
INSIDE INFORMATION

My conscience . . . bearing me witness in the Holy [Spirit].

The Holy Spirit bears witness to our consciences. Here, Paul is attesting to a truth the Holy Spirit has made known to him about his zeal for his Jewish brothers. It is as if Paul was swearing to the fact because the Holy Spirit told him: "I am speaking the truth in Christ. I am not lying; my conscience [enlightened and prompted] by the Holy Spirit, bearing witness with me" (Romans 9:1, AMPLIFIED).

Along with our minds or souls, the Holy Spirit also bears witness with our spirits, in our hearts. God has "set his seal of ownership on us, and put his Spirit in our hearts as a deposit" (2 Corinthians 1:22, NIV).

This is why Paul was so bold in his declarations. He spoke as the oracles of God because he had an inner witness of the Spirit to lean on. He was positive he was not lying and said so. "I am ordained a preacher, and an apostle, (I speak the truth in Christ, and lie not;) a teacher of the Gentiles in faith and verity [truth]" (1 Timothy 2:7).

Paul had the same sure witness for what he wrote. To the Galatians he wrote, "the things . . . I write unto you, behold, before God, I lie not" (Galatians 1:20).

Paul's conscience was clear. He was honest with God and with men because he yielded to the Holy Spirit. He declared, "Our rejoicing is this, the testimony of our conscience, that in simplicity and godly sincerity, not with fleshly wisdom, but by the grace of God, we have had our conversation in the world" (2 Corinthians 1:12).

When the world questions who we are, what our purpose is, it is imperative that we have this witness in the Spirit to walk boldly by faith in the things of God. We know who we are. We know why we are here. We know what we want to do, and by God's grace, how to do it. "For God hath not given us the spirit of fear; but of power, and of love, and of a sound mind" (2 Timothy 1:7).

A conscience under the protection of the Holy Spirit is a divine vindication that keeps the heart and mind in Christ Jesus. The Spirit forewarned us that "in later times some will abandon the faith and follow deceiving spirits and things taught by demons. Such teachings come through hypocritical liars, whose consciences have been seared as with a hot iron" (1 Timothy 4:1–2, NIV).

What a privilege to say, "My conscience bears me witness in the Spirit." We can draw near to God; our minds having been sprinkled from an evil conscience by the blood of Jesus.

> By this we shall come to know—perceive and recognize and understand— that we are of the Truth, and can reassure (quiet, conciliate and pacify) our hearts in His presence. In whatever our hearts in [tormenting] self-accusation make us feel guilty and condemn us. For [we are in God's hands]; He is above and greater than our consciences (our hearts), and He knows (perceives and understands) everything—nothing is hidden from Him. And, beloved, if our consciences (our hearts) do not accuse us—if they do not make us feel guilty and condemn us—we have confidence (complete assurance and boldness) before God.
>
> 1 John 3:19–21, AMPLIFIED

O Spirit of God,
now I know why You search me:
to know my heart.
And try me: to know my thoughts.
You give me inside information.

77

HOPE

Abound in hope, through the power of the Holy [Spirit].

ROMANS 15:13

One of the sure evidences of the Holy Spirit at work in a believer is the abundance of hope. This "hope" could be defined as the strong, confident, mental expectation of future good based upon God and the encouragement of the Scriptures. "For whatsoever things were written aforetime were written for our learning, that we through patience and comfort of the scriptures might have hope" (Romans 15:4).

The psalmist wrote about this hope with great emotion. "My soul faints with longing for your salvation, but I have put my hope in your word" (Psalm 119:81, NIV).

Scriptural hope differs from the dictionary definition of hope, which is "wishful thinking." The hope of the world comes from the self and originates in the imagination or wishes. This is not the hope we overflow with by the power of the Holy Spirit. Hope differs from faith although it is based on faith. Faith is in the present; hope is in the future. Faith is today's proof of what we hope for in the future. For this reason, hope must be strong enough to endure until we *see* what we hope for: our resurrection bodies.

This kind of hope saves us from despair as it produces patience. Scripture declares that "in this hope we were saved. But hope that is seen is no hope at all. Who hopes for what he already has? But if we hope for what we do not yet have, we wait for it patiently" (Romans 8:24–25, NIV).

There is another difference between hope and faith. Hope is in the mind (soul); faith is in the heart. Both are necessary and work together with love. Faith and love are described as armor that protects the heart. Hope is described as a helmet that protects the head (the mind, the soul), to endure to the end. It is a spiritual helmet we are admonished to wear. We are to "be sober, putting on the breastplate of faith and love; and for an helmet, the hope of salvation" (1 Thessalonians 5:8).

The Spirit of hope anchors us to the Rock. "This certain hope of being saved is a strong and trustworthy anchor for our souls, connecting us with God himself behind the sacred curtains of heaven" (Hebrews 6:19, TLB).

And while we wait for the appearing of our Lord Jesus Christ, faith, hope and love still abide. The Christian cannot do without these three spiritual realities. To be void of any one of them is to be without Christ as we were before we were saved. "[In time past] ye were without Christ, being aliens from the commonwealth of Israel, and strangers from the covenants of promise, having no hope and without God in the world" (Ephesians 2:12–13).

Without hope, the soul is sick. Without hope, there is nothing to rejoice about. Without hope, we would be ashamed and disillusioned. Without hope, we would sorrow as others who have no hope.

Hope is essential to salvation.

Hope purifies us while we wait.

Hope is a Person. It is Christ in us, our hope of glory.

Holy Spirit,
with You, I can give
a reason for the hope that is in me.

78
SANCTIFICATION

Acceptable [to God], being sanctified by the Holy [Spirit].
ROMANS 15:16

anctification means to be set apart for God.

God is the sanctifier, the One who sets apart the person, place or thing for Himself. Therefore, whatever or whoever is sanctified is destined to become holy, for God is holy. This is the work of the Holy Spirit. Without His help, we would be left alone and fail utterly. No Holy Spirit, no sanctification.

For example, God set apart a people for Himself when He chose the nation of Israel. Abraham, Isaac, Jacob and their seed were to become His holy, covenant people on the earth. Through keeping the Law of ordinances and the shedding of blood of bulls and goats, they were made acceptable to God until a better way came.

All the other nations (Gentiles), not chosen by God, were under a curse. Paul reminded the Gentiles of this fact. "Never forget that once you were heathen, and that you were called godless and 'unclean' by the Jews" (Ephesians 2:11, TLB).

The Gentiles were not set apart for God until the resurrection of Jesus and the Gospel was preached to them. Then, under a New Covenant, it was possible for the whole world—every kindred, every people, every tribe, every nation—to become holy, sanctified people of God. Paul explained it to the Romans this way: "God gave me to be a minister of Christ Jesus to the Gentiles with the priestly duty of proclaiming the gospel of God, so that the Gentiles might become an offering acceptable to God, sanctified by the Holy Spirit" (Romans 15:15–16, NIV).

Our sanctification is under the charge of the Holy Spirit. We become acceptable to God as He changes the sinner to saint, the reprobate to righteous, the depraved sons of the devil to dedicated sons of God. "For whom He foreknew, He also predestined to be conformed to the image of His Son. . . . Whom He predestined, these He also called; whom He called, these He also justified; and whom He justified, these He also glorified" (Romans 8:29–30, NKJV).

God, the Holy Spirit, works in us to make us holy like Jesus. He works in secret upon our hearts with the Word of Truth. His authority demolishes every stronghold. It is the omnipotence that put the universe in space and sustains it. In God's Word there is spirit and power to transform us within and without until we "become blameless and pure, children of God without fault in a crooked and depraved generation, in which you shine like stars in the universe as you hold out the word of life" (Philippians 2:15–16, NIV).

Holy Spirit,
thank You for guaranteeing our destiny.
Without You, we can do nothing.

79
SIGNS AND WONDERS

Mighty signs and wonders . . . of the Spirit.
ROMANS 15:19

The mighty signs and wonders done by Paul were administered by the power of the Holy Spirit. Paul gave Him credit for the success he had had in evangelizing the Gentiles, saying, "I have won them by my message and by the good way I have lived before them, and by the miracles done through me as signs from God—all by the Holy Spirit's power. In this way I have preached the full Gospel of Christ" (Romans 15:19, TLB).

In other words, the "full Gospel" of Jesus Christ included miracles—visible signs of God's power. It brought the ungodly to repentance, for signs and wonders proved that God's Kingdom had invaded their space.

Faith is not always founded on words alone. Indeed, the Kingdom of God is not in word, but in power, too. It is often suggested, "Talk is cheap," or "Show me." Therefore, God allows Himself to be proven. Paul emphasizes again that "my speech and my preaching was not with enticing words of man's wisdom, but in demonstration of the Spirit and of power; that your faith should not stand in the wisdom of men, but in the power of God" (1 Corinthians 2:4–5).

The power of the Almighty will eventually settle any argument. He has the last word.

Jesus gave every believer the permission to do miracles when He said, "He that believeth on me, the works that I do shall he do also; and greater works than these shall he do; because I go to the Father" (John 14:12).

Miracles done by believers prove three things: that they believe in Jesus Christ, that Jesus is with the Father and that the Holy Spirit is here with us, even as He was with Jesus.

However, the world's reaction to the supernatural today is the same as in Jesus' day. Not everyone believed the miracles Jesus did. In some cases, the signs and wonders caused hatred and rebellion, which prompted Jesus to say, "If I had not done among them the works which no one else did, they would have no sin; but now they have seen and also hated both Me and My Father. But this has happened that the word might be fulfilled which is written in their law, 'They hated Me without a cause'" (John 15:24–25, NKJV).

Those who refuse to believe the truth believe a lie. Satan is the spirit behind the "lying" wonders by which they are deceived. "And he [false prophet] doeth great wonders, so that he maketh fire come down from heaven on the earth in the sight of men. And deceiveth them that dwell on the earth by the means of those miracles which he had power to do" (Revelation 13:13–14).

As the Second Coming of Jesus draws near, mankind will see many more signs and wonders done by the power of the Holy Spirit. For God declared that as He poured out His Spirit upon all flesh, He would "show wonders in heaven above, and signs in the earth beneath; blood, and fire and vapour of smoke: The sun shall be turned into blood, before that great and notable day of the Lord come . . . and whosoever shall call on the name of the Lord shall be saved" (Acts 2:19–21).

The Holy Spirit's demonstration of miracles in our midst proves the power of the Godhead. It continues the Kingdom of God upon the earth, which Jesus began. Christians, by faith in the name of Jesus, rule and overrule powers and authorities of a different world by divine intervention. This authenticates us. This is our verification. It establishes our claim that Jesus Christ is truly our Lord.

The competition for miracles resides in the heavenlies. It rages between the Kingdom of light and the kingdom of darkness. We know because we were forewarned by Jesus not to believe every spiritual phenomenon. He prophesied that "false Christs and false prophets shall arise, and shall shew signs and wonders, to seduce, if it were possible, even the elect" (Mark 13:22).

We need to discern the difference between the true and the false. But we are not to refuse the gifts of miracles by the work of the Holy Spirit. Through them, the Church of God is still renewed today. "For his miracles demonstrate his honor, majesty, and eternal goodness" (Psalm 111:3, TLB).

Holy Spirit,
it is true, no one
who does miracles by Your power
speaks evil of Jesus!

80
SEARCHING

The Spirit searcheth all things.
1 CORINTHIANS 2:10

The Holy Spirit's work is to search *all* things. The emphasis is on the word *all*. And since He searches out everything, there is absolutely nothing that He does not know. He is eternally omniscient. That is, both His Person and His work are one and the same: knowing all things.

To know everything, the Holy Spirit has access to both the spiritual heart of man and the very heart of God. For "the Spirit searches all things, even the deep things of God" (1 Corinthians 2:10, NIV).

The deep things of God are not available to man without the help of the Holy Spirit. He alone understands the mind and will of God, because He is God's Spirit. "For who among men knows the thoughts of a man except the man's spirit within him? In the same way no one knows the thoughts of God except the Spirit of God" (1 Corinthians 2:11, NIV).

For this reason, Isaiah the prophet made this plea to the people of his day, and ultimately, to us.

Let the wicked forsake his way and the evil man his thoughts. Let him turn to the LORD, and he will have mercy on him, and to our God, for he will freely pardon. "For my thoughts are not your thoughts, neither are your ways my ways," declares the LORD. As the heavens are higher than the earth, so are my ways higher than your ways and my thoughts than your thoughts. As the rain and the snow come down from heaven, and do not return to it without watering the earth and making it bud and flourish, so that it yields seed for the sower and bread for the eater, so is my word that goes out from my mouth: It will not return to me empty, but will accomplish what I desire and achieve the purpose for which I sent it.

Isaiah 55:7–11, NIV

The Word of God and the Spirit of God are in agreement. The Spirit performs the Word. That is how we are born of the Spirit by the Word from God's mouth. The Word achieves the purpose for which God sent it, and something wonderful happens. We have a change of spirit. "Now we have received, not the spirit of the world, but the spirit which is of God" (1 Corinthians 2:12).

The world—with all its wisdom—can never search out God and know Him because God will not give His glory to another spirit. "Where is the wise man? Where is the scholar? Where is the philosopher of this age? Has not God made foolish the wisdom of the world?" (1 Corinthians 1:20, NIV).

The answer is yes, He has. The counsel of the Godhead is privileged information imparted under the direction of the Holy Spirit.

O Holy Spirit,
through You we not only seek for
God and search for Him
with all our hearts:
We find Him!

81
REVELATION

God hath revealed them unto us by his Spirit.
1 CORINTHIANS 2:10

Is there revelation knowledge apart from God's written Word? Has everything we need to know been recorded? Do we know all we can about things to come? Is it possible to remember what we have learned and forgotten? These questions deal with the need for the revelation work of the Holy Spirit.

Sometimes God's people question their privilege to understand. They throw up their hands and say, "We just can't know everything"—and they quote the verse, "It is written, eye hath not seen, nor ear heard, neither have entered into the heart of man, the things which God hath prepared for them that love him" (1 Corinthians 2:9).

But Scripture does not agree with that. They stopped too soon. Read on—there is more. The next verse contains an important *"but"* that shows the work of the Holy Spirit: "But God hath revealed them unto us by his Spirit" (1 Corinthians 2:10).

What has God revealed to us by His Spirit? Things beyond our senses, beyond our natural ability to comprehend. God prepared these *things,* called "the hidden wisdom of God," for our glory before the world began. Thus they did not come from the rulers of this age, nor were they even known by them. What then is the hidden wisdom of God revealed by the Holy Spirit? The revelation is a Person. It is *Jesus Christ!* For "in him lie hidden all the mighty, untapped treasures of wisdom and knowledge" (Colossians 2:3, TLB).

Had the rulers of this age known the secret plan of God's eternal wisdom, they never would have crucified Jesus. They (and Satan) missed it right there. And anyone or anything that proposes to teach hidden wisdom today is false, unless it reveals Jesus Christ—crucified, dead, buried, risen, ascended and coming again.

The work of the Holy Spirit enables us to receive revelation knowledge apart from the written Word of God. His voice is heard in our hearts. Otherwise, the wisdom of the cross would be utter foolishness to us as it is to the world.

Because the Holy Spirit imparts the deep things of God, the revelation of Jesus never stops. And "whoever has [spiritual knowledge], to him will more be given and he will be furnished richly, so that he will have abundance; but from him who has not, even what he has will be taken away" (Matthew 13:12, AMPLIFIED).

This is why Jesus taught in parables. It fulfills Isaiah's prophecy about those who refuse to believe and, therefore, cannot receive revelation. It is still true today. Jesus said, "This is the reason that I speak to them in parables, because having the power of seeing they do not see, and having the power of hearing they do not hear, nor do they grasp and understand. In them indeed is the process of fulfillment of the prophecy of Isaiah, which says: You shall indeed hear and hear, but never grasp and understand; and you shall indeed look and look, but never see and perceive" (Matthew 13:13–14, AMPLIFIED).

Jesus sent the Revelator to reveal *Him*. For "when the Comforter is come . . . he shall testify of me" (John 15:26).

Jesus sent the Remembrancer to remind us of what He said: "He shall . . . bring all things to your remembrance, whatsoever I have said unto you" (John 14:26).

Jesus sent the Oracle to reveal things heard in the councils of the Godhead, and to make known the future. For "he shall not speak of himself; but whatsoever he shall hear, that shall he speak: and he will shew you things to come. He shall glorify me: for he shall receive of mine, and shall shew it unto you" (John 16:13–14).

Revelation knowledge glorifies God. And God's only agent for it is the Holy Spirit. We cannot bypass the Holy Spirit and know the things of God.

But we who love God *can* know God's plans for sure, without any doubt. We can be eyewitnesses of Jesus' glory in our spirit. How faithful God is not to let us be ignorant!

Our spiritual eyes and ears are blessed
by You, Holy Spirit, every time You make
known the unsearchable riches of Christ.

82
SPIRITUAL EDUCATION

The Holy [Spirit] teacheth. . . .
1 CORINTHIANS 2:13

*T*he Holy Spirit is the one who teaches us "revealed things." It stands to reason that since the Spirit of God knows the thoughts of God, He is able to teach them. And when He does so, He uses His own words.

Paul explains this to the Corinthian believers by describing *how* the Holy Spirit teaches through him. "We speak, not in words taught us by human wisdom but in words taught by the Spirit, expressing spiritual truths in spiritual words" (1 Corinthians 2:13, NIV).

Some people object to the words "born again" to describe the Christian's experience. Yet that is a good example of spiritual truth expressed in spiritual words. Jesus spoke in the Holy Spirit's language to teach what happens when we receive Him and are made alive by the Spirit. Those two words perfectly illustrate truth with a minimum of verbiage. They cannot be improved upon.

The Holy Spirit never distracts from the simplicity of the cross with complicated rhetoric. Thus Paul imitated Christ when he preached, using Spirit words everyone could understand, saying, "I do not fill my sermons with profound words and high sounding ideas, for fear of diluting the mighty . . . message of the cross of Christ" (1 Corinthians 1:17, TLB).

So it can be said that the Holy Spirit makes us teachable and then teaches us by "combining and interpreting spiritual truths with spiritual language [to those who possess the (Holy) Spirit]" (1 Corinthians 2:13, AMPLIFIED).

The Holy Spirit does not teach the person who is not born again because his spirit is dead and he cannot receive the things of the Spirit. The Scriptures are *burglar proof* to those who do not have the "spiritual combination." Why? Because "the man who isn't a Christian can't understand and can't accept these thoughts from God, which the Holy Spirit gives us. They sound foolish to him, because only those who have the Holy Spirit within them can understand what the Holy Spirit means. Others just can't take it in" (1 Corinthians 2:14, TLB).

Paul said he was not ashamed of this kind of teaching. While unacceptable to the man of the world, it does not embarrass those who are born again. Boldly he declared, "I am not ashamed of the gospel of Christ: for it is the power of God unto salvation to everyone that believeth; to the Jew first and also to the Greek. For therein is the righteousness of God revealed" (Romans 1:16–17).

When the Holy Spirit's words are used to teach the Holy Spirit's facts to men and women of God, this gives them power to understand the righteousness of God and be saved.

Holy Spirit,
You make it exciting to learn.
Even a child can understand.

83

ABIDING WITHIN

Know ye not that . . . the Spirit of God dwelleth in you?
1 CORINTHIANS 3:16

he Holy Spirit inhabits each believer in the Lord Jesus Christ. This is one of the "revealed things" the Holy Spirit teaches so well. To the natural mind this would be foolishness, but to the spiritual mind it is understood by revelation knowledge. That is, we believe what the Word says the Holy Spirit does. The Holy Spirit *indwells* believers. "Know ye not that ye are the temple of God, and that the Spirit of God dwelleth in you?" (1 Corinthians 3:16).

The indwelling presence of the Holy Spirit did not exist in the days of the Old Testament saints. During that time, the Holy Spirit came upon men and women but did not abide in them permanently. The Spirit of God indwelt believers from the Day of Pentecost onward.

In this work the Holy Spirit joins Himself to us in our spirits and we become one. Just as a physical union makes two people one flesh, a spiritual union with God makes us one spirit with God. Scripture states that "he who is joined to the Lord is one spirit with Him" (1 Corinthians 6:17, NKJV).

It would not make sense to say that he who is joined to the Lord is one soul with Him; for God is Spirit. The soul can know about God as doctrine or theology, but it is the spirit of man indwelt by the Holy Spirit that is intimately joined with God.

This is why we are commanded not to be unequally yoked together with any other god or unbeliever. We do not mix. Because the Holy Spirit has taken up residence in us, we are declared holy and belong only to God. God has first rights to us. He paid for us with the blood of His Son. "Know ye not that your body is the temple of the Holy [Spirit] which is in you, which ye have of God, and ye are not your own?" (1 Corinthians 6:19).

We are to be like the Father and the Son. They spoke the same thing. They agreed together. They were *one*. Paul exhorted the believers to do likewise: "All speak the same thing. . . . Be perfectly joined together in the same mind and in the same judgment" (1 Corinthians 1:10, TLB).

184

Let it be well known among all believers that we are the temples of the living God through the habitation of the Holy Spirit. Yes, God *has* said, "I will dwell in them, and walk in them; and I will be their God and they shall be my people" (2 Corinthians 6:16).

The time has come for true worshipers to praise Him from the temple within.

Holy Spirit,
how dependent we
are upon Your presence within us.
We worship You,
Father, in the Holy Place.

84
COMPLETE SALVATION

Washed . . . sanctified . . . justified . . . by the Spirit of our God.
1 CORINTHIANS 6:11

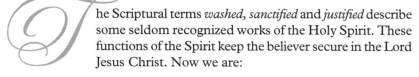

he Scriptural terms *washed, sanctified* and *justified* describe some seldom recognized works of the Holy Spirit. These functions of the Spirit keep the believer secure in the Lord Jesus Christ. Now we are:

- *Washed: cleansed.* The Holy Spirit as living water flows within the redeemed for continual cleansing from sin.
- *Sanctified: consecrated.* The anointing of the Holy Spirit sets us apart for God's use.
- *Justified: declared righteous.* By God's great mercy and grace we are forgiven and our sins blotted out. The Holy Spirit watches over us for our good, just as if we had never sinned.

Meditating upon these three mighty works brings a new appreciation of the fact that God has not left us alone to work out our own salvation. Rather, it is the Spirit of God who works in us so that we are ready, willing and able to do God's will.

Because the Holy Spirit cares for us so well, He could be likened to a sponsor, an advocate, a supporter. He continually helps us. We need Him, for we were once in rebellion against God and totally disabled. "Such [ungodly] were some of you: but ye are washed, but ye are sanctified, but ye are justified in the name of the Lord Jesus, and by the Spirit of our God" (1 Corinthians 6:11).

A sponsor makes a formal promise or pledge on behalf of another. The Scripture says "you . . . were stamped with the seal of the long-promised Holy Spirit. That [Spirit] is the guarantee of our inheritance—the first fruit, the pledge and foretaste" (Ephesians 1:13–14, AMPLIFIED).

A sponsor is a person who arranges or promotes an organization or meeting. "For by (means of the personal agency of) one (Holy) Spirit we were all . . . baptized . . . into one body, and all made to drink of one (Holy) Spirit" (1 Corinthians 12:13, AMPLIFIED).

His threefold work fashions us into one organism: the Church, the Body of Christ. It is the Holy Spirit who will present the Church as a chaste virgin to Christ: holy, without spot, wrinkle or blemish.

How the Holy Spirit does His work is the great mystery of godliness. But because He works in us to will and to do of God's good pleasure, we are encouraged to press on toward that high calling of God, who chose us for Himself. Meanwhile, we testify as Paul did: "I don't mean to say I am perfect. I haven't learned all I should even yet, but I keep working toward that day when I will finally be all that Christ saved me for and wants me to be" (Philippians 3:12, TLB).

Yes, God the Father and God the Son would say to us, this is why we sent the Holy Spirit. He never fails. Trust Him.

We trust You, Holy Spirit,
to perfect the saints.

85

CONTROLLING MY SPEECH

No man can say that Jesus is the Lord, but by the Holy [Spirit].

1 CORINTHIANS 12:3

How can it be that no one is able to say "Jesus is Lord" but by the power of the Holy Spirit? Those wanting to show that God is a liar would laugh at this and prove Him wrong by using their own mouths to say "Jesus is Lord." What the Scripture means here is that no one can say Jesus is Lord and really believe it unless the Holy Spirit helps him. An amplified reading of the text explains it well: "No one can [really] say, Jesus is [my] Lord, except by and under the power and influence of the Holy Spirit" (1 Corinthians 12:3, AMPLIFIED).

Conversely, the demons and all the host of hell declare who Jesus is to them. They believe—and tremble—saying, "What have we to do with thee, Jesus, thou Son of God? art thou come . . . to torment us before the time?" (Matthew 8:29).

They know "Jesus, Son of the Most High God" (Mark 5:7; Luke 8:28), but He is not their Lord. For to claim Jesus as your Lord means you are His servant. Demons serve their lord—Beelzebub, the prince of demons, Satan.

But what does this have to do with us today? Can people say that Jesus is their Lord and fake it? They can, yet they cannot. They lie. It is not the truth. And the Holy Spirit knows what is truth and what is not. It is His breath they use in lying to Him if Jesus is not their Lord, and He brings just judgment.

It is possible to lie to men but it is not possible to lie to the Holy Spirit. Ananias and Sapphira tried that; it did not work. Look at the father of their lie: "Why hath Satan filled thine heart to lie to the Holy Spirit[?] . . . Why hast thou conceived this thing in thine heart? thou hast not lied unto men, but unto God" (Acts 5:3–4).

In Jesus' earthly ministry both Jews and Gentiles disowned, blasphemed and cursed Him as an imposter. The Spirit of God would never speak that way. "Therefore I tell you that no one who is speaking by the Spirit of God says, 'Jesus be cursed,' and no one can say, 'Jesus is Lord,' except by the Holy Spirit" (1 Corinthians 12:3, NIV).

This "speech control" of the Holy Spirit is important to us in other ways, too. It helps us discern whether or not those who say they speak messages from God are true or false:

> You will remember that before you became Christians you went around from one idol to another, not one of which could speak a single word. But now you are meeting people who claim to speak messages from the Spirit of God. How can you know whether they are really inspired by God or whether they are fakes? Here is the test: no one speaking by the power of the Spirit of God can curse Jesus, and no one can say, "Jesus is Lord," and really mean it, unless the Holy Spirit is helping him.
>
> 1 Corinthians 12:2–3, TLB

Thank You, Holy Spirit,
for letting the redeemed of the
Lord know why they can say so.
Yes, Jesus Christ is my Lord!

86
SPIRITUAL GIFTS

There are diversities of gifts, but the same Spirit.
1 CORINTHIANS 12:4

ince we are not to be ignorant concerning spiritual gifts, exactly what are they? A "spiritual gift" is God's grace, favor and kindness freely bestowed upon us. The Greek word used in the text for gift is the familiar word *charisma*. It denotes God's supernatural abilities given through the inward working of the Holy Spirit.

The act of giving originated in God. He was the first to give anything. God so loved the world that He gave—Jesus is God's gift. The Holy Spirit is a *charisma* from both the Father and Son. In other words, the "gift" God gave is a Person: Himself. *Emmanuel!*

Every gift received from God is part of God, for He cares enough to impart the very best. And since God is Spirit, the gifts He gives are named "spiritual gifts." Like Him, they are alive, powerful and full of His Spirit. So it can be said, "Every good gift and every perfect gift is from above, and cometh down from the Father of lights with whom is no variableness neither shadow of turning" (James 1:17).

There is no end to the good gifts of God just as there is no end to God. But there is only one Spirit through whom they are given. "Now God gives us many kinds of special abilities, but it is the same Holy Spirit who is the source of them all" (1 Corinthians 12:4, TLB).

Spiritual gifts are the responsibility of the Holy Spirit. His work is to distribute them as He deems necessary. He knows *who* should have *what* gift, *why, when* and *where*. "All these [achievements and abilities] are inspired and brought to pass by one and the same (Holy) Spirit, Who apportions to each person individually [exactly] as He chooses" (1 Corinthians 12:11, AMPLIFIED).

There is an Old Testament picture of giving gifts in Genesis 24, which beautifully typifies this work of the Holy Spirit. When it came time for Abraham to choose a bride for his son Isaac, he sent his chief steward back to his kindred for that purpose.

Setting out with ten camels laden with gifts, the steward pondered these questions. "How will I know I have found the right woman? What if she is not willing to follow me home to my master's house and to be Isaac's bride?" He then prayed that the one who gave him water to drink and provided water for his camels also, would be the one.

Rebekah did just that. And as soon as she did, Abraham's steward gave her gifts: an earring and bracelets.

After meeting her family and explaining his mission to them, they gave their permission for the marriage. And when Rebekah agreed to be Isaac's bride, Abraham's steward unloaded *all* the gifts he had brought. He withheld nothing. Jewels of silver and gold, fine raiment and costly garments of beauty he lavished upon Rebekah and all her family.

The next day Rebekah left her familiar world and went with the trusted servant, who led her back to be joined to Isaac.

In the story, Abraham is a type of God the Father. Isaac is a type of Jesus the Son. The steward, nameless in the Scripture, is a type of the Holy Spirit. Rebekah, the bride, is a type of the Church—those "called out ones" who are given the gifts, who receive them with joy and use them.

Paul understood the importance of spiritual gifts. He praised God for their abundance in the church at Corinth saying, "I can never stop thanking God for all the wonderful gifts he has given you, now that you are Christ's: he has enriched your whole life. . . . Now you have every grace and blessing; every spiritual gift and power for doing his will are yours during this time of waiting for the return of our Lord Jesus Christ" (1 Corinthians 1:4–5, 7, TLB).

It is true. While we wait for the return of our heavenly bridegroom, we are richly dressed and richly blessed. Every grace and blessing, every spiritual gift and power, are ours to do God's will. They belong to the Church. We should not allow ourselves to be robbed of them by anyone. Nor should we make excuses for the lack of them if we have not accepted them.

When the Holy Spirit ushers out the Church to meet the Lord in the air, the beast, the false prophet and the dragon will counterfeit the gifts to deceive the whole world. This will fulfill the prophecy of Jesus. "I am come in my Father's name, and ye receive me not: if another shall come in his own name, him ye will receive" (John 5:43).

Precious Holy Spirit,
You and Your gifts I do receive.
They are good, perfect, full and free.
I'm glad You know what is best for me.

87

DAILY BENEFITS

The Spirit is given to every man to profit.
1 CORINTHIANS 12:7

The work of the Holy Spirit, as He apportions the gifts, helps *everyone*—both the one through whom the gift is flowing and those upon whom the gift is bestowed. "To each one is given the manifestation of the (Holy) Spirit—that is, the evidence, the spiritual illumination of the Spirit—for good and profit" (1 Corinthians 12:7, AMPLIFIED).

Activating the gifts became possible when Jesus returned to heaven after His resurrection. It is written of Him, when He ascended to the Father in heaven, "Thou hast ascended on high . . . thou hast received gifts for men; yea, for the rebellious also, that the LORD God might dwell among them. Blessed be the Lord, who daily loadeth us with benefits, even the God of our salvation" (Psalm 68:18–19).

That storehouse of gifts He received for us was unloaded upon us through the Holy Spirit in the form of men. "His (Christ's) gifts were [varied; He Himself appointed and gave men to us,] some to be apostles (special messengers), some prophets (inspired preachers and expounders), some evangelists (preachers of the Gospel, traveling missionaries), some pastors (shepherds of His flock) and teachers" (Ephesians 4:11, AMPLIFIED).

These special messengers through whom the gifts flow bless the whole church, worldwide, in each generation. They are "building up the church, the Body of Christ, to a position of strength and maturity; until finally we all believe alike about our salvation and about our Savior, God's Son, and all become full-grown in the Lord—yes, to the point of being filled full with Christ" (Ephesians 4:12–13, TLB).

Just as Jesus was filled with all the fullness of the Godhead in His body, even so we can be filled with Christ's fullness. Under the leadership of the Holy Spirit we are weaned from being children who keep changing their minds about what they believe.

The gifts are necessary tools to equip God's people to do His work, but do we really appreciate them? If we did, wouldn't there be more evidence of the gifts functioning in each individual life? Spiritual gifts should be the things we "hold in common." That is why Christians are admonished to covet the best gifts and lovingly share them. "As each of you has received a gift (a particular spiritual talent, a gracious divine endowment), employ it for one another as [befits] good trustees of God's many-sided grace—faithful stewards of the extremely diverse [powers and gifts granted to Christians by] unmerited favor" (1 Peter 4:10, AMPLIFIED).

In the Old Testament, Esau is an example of one who despised the gifts that belonged to him as the eldest son. He attached no importance to his rightful inheritance from Isaac and sold it to his brother Jacob for a bowl of lentil stew. Afterward, "when he wanted [to regain title to] his inheritance of the blessing, he was rejected (disqualified and set aside), for he could find no chance to recall the choice he had made—although he sought for it carefully with [bitter] tears" (Hebrews 12:17, AMPLIFIED).

Esau had made a decision he had no power to reverse. God judged him as a profane (godless and sacrilegious) man for what he did.

Every moving of the Spirit is beneficial. From the beginning of time we see the Holy Spirit making order out of chaos, and so He does in the Church. He is the same, yesterday, today and forever. "Thus saith the LORD, thy Redeemer, the Holy One of Israel; I am the LORD thy God which teacheth thee to profit, which leadeth thee by the way that thou shouldest go" (Isaiah 48:17).

Holy Spirit,
we thank You for the gifts,
which profit us. Forgive us for despising
them when You mean them for our good.

88
WISDOM, KNOWLEDGE, DISCERNING OF SPIRITS

By the Spirit [is given] . . . wisdom . . . knowledge . . . discerning of spirits.

1 CORINTHIANS 12:8, 10

Listed in this chapter are nine specific spiritual gifts given by the Holy Spirit. Since much has been written about them, the emphasis here will be on the definition of the gifts—what they are and are not—with examples from Scripture to illustrate them.

The word of wisdom, the word of knowledge and the discerning of spirits are best described as "revelation gifts." They reveal truth not known. It is important to recognize that the Holy Spirit is the channel for their operation. "For to one is given by the Spirit the word of wisdom; to another the word of knowledge by the same Spirit . . . to another discerning of spirits" (1 Corinthians 12:8, 10).

Wisdom

The word of wisdom is supernatural direction from God to work out our salvation and carry out His will. It comes from the heart of God as part of His omniscience. Note: It is a word, not the whole counsel of God. It is the right word for the right time to remedy a problem.

This wisdom gift is beyond man's understanding or intuition. Nor is it found in a god or goddess. It is totally under the control of the Holy Spirit, who gives it for the common good of all concerned. The word of wisdom influences future behavior.

The Spirit of wisdom moved upon every prophet in Old Testament times. They often spoke wisdom in mysteries they did not fully understand. Sometimes the wisdom spoken to them was not heeded. Other times the wisdom imparted to them enabled them to do exploits beyond their own knowledge.

For example, God's wisdom shared with Bezaleel gave him understanding to build a special dwelling place (Tabernacle) for God on the earth. Bezaleel received craftsmanship abilities and supernatural wisdom to follow God's perfect pattern for the Tabernacle. The Lord "filled him with the spirit of God, in wisdom, in understanding, and in knowledge, and in all manner of workmanship" (Exodus 35:31) to create things unseen before.

Isaiah spoke and wrote as he was moved by the Holy Spirit to reveal truth about the coming Messiah. Isaiah 53 stands out as an example of indisputable wisdom about Jesus Christ which, many years later, was fulfilled to the letter.

Today, wisdom comes through the Holy Spirit in a variety of ways. In dreams, in visions, by taking individuals up into the Spirit realm supernaturally to see things out of this world, or just in speaking through them. As they open their mouths, He fills them.

For example, when uneducated Peter was asked to explain the momentous events on the Day of Pentecost, he spoke forth wisdom that did not come from his own understanding. His word was, "This is that which was spoken through the prophet Joel. . . . I will pour out . . . my Spirit; and they shall prophesy" (Acts 2:16, 18).

Knowledge

The word of knowledge is informative. It works closely with the word of wisdom by understanding how to put it into effect. This gift is God's knowledge of things present. Again, the Holy Spirit controls its dispensing and use.

The Spirit of knowledge is not an educated guess. Nor is it knowledge acquired through means of extrasensory perception. It is spiritual knowledge given for guidance, to meet a need or to build up the Church.

The apostle Paul spoke a word of knowledge when a severe storm threatened the lives of all those sailing with him. He warned, "You will all die unless everyone stays aboard" (Acts 27:31, TLB). He further instructed the soldiers and the commanding officer not to use the lifeboats but to let those who were able swim to shore and the rest use planks and debris from the broken ship. As a result everyone was saved.

To settle an argument regarding the daily distribution of food between Greek and Hebrew women, the first apostles used this word of knowledge. "It would not be right for us to neglect the ministry of the word of God in order to wait on tables. Brothers, choose seven men from among you who are known to be full of the Spirit and wisdom. We will turn this responsibility over to them and will give our attention to prayer and the ministry of the word" (Acts 6:2–4, NIV). This word of knowledge pleased both sides, and the solution brought about the ministry of deacons in the church.

God, the Holy Spirit, does not give a word of knowledge in vain. It is always profitable. It always accomplishes what He pleases.

Discerning of Spirits

The discerning or distinguishing of spirits is the God-given ability to recognize, identify and discern various kinds of spirits we come in contact with.

It is not the discerning of times and seasons, a hunch, a suspicion or feelings. Nor is it obtained through means of occult mediums in a seance. It is the discerning of spirits: God's Spirit, angelic spirits, the human spirit or demonic spirits.

When the gift of discerning spirits is working, those with the gift can differentiate the various spirits. This guards against deception, lies, false doctrine and unholy spirits. The Holy Spirit, being spirit, cannot be fooled. That is why the apostle John warned the Church saying, "Beloved, believe not every spirit, but try the spirits whether they are of God: because many false prophets are gone out into the world" (1 John 4:1).

An example of the discerning of spirits occurs in the Old Testament story of Elisha and his servant Gehazi. After Elisha healed King Naaman's leprosy, the king offered him gifts, which Elisha refused to accept. But Gehazi secretly ran after Naaman saying his master had sent him for 75 pounds of silver and two sets of clothing. When Gehazi went back to Elisha, he lied about where he had been and what he had done. But Elisha said to him, "Was not my spirit with you when the man got down from his chariot to meet you? Is this the time to take money, or to accept clothes . . . ? Naaman's leprosy will cling to you and your descendants forever" (2 Kings 5:26–27, NIV).

In the first church, Peter discerned the spirits of Ananias and Sapphira when they told him they gave the church *all* the money they had gotten from selling a possession. Without being told, Peter knew Ananias was lying and said, "Ananias, how is it that Satan has so filled your heart that you have lied to the Holy Spirit and have kept for yourself some of the money you have received for the land? . . . You have not lied to men but to God" (Acts 5:3–4, NIV). Ananias died.

Later on, Paul discerned the spirit in Elymas, a sorcerer, who was opposing Paul's preaching of Jesus. Paul looked straight at Elymas and announced, "You are a child of the devil and an enemy of everything that is right! You are full of all kinds of deceit and trickery. Will you never stop perverting the right ways of the Lord?" (Acts.13:10, NIV). Elymas became blind.

The gifts of wisdom, knowledge and discerning of spirits cannot be entered into with human reasoning nor comprehended by the senses. They may at times overlap, or there may be a combination of all three.

How do we recognize the moving of the Spirit in the revelation gifts? By faith. His manifestation is like that still, small voice described by Elijah that you begin to know on the inside. Or that Isaiah likened to our ears hearing a word spoken behind us that says "this is the way, walk in it," when we do not know whether to turn left or right. Our work is simply to wait and be ready and willing.

Holy Spirit,
without You we could not
possibly know that we know that we know.

89

FAITH, HEALING, MIRACLES

By the Spirit [is given] . . . faith . . . the gifts of healing . . . the working of miracles.

1 CORINTHIANS 12:8–10

he gift of faith, gifts of healing and the working of miracles are often described as "power gifts" because they *do* something. "To another faith by the same Spirit; to another the gifts of healing by the same Spirit; to another the working of miracles" (1 Corinthians 12:9–10).

Faith

The gift of faith is a supernatural surge of *God's faith* to accomplish His purposes. It requires God's omnipotence, which produces faith so full of power it can usually be demonstrated.

The gift of faith is not the *natural* faith that every man has. Nor is it *saving* faith, which every man can be *reborn* with. Nor is it the faith a Christian lives by daily. Neither is it faith in curses or black magic.

The gift of faith is the ability to believe God and act supernaturally, beyond human doubts, reasoning or questioning. Like Peter walking on the water. The gift of faith is usually activated by speaking. For instance, demons can be commanded to come out of willing people once they are discerned by revelation gifts.

When the gift of faith begins to operate it can usher in the gifts of healing and the working of miracles too. Sometimes it is difficult to say where one gift stops and another starts, but the Holy Spirit gives them as He wills to get the job done.

Jesus' ministry is the best example of the authority and power operating in these gifts. Seeing a fig tree without any fruit, He spoke the word that fruit should not grow upon it again. The disciples saw how soon the fig tree withered away and were amazed. Jesus assured them, "If you have faith and do not doubt, you will not only do what was done to the fig tree, but also if you say to this mountain, 'Be removed and be cast into the sea;' it will be done" (Matthew 21:21, NKJV).

Hebrews 11 lists many examples of the gift of faith accomplishing feats beyond any natural potential in individuals. Some of these heroes of faith in the Old Testament "stopped the mouths of lions, quenched the violence of fire, escaped the edge of the sword, out of weakness [they] were made strong. . . . Women received their dead raised to life again: and others were tortured, not accepting deliverance; that they might obtain a better resurrection" (Hebrews 11:33–35).

The gift of faith is in operation every day.

Healing

Gifts of healing are by the same Spirit. Again, it is all of God and none of man. It is the extraordinary power to heal sickness and disease without human aid or medical science.

The gifts of healing are *not* healing through drugs, potions or mind science. Nor are they the sometimes-gradual healings manifested when the elders of the church pray for the sick and anoint them with oil.

Gifts of healing through the anointing of the Holy Spirit are instantaneous and verifiable. They may be physical or spiritual in form. The infirmity is replaced with health.

Jesus was the only one who never failed to heal all manner of sickness and disease. Sometimes He spoke forth the healing with words, or touched the person, or they touched Him.

The woman with an issue of blood had seen doctors for twelve years and spent all she had. She was desperate. She believed that if she just touched His clothes, she would be made whole. Her faith rose to meet the occasion. The results were supernatural. She knew it and Jesus knew it. Healing power had gone out from Him, and she was instantly cured. Jesus commented to her, "Daughter, your faith has healed you. Go in peace and be freed from your suffering" (Mark 5:34, NIV).

Soon after Pentecost and the arrival of the Holy Spirit, Peter and John released the gift of healing upon a man born lame. The man had requested silver and gold, but Peter gave him Jesus and health when he said, "Silver or gold I do not have, but what I have I give you. In the name of Jesus Christ of Nazareth, walk" (Acts 3:6, NIV).

As Peter took hold of the man's hand, the man leaped to his feet, began to walk and praised God. He knew the source of his healing.

Paul moved in the gifts of healing, too. On the island of Malta, Publius' father was sick in bed, "suffering from fever and dysentery. Paul went in to see him and, after prayer, placed his hands on him and healed him. When this had happened, the rest of the sick on the island came and were cured" (Acts 28:8–9, NIV).

Notice that the rest of the sick were healed too. The healing gifts manifested that day were numerous enough for all. There is no lack of supply in the Godhead.

Healing gifts are for today.

Miracles

The working of miracles is the supernatural intervention of God through the Holy Spirit in the ordinary course of nature. It sets aside the normal laws of the universe and supersedes them with God's divine order.

The working of miracles is not associated with witchcraft, sorcery or magical arts.

The working of miracles is closely related to the healing gifts, yet is different. Gifts of healing have to do with human physiology while miracles invade the laws of physics. Miracles must be seen to be proven. Healing gifts can be visible and invisible.

If we witness a miracle, we know a mighty God has intervened in the course of human events. The very purpose of miracles is to capture the attention of people and cause them to know that God *is* God!

On the island of Malta, Paul was bitten by a poisonous snake. The people who saw it were sure he would die. Instead, Paul shook off the snake and was unharmed. It so impressed the people that they thought he was a god (see Acts 28:1–6). The Holy Spirit makes supermen out of ordinary men through the working of miracles.

Jesus is the best pattern for miracles. The unruly winds and seas obeyed His rebuke and calmed down. Five loaves and two fishes multiplied to feed five thousand men plus the women and children. Jesus resurrected Lazarus, dead for four days, because the Spirit of the Lord had so highly anointed Him.

Jesus promised that we too would do these works, and even greater miracles than He did. Not greater in *quality*, but greater in *quantity*. Every time, this would bring glory to the Father.

Therefore, Peter, in fulfilling Jesus' prophecy, raised a dead woman to life in Joppa. Her friends had already prepared her for burial. Peter, turning toward the body, said, "'Get up, Dorcas,' and she opened her eyes!

And when she saw Peter she sat up! . . . The news raced through the town, and many believed in the Lord" (Acts 9:40, 42, TLB).

The gifts are given for the Church to use. We must receive them, acknowledge the giver and make use of them.

And we shall. Before this age comes to a close, more mighty works will again be evident throughout the whole earth, making hell's foundations quiver!

Holy Spirit,
You won't be finished with
us until we use Your gifts the right way.
Keep stirring us up!

90

PROPHECY, TONGUES, INTERPRETATION OF TONGUES

By the same Spirit [is given] . . . prophecy . . . tongues . . . the interpretation of tongues.

1 CORINTHIANS 12:9–10

The gifts of prophecy, tongues and interpretation of tongues are frequently called "inspiration gifts," or vocal gifts. They are gifts that *say* something.

All these gifts are like a partnership. They require both the inspiration of the Holy Spirit and the use of our vocal cords. As someone aptly put it, "Without the Holy Spirit we cannot, and without us the Holy Spirit will not."

Prophecy

The gift of prophecy is the supernatural ability to speak forth words that come from God.

What kind of words? Paul defined prophecy to the church at Corinth by saying, "He who prophesies speaks edification and exhortation and comfort to men" (1 Corinthians 14:3, NKJV).

In other words, correctly used, the gift of prophecy should build up, stir up and cheer up the church.

The gift of prophecy does not come from man's thoughts or feelings. Nor is it learned through soothsayers or divination. But there are rules to govern its use. Scripture tells us to "quench not the Spirit. Despise not prophesyings. Prove all things; hold fast that which is good" (1 Thessalonians 5:19–21).

To do that, there is often more than one prophet. Prophets should work in harmony with each other and control their speaking. Two or three may speak while the others are to judge what is said; for at the mouth of two or three witnesses everything is to be established, even the things of God. Judgment is the built-in protection for holding fast that which is good.

The value of prophecy is that it is spoken to the Church in the language of the people. Therefore, "if an unbeliever or someone who does not understand comes in while everybody is prophesying, he will be convinced by all that he is a sinner and will be judged by all, and the secrets of his heart will be laid bare. So he will fall down and worship God, exclaiming, 'God is really among you!'" (1 Corinthians 14:24–25, NIV).

Prophecy was the gift flowing through Paul to edify young Timothy in the early Church. He told him, "Do not neglect your gift, which was given you through a prophetic message when the body of elders laid their hands on you. Be diligent in these matters; give yourself wholly to them, so that everyone may see your progress. Watch your life and doctrine closely. Persevere in them, because if you do, you will save both yourself and your hearers" (1 Timothy 4:14–16, NIV).

Prophesying is alive and well today.

Tongues

The gift of tongues is a supernatural utterance that comes from God through the Holy Spirit for the Church. This gift comes through the person speaking it in a language unknown to him, but occasionally known to others who hear it. It is sometimes sung.

Tongues may be spoken in the church by several individuals who speak out the utterances the Holy Spirit gives them. The church then waits to hear the interpretation.

Used in public ministry, the unknown language is meant to get the attention of those who do not believe. Paul wrote that "tongues are for a sign, not to them that believe, but to them that believe not" (1 Corinthians 14:22).

All believers may pray with the Spirit and with their understanding. But the gift of tongues spoken publicly in church requires the additional prompting of the Holy Spirit. It is a step of faith beyond the private use of praying in the Spirit.

Paul refers to the benefits of praying in the Spirit alone. There are at least four things that happen.

One: We speak mysteries to God in our spirit. "He that speaketh in an unknown tongue speaketh not unto men, but unto God. . . . In the spirit he speaketh mysteries" (1 Corinthians 14:2).

As we give our tongues over to the control of the Holy Spirit, He speaks through us to God in the language of the Godhead. Our Father ordained it that way. We may not understand what is said, but God does. God understands the mysteries uttered as we become aware of the glory of His presence. For "we speak the wisdom of God in a mystery, even the hidden wisdom, which God ordained before the world unto our glory" (1 Corinthians 2:7).

Two: We edify ourselves. "He that speaketh in an unknown tongue edifieth himself" (1 Corinthians 14:4).

We personally grow spiritually when we speak in tongues, just as the whole church is strengthened through prophecy.

Three: We pray and sing with the Spirit. "If I pray in an unknown tongue, my spirit prayeth, but my understanding is unfruitful. . . . I will pray with the spirit, and I will pray with the understanding also: I will sing with the spirit, and I will sing with the understanding also" (1 Corinthians 14:14–15).

None of us should say we do not know *how* to pray when the Holy Spirit is available to pray with us. Paul depended upon the Holy Spirit and explained to the Corinthian believers that he prayed with his understanding *and* with his spirit. He sang with his understanding *and* with his spirit. It was as if Paul allowed the Holy Spirit to set up a prayer and praise meeting inside of him. When he came to the end of his understanding, he yielded to the Holy Spirit and joined Him in spiritual language and music that went beyond his own expressions. How Satan must hate this, for he is totally ignored!

Four: We bless with the spirit and give thanks with the spirit. "You praise and thank God with the spirit" (1 Corinthians 14:16, TLB).

Although we speak mysteries to God, edify ourselves, sing and pray in the spirit, bless with the spirit and give thanks with the spirit, Paul reminds us to benefit the whole church by speaking with our understanding so everyone can join in saying "Amen!"

Tongues, interpretation and prophecy have their rightful place whenever the Body of Christ gets together. They are to operate freely to inspire the whole assembly. Everyone has something to contribute. "What then shall we say, brothers? When you come together, everyone has a hymn, or a word of instruction, a revelation, a tongue or an interpretation. All of these must be done for the strengthening of the church" (1 Corinthians 14:26, NIV).

Can tongues be faked? Yes, anything God does, Satan will attempt to counterfeit. Words can be stammered out under demonic power; but for those words, there can be no Holy Spirit-inspired interpretation.

Tongues should not be spoken against, especially since they are part of the Great Commission to the Church. Jesus' last words to His disciples were, "Go ye into all the world, and preach the gospel to every creature. He that believeth and is baptized shall be saved; but he that believeth not shall be damned. And these signs shall follow them that believe; In my name shall they cast out devils; they shall speak with new tongues" (Mark 16:15–17).

Tongues too are for today. They will not cease until *all* the gifts have ceased. When the Church is with God, none of the gifts of the Spirit will be needed. For we shall know as God knows and speak with the tongues of angels in the language of heaven.

Interpretation of Tongues

The gift of tongues necessarily *precedes* the interpretation of tongues. If tongues were not spoken there would be nothing to interpret.

Interpretation of tongues is the ability to interpret in a *known* language something previously spoken in an *unknown* language. Tongues and the interpretation of the tongues together are equal to prophecy because they edify the Church.

The one who speaks in tongues is encouraged to pray for the interpretation. Thus, the person who interprets may be the same one who spoke the unknown language, operating in two of the gifts. Or it may be a different person. The Holy Spirit decides.

The interpretation is not a literal translation. Therefore, there can be more than one interpretation to a single message in tongues. Each reveals what God wants us to know and not the thoughts of the person speaking.

Again, Paul laid down guidelines to keep order, saying, "If anyone speaks in a tongue, two—or at the most three—should speak, one at a time, and someone must interpret. If there is no interpreter, the speaker should keep quiet in the church and speak to himself and God" (1 Corinthians 14:27–28, NIV).

All the gifts operated in the Old Testament and the life of Jesus except tongues and interpretation of tongues. These two gifts were born with the Church.

In summarizing the gifts, it would seem that the revelation gifts of wisdom, knowledge and discerning of spirits are found in God the Father. The power gifts of faith, healing and miracles are found in Jesus the Son. And the vocal gifts of prophecy, tongues and interpretation are found in the Holy Spirit.

All the gifts are helping to write the last, still unfinished chapter of the book of Acts—and will, until He who is perfect is come.

We give thee back thine own, Eternal Spirit,
whate'er that gift may be, for all we have
is thine alone, a gift, O Lord, from thee.

91
BODY BAPTISM

For by one Spirit are we all baptized into one body . . . and have been all made to drink into one Spirit.

1 CORINTHIANS 12:13

The Holy Spirit's primary work on the earth today centers on the Body of Christ—all who are redeemed by the blood of Jesus. The Holy Spirit transforms and transfuses us with His Spirit until we become one living organism. In doing this, the Holy Spirit baptizes us into the Body of Christ. "For by one Spirit are we all baptized into one body" (1 Corinthians 12:13).

The Holy Spirit is the agent who does the baptizing. The element into which the Holy Spirit baptizes is Christ's body. Those baptized include everyone whom the Lord has chosen out of the world to come to Him.

When the Holy Spirit baptizes us, He plunges us into Christ. It is a total identification or transformation into the corporate Body of Christ, for "he that is joined to the Lord is one spirit" (1 Corinthians 6:17).

The Greek word *baptizo* means "to dye a cloth by dipping, or the *drawing of water by dipping one vessel into another.*"

Think about Jesus at the wedding in Cana when they ran out of wine. He told the servants to fill six pots, twenty or thirty gallons each, with water. "Dip some out and take it to the master of ceremonies," he instructed them. When the master of ceremonies sampled the *water,* he said it was the best *wine* he ever tasted. For Jesus had changed the water into wine—and set into motion a miracle that has never ceased.

The purpose of the Holy Spirit's dipping one vessel into another is oneness. Only the Holy Spirit could take people from every kindred, tribe and nation, and perfectly join them, the Body, to the Head in heaven. Thus we become one, sharing the divine nature of the Godhead (see 2 Peter 1:4, AMPLIFIED) by drinking the same Spirit of Life. "For by (means of the personal agency of) one (Holy) Spirit we were all, whether Jews or Greeks, slaves or free, baptized [and by baptism united together] into one body, and all made to drink of one (Holy) Spirit" (1 Corinthians 12:13, AMPLIFIED).

Just as God made the *human* body with many different parts and functions, so is the *spiritual* Body of Christ: "For just as the body is a unity and yet has many parts, and all the parts, though many, form [only] one body, so it is with Christ, the Messiah, the Anointed One" (1 Corinthians 12:12, AMPLIFIED).

To be members of Christ's body is so unique it has never before been conceived, nor has it entered into the heart of man to imagine such a wondrous thing. Believers, baptized by the Holy Spirit into Christ's body, come forth a *new creation.*

Paul had some idea of how glorious this new creation was when he was inspired by the Holy Spirit to describe a "chaste virgin." Writing to the church at Corinth he states, "I am jealous over you with godly jealousy: for I have espoused you to one husband, that I may present you as a chaste virgin to Christ" (2 Corinthians 11:2).

We are like a bride prepared for Christ by the work of the Holy Spirit. The proof of our virginity is left in the hands of the Holy Spirit. Our heavenly Baptizer, present among us, continues to fashion this new creation until at last we are complete in Christ.

Baptizing Holy Spirit,
thank You for putting us into one body
and making us "one spirit" with You.

92

OUR GUARANTEE

God has given us "the earnest of the Spirit."
2 CORINTHIANS 1:22

The Greek word for *earnest* is very special. It means "surety, a pledge, a guarantee." In this verse the "earnest" is a Person: the Holy Spirit.

It could be said that the earnest—the Holy Spirit—*is* the promise. Like an engagement ring for the bride to be, He is the tangible evidence of things not seen but hoped for. God "put his Spirit in our hearts as a deposit, guaranteeing what is to come" (2 Corinthians 1:22, NIV).

It is as if reservations have been made in advance for us, and the Holy Spirit is our down payment. He owns us. As proof, we carry Him around in that inner place of our hearts where we know God. There the guarantee rests secure, written not in ink "but with the Spirit of the living God, not on tablets of stone but on tablets of human hearts" (2 Corinthians 3:3, NIV).

If or when our hearts might condemn us, we have the assurance that our God is greater than our hearts. For when God is for us, who could possibly be against us? Remember: He spared not His own Son but delivered Him up for us all so that, with Him, He might freely give us all that He promised.

He did not leave us or forsake us. He came as promised to stay with us forever. The Holy Spirit in our hearts is our guarantee and God's guarantee that we belong to Him. Such surety brings that peace that passes all understanding. Yes, "the foundation of God standeth sure, having this seal, The Lord knoweth them that are his. And, Let every one that nameth the name of Christ depart from iniquity" (2 Timothy 2:19).

Do you have the earnest of the Spirit in your heart, confirming your destiny? Do you really believe God is able to keep you from falling, and to present you faultless before His throne in a resurrected body? Read it one more time. "We know that . . . when we die . . . we will have wonderful new bodies in heaven, homes that will be ours forevermore, made for us by God. . . . This is what God has prepared for us and, as a guarantee, he has given us his Holy Spirit" (2 Corinthians 5:1, 5, TLB).

Holy Spirit,
You are more than blind faith.
You are a foretaste of glory divine
living so deeply in our hearts. Amen.

93
GIVING LIFE

The spirit giveth life.
2 CORINTHIANS 3:6

Because of the work Christ did, the Spirit can work in and through us. The Holy Spirit's work is to give us life! Our work is to accept it and share it.

Paul, under the influence of the Holy Spirit, made sure the Corinthians understood where their life came from. He said God had helped the apostles to be "competent as ministers of a new covenant—not of the letter but of the Spirit; for the letter kills, but the Spirit gives life" (2 Corinthians 3:6, NIV).

Paul referred to the Old Testament (covenant) as the "letter" and the New Testament (covenant) as the "Spirit." He emphasized the old letter brought "condemnation" and death, but the Spirit brought "righteousness" and eternal life. It stands to reason that "if there had been a law given which could have given life . . . righteousness would have been by the law" (Galatians 3:21, NKJV).

The purpose of the Law was to bring the knowledge of sin and death. But it had no remedy. The purpose of Christ's coming was to bring life. Christ's life is the remedy the Holy Spirit gives us. If the Law could have given life, then Christ would not have had to die.

The old covenant of written law versus the New Covenant of a life-giving Spirit is not such a big stumbling block in this age of grace. But back then the new way was just beginning, and many misunderstood it. This transition from death to life needed to be taught so that people could be saved from their own deadly works of righteousness. Paul explained, "We do not tell them that they must obey every law of God or die; but we tell them there is life for them from the Holy Spirit. The old way, trying to be saved by keeping the Ten Commandments, ends in death; in the new way, the Holy Spirit gives them life" (2 Corinthians 3:6, TLB).

When was the legal written code of law replaced? By what and by whom? The written code of law was replaced by the living, spoken Word—Jesus

Christ—so that from the time of Jesus' resurrection it could be said, "Christ is the end of the law . . ." (Romans 10:4, NIV).

That is what the gospel is all about: Christ ending the Law! The old system of law was only enforced until Christ fulfilled it. Under the law, no one made it. *All* died and *all* fell short of God's righteous standard for life. But when the promised Messiah came, He offered the world an exchange for the laws no one could keep: His righteous life!

Using metaphoric language, Paul said "we are the sweet fragrance of Christ [which exhales] unto God, [discernable alike] among those who are being saved and among those who are perishing; to the latter it is an aroma [wafted] from death to death—a fatal odor, the smell of doom; to the former it is an aroma from life to life—a vital fragrance, living and fresh" (2 Corinthians 2:15–16, AMPLIFIED).

How does the Holy Spirit give life? No one knows that. But we share the evidence in ourselves by faith. He is life, and He gives life to those in Christ. It is the same eternal life shared by the Godhead.

How do we know we have never-ending life? God said so. And He cannot lie.

When did the Holy Spirit give us this life? The moment we came to Jesus. By the supernatural work of the Holy Spirit it is there now!

How can we be sure we are not still dead? There is a test. "We know that we have passed over out of death into the Life by the fact that we love the brethren, [our fellow Christians]. He who does not love abides—remains, is held and kept continually—in [spiritual] death" (1 John 3:14, AMPLIFIED).

Loving the brethren is not hard to do, for the same Holy Spirit who gives life has also flooded our hearts with God's love for one another.

Holy Spirit,
I'm alive! You do everything.
What excuse do I have
for not being like Christ?

94

LIBERTY

Where the Spirit of the Lord is, there is liberty.
2 CORINTHIANS 3:17

Liberty, in this Scripture, is a Person. The Spirit of the Lord Himself is liberty. Therefore, it can be said that where the Spirit of the Lord is, men's souls have been set free (see 2 Corinthians 3:17).

In the Old Testament this spirit of freedom was partially foreseen in the holy days God commanded the children of Israel to keep. The Sabbath day, celebrated once a week, represented physical freedom as a day of rest from work. And just as every seventh *day* was a Sabbath, every seventh *year* was a Sabbatical year of rest. But even more glorious was the multiple of seven Sabbatical years—Jubilee.

The celebration of Jubilee constituted three years when the Israelites did not have to work (sow or reap), for the land would yield its own increase. It began every fiftieth year, on the Day of Atonement. Liberty was proclaimed throughout the land, canceling all debts—both private and public—and restoring all original inheritances to their rightful owners. Every person was free to return to his own possessions and to his own family.

God instituted the economy of His nation Israel after these principles and guaranteed that it would work *if* they kept the Sabbaths. According to written history, Israel never enjoyed their liberty. They rarely kept the Sabbatical year, let alone the Jubilee at the end of the forty-ninth year.

Under the Law Jubilee was three years long, but when Jesus came He ushered in a perpetual Jubilee. He began His ministry by announcing this to Israel when He stood up in the Temple to read from Isaiah. It was as if He was saying, "You have another opportunity to be free at last and return to God!" Jesus declared, "The Spirit of the Lord is upon me, because he has anointed me to preach good news to the poor. He has sent me to proclaim freedom for the prisoners and recovery of sight for the blind, to release the oppressed, to proclaim the year of the Lord's favor" (Luke 4:18–19, NIV).

Many believe that announcement came in the year of Jubilee. That day, the Spirit of the Lord upon Jesus began to fulfill the conditions of Jubilee in every way, spiritually and physically. Everything Jesus said and did loosed them from the bondage of condemnation, sin and death. The miracles proved it. Jesus fulfilled all the righteous requirements of the Law that they could not. The Israelites received God's favor without having to work for it. Then at Pentecost, He passed on the same Spirit of the Lord that was upon Him to the new believers and to us.

This liberty that the Spirit imparted was such "good news" that Paul had to warn the Galatians of "false brethren" who would take it away if they could. He said, "[They] came to spy on us and see what freedom we enjoyed in Christ Jesus, as to whether we obeyed the Jewish laws or not. They tried to get us all tied up in their rules, like slaves in chains. But we did not listen to them for a single moment, for we did not want to confuse you into thinking that salvation can be earned by being circumcised and by obeying Jewish laws" (Galatians 2:4–6, TLB).

This is just as true today as it was then. Satan, through false brethren, is ever at work luring freed Christians back into religious bondage of being saved by another set of laws (rules) made up to inflate the ego. "Such rules are mere human teachings. . . . [They] may seem good, for rules of this kind require strong devotion and are humiliating and hard on the body, but they have no effect when it comes to conquering a person's evil thoughts and desires. They only make him proud" (Colossians 2:22–23, TLB).

So while it is true that whomever the Son sets free is truly free, our freedom is not given to add to the work of the cross. Our freedom is to do God's will, not alter it or substitute our own.

Paul also warned the Christians about losing their freedom through lack of self-control. "Everything is permissible for me—allowable and lawful; but not all things are helpful—good for me to do, expedient and profitable, when considered with other things. Everything is lawful for me, but I will not become the slave of anything or be brought under its power" (1 Corinthians 6:12, AMPLIFIED).

Only where the Spirit of the Lord is, is there true freedom. And only a truly liberated man or woman can be led of the Spirit.

Because of You, Holy Spirit, we
stand fast in the liberty
wherewith Christ has made us free.

95

CHANGING US

[We] are changed into the same image . . . by the Spirit of the Lord.

2 CORINTHIANS 3:18

*T*hose who turn to the Lord undergo a remarkable transformation wrought by the Holy Spirit—they are changed into the image of Jesus.

The amplification of the word *change* is interesting. The Greek word *metamorphoo* means "to change the form." This "change of form" is illustrated at least three times in Scripture: the transfigurations of Moses, Jesus and Stephen the martyr.

When Moses came down from Mt. Sinai with the Ten Commandments after forty days and forty nights with God, "the skin of his face shone" (Exodus 34:29).

The shining of Moses' face is very vivid in the Hebrew. *Shine* means "to push; to shoot out horns; to send out rays; to shine out or dart forth as lightning flashes." Because Moses had been in God's presence for so long, His glory made Moses' face as bright as the sun. Aaron and the Israelites were afraid to go near him so Moses put a veil over his face while speaking to them.

A similar experience happened to Peter, James and John when they suddenly saw Jesus transfigured before them. They, too, were frightened at the sight! Jesus' face "began to shine with glory, and his clothing became dazzling white, far more glorious than any earthly process could ever make it!" (Mark 9:2–3, TLB).

Stephen, in the early church, was on trial for his life. As he was brought before the Sanhedrin council of false witnesses, God's glory shone on his face and "everyone in the Council chamber saw Stephen's face become as radiant as an angel's!" (Acts 6:15, TLB).

Can we also be transformed inside and outside by the same glory? Of course we can. It is a work of the Holy Spirit. From glory to glory He is changing us, for our God is the Spirit of glory. As He was in the days of Moses, Jesus and Stephen, so is He in our day.

Where do we behold God's glory today? In His Word. When we renew our minds with the presence of God in His Word, the Holy Spirit overcomes us with change. We "are constantly being transfigured into His very own image in ever increasing splendor and from one degree of glory to another; [for this comes] from the Lord [Who is] the Spirit" (2 Corinthians 3:18, AMPLIFIED).

The metamorphosis that transforms and transfigures us is so spiritually natural that we gradually emerge into the very same image of God the Son.

This is just the beginning. Not only are we changed, but one day the whole earth will be changed and filled with His glory. In the age to come known as the Millennium, the sevenfold light of God's glory will be upon Israel for all the nations to see. At last, everyone will know the fulfillment of the prophets' predictions: "Arise, shine; for thy light is come, and the glory of the LORD has risen upon thee. The sun shall be no more thy light by day; neither for brightness shall the moon give light unto thee: but the LORD shall be unto thee an everlasting light, and thy God thy glory" (Isaiah 60:1, 19).

Holy Spirit,
what a blessing to know who the "changer" is.
No wonder God can be all in all!

96
COMMUNION

The communion of the Holy [Spirit] . . .
2 CORINTHIANS 13:14

he "communion of the Holy Spirit" is vital to the Church. Paul confirmed this when he ended his second letter to the Corinthian church with his blessing: "The grace of our Lord Jesus Christ, and the love of God, and the communion of the Holy [Spirit] be with you all. Amen" (2 Corinthians 13:14).

Paul rates the *communion* of the Holy Spirit with the *love* of God and the *grace* of our Lord Jesus Christ. This Scripture makes a clear reference to the three separate Persons of the Godhead and the part each plays in our salvation.

Communion is the Greek word *koinonia.* It means "fellowshipping with one another by communicating, sharing together, partaking together and being one." It describes the closeness produced in the divine union between God and man when the believer receives God's *love* and Christ's *grace.* It is only then that we share the intimacy of the Holy Spirit's presence.

God agreed to make us in His likeness and image for the very purpose of this companionship. Adam and Eve were the first to enjoy it. God walked and talked with them in the Garden in the cool of the day. Enoch, too, walked with God, and his conversation so pleased the Lord that He took Enoch home with Him. Noah walked and talked with God. God withheld nothing from Abraham, His friend. With Moses, He spoke face-to-face. God enjoys our company. He has allowed Himself to be known by all His children down through the ages, from the least to the greatest.

And He is still the same. Jesus told the disciples He had much more to say to them before He left, but they could not grasp it all then. That is why He promised to send the Holy Spirit, who would be with them forever and tell them everything Jesus was saying and doing.

It is this sweet communion the first apostles—so intimate with Jesus—yearned to pass on to us. They encouraged us to share it, too: "What we have seen and [ourselves] heard we are also telling you, so that you too may realize and enjoy fellowship as partners and partakers with us. And [this] fellowship that we have (which is a distinguishing mark of Christians) is with the Father and His Son Jesus Christ, the Messiah. And we are now writing these things to you so that our joy [in seeing you included] may be full—and your joy may be complete" (1 John 1:3–4, AMPLIFIED).

The proof of real communion and fellowship with God is overflowing *joy*. It comes from being welcomed into the secret place of the Most High God while still in this body of clay. And because our real citizenship is in heaven, the Holy Spirit ushers us "right up into Mount Zion, to the city of the living God, the heavenly Jerusalem, and to the gathering of countless happy angels; and to the church, composed of all those registered in heaven; and to God who is Judge of all; and to the spirits of the redeemed in heaven, already made perfect; and to Jesus himself" (Hebrews 12:22–24, TLB).

What is the communion of the Holy Spirit all about? What does the Holy Spirit communicate to us? In a word, it is Jesus Himself. The Spirit communicates to the Church the revelation of Jesus Christ. Through Him, we know the realities of the Kingdom of heaven.

Sunday morning finds many Christians in churches confidently affirming, "I believe in the Holy Spirit; . . . the communion of the saints; the forgiveness of sins; the resurrection of the body, and the life everlasting. Amen." The "communion of the saints" is made possible through union with the Holy Spirit. It is a work of the Holy Spirit seldom emphasized, yet without Him we could not enter into this holy privilege.

Thank You, Holy Spirit,
for being the tie that binds our hearts
into fellowship with those above.

97
WAITING

We through the Spirit wait....
GALATIANS 5:5

Who of us is not acquainted with waiting? Waiting is the chief complaint of the human race every day. Everyone waits for some*thing,* some*time* or some*one.*

Waiting is one of the hardest things we do. Our impatience makes it so, along with our desire to have everything we want—right now!

Solomon analyzed this problem by pointing out the waiting season for everything and every purpose under the sun. In Ecclesiastes 3, he observes that one has to wait to be born and wait to die; wait to plant and wait to harvest; wait to kill and wait for healing; wait to tear down and wait to build up. There is an appointed time to weep and a time to laugh; a time to mourn and a time to dance; a time to scatter stones and a time to gather them; a time to embrace and a time to refrain from embracing; a time to gain and a time to lose; a time to keep and a time to throw away; a time to tear and a time to mend; a time to be silent and a time to speak; a time to love and a time to hate; a time for war and a time for peace. The list is endless. The point is that the things we wait for are right only when the time is right. Therefore, it is important for us not only to wait, but to know the times as well.

Waiting is universal. It governs the heavens and the earth. And just as all creation waits for times and seasons under the *sun,* so do all Christians wait for times and seasons under the *Son.* Heaven waits. Earth waits. Man waits. And God waits.

Waiting is a divine attribute. How then can we complain? God has waited longer than any of His creation for the pleasure of His will. It is the end of the book: "When everything is subjected to Christ, then the Son Himself will also subject Himself to [the Father] Who put all things under Him, so that God may be all in all—that is, be everything to everyone, supreme, the indwelling and controlling factor of life" (1 Corinthians 15:28, AMPLIFIED).

God has His own reasons for controlling the times and seasons of our lives. He waits to be merciful to each one who accepts His love, and then asks us to wait *with Him* for others to come. The Lord knows those who are His; we do not. That is why we cannot judge anyone's spiritual destiny before the time of the Lord's coming, when the court of heaven will issue the verdict. "Therefore the LORD will wait, that He may be gracious to you; and therefore He will be exalted, that He may have mercy on you. For the LORD is a God of justice; blessed are all those who wait for Him" (Isaiah 30:18, NKJV).

We could not survive this long wait without the Holy Spirit's help. We would be too exhausted and give up, "but those who wait on the LORD shall renew their strength; they shall mount up with wings like eagles, they shall run and not be weary, they shall walk and not faint" (Isaiah 40:31, NKJV).

Waiting for God has to be learned. Can you name one servant of God who did not have to wait? Waiting makes us dependent upon the Lord. It deals with our pride. Although it is humbling, waiting has its rewards. Waiting rejuvenates and strengthens us. It keeps us from presumptuous sin that could arise from leaning on our own understanding. Waiting through the Holy Spirit is better than all the self-action doctrines that burn us out prematurely and often provoke us to blame God.

The Holy Spirit encourages us to wait patiently by eliminating our excuses. "You do not lack any spiritual gift as you eagerly wait for our Lord Jesus Christ to be revealed. He will keep you strong to the end, so that you will be blameless on the day of our Lord Jesus Christ" (1 Corinthians 1:7–8, NIV).

Is there an end to waiting? Yes, but not until the fullness of time ordained by God—which means, not until God is ready. The "things I plan won't happen right away. . . . If it seems slow, do not despair. . . . Just be patient! They will not be overdue a single day!" (Habakkuk 2:3, TLB).

While we wait, we could be frustrated and lonely if not for the companionship of the Holy Spirit. Because of Him we are not left as orphans, nor are we left ignorant of the vision we wait for. We "through the Spirit eagerly wait for the hope of righteousness by faith" (Galatians 5:5, NKJV).

There is an old, orthodox Jewish confession that sums up the whole process of waiting. It states: "I believe with a perfect faith in the coming of the Messiah, and though he tarry, I will wait for him every day." Amen!

In every generation, God's people are a waiting people. The promised Righteous Branch is coming to all who eagerly wait for Him: both Israel and the Church. They will not be ashamed, for in the end all God's promises are well worth waiting for. They are like seeds that require time to germinate, which God makes beautiful *in His time.*

Abiding Holy Spirit,
I rest. My times are safe in Your
hands. Thank You for waiting with
me till the end of time.

98
SPIRITUAL FRUIT

The fruit of the Spirit . . .
GALATIANS 5:22

hat is the "fruit" of the Spirit? In Scripture, fruit is what is produced from being in union with God and Christ. It is the character of Christ reproduced in vessels of clay. Just as Jesus came to earth and we beheld the fruit of the Father in Him, so we are here to reflect the fruit of Christ in ourselves.

Spiritual fruit is absolutely essential in the Christian life. In fact, without it there is no Christian life. The fruit of the Spirit is evidence of the life of Christ within us. Without fruit—we are dead.

To bear fruit is the reason we exist. Jesus stated emphatically to His disciples, "Ye have not chosen me, but I have *chosen* you, and *ordained* you, that ye should go and bring forth fruit, and that your fruit should *remain*" (John 15:16, emphasis added).

Jesus chose (called) us and ordained (appointed) us to bring forth fruit that would endure. To do this, we are provided with the fruit of the Spirit.

The *fruit of the Spirit* is the unique work of the Holy Spirit because:

- The fruit of the Spirit comes from spiritual Seed—the Word of God.
- The Seed is in itself (the Word), as the Law in Genesis states, and brings forth fruit after its own kind.
- Spiritual Seed grows into spiritual fruit because of the life-giving Spirit abiding in it.
- The fruit is grown in the ground of the heart prepared for the Seed by the Holy Spirit.

The purpose of the fruit bearer is to be "fruitful and multiply and replenish the earth"—with the likeness and image of the original Firstfruit.

The fruit the Holy Spirit produces has life within itself—Christ, the Word of God. It is His life, His character, His nature, *Himself.* The objective of

God is to get this same life reproduced in all those called by Christ's name. God will have many sons and daughters like Christ. Nothing less is acceptable to Him. Therefore, whenever the attributes of Jesus leak out from us, it is evidence of the Holy Spirit working within. It is fruit that the Father enjoys. "(For the fruit of the Spirit is in all goodness and righteousness and truth); proving what is acceptable unto the Lord" (Ephesians 5:9–10).

God will only accept fruit born from the Seed of God's Word. It is incorruptible Seed that must be received by us who have been prepared in advance by the Holy Spirit. Then it is possible to have this treasure in earthen vessels. For we "have been regenerated—born again—not from a mortal origin (seed, sperm) but from one that is immortal by the ever living and lasting Word of God" (1 Peter 1:23, AMPLIFIED).

Jesus explained to His disciples how the Seed grows into fruit for God by using the illustration of a vineyard. Jesus is the Vine, God is the Gardener and we are the branches. "I Am the True Vine and My Father is the Vinedresser. Any branch in Me that does not bear fruit—that stops bearing—He cuts away (trims off, takes away). And He cleanses and repeatedly prunes every branch that continues to bear fruit, to make it bear more and richer and more excellent fruit" (John 15:1–2, AMPLIFIED).

Notice two things. Our Heavenly Gardener prunes even the fruitful branches for greater strength and usefulness. And, God's pruning shears are the Word. "You are cleansed and pruned already, because of the Word which I have given you—the teachings I have discussed with you" (John 15:3, AMPLIFIED).

Jesus told the disciples they were *already* clean through the Word He had taught them. All but one: Judas.

Then He taught them the importance of staying attached to the Vine. "Just as no branch can bear fruit of itself without abiding in (vitally united to) the vine, neither can you bear fruit unless you abide in Me" (John 15:4, AMPLIFIED).

Abide? How is it possible for us, the branches, to "abide" in Jesus, the Vine? By abiding in Jesus, the Word. That keeps life flowing into us. Senior saints, who have lived in the Word lo these many years, seem to be living proof of that, because fruit matures slowly.

Constant abiding has promise of great reward, both for us and for our Father. "If ye abide in me, and my words abide in you, ye shall ask what ye will, and it shall be done unto you. Herein is my Father glorified, that ye bear much fruit" (John 15:7–8).

Our Father is glorified by *much* fruit. The more we ingest the Word, the more fruit we bear. But note the fine print: Only those bearing the fruit of the Spirit may *ask* the Father for favor and blessings.

There is another witness to what Jesus said. David tells us why spiritual fruit is profitable: "He shall be like a tree planted by the rivers of water, that bringeth forth his fruit in his season; his leaf also shall not wither; and whatsoever he doeth shall prosper" (Psalm 1:3).

We prosper by bringing forth fruit in season and out of season because it yields everything we need—to be like Him.

The work of the Holy Spirit is to make us fruitful.

Now I know the beauty of Jesus
can be seen in me.
Thank You, Holy Spirit.

99

LOVE, JOY, PEACE

The fruit of the Spirit is love, joy, peace. . . .
GALATIANS 5:22

Galatians 5 lists nine specific fruit of the Spirit. Notice that the word *fruit* of the Spirit is singular. There are nine segments in one fruit, and they are so closely related they are not meant to be separated: love, joy, peace, longsuffering, gentleness, goodness, faith, meekness and temperance. This is the sum of the divine nature shared with us.

The fruit of the Spirit is solely the work of the Holy Spirit. Since much has been written about them, the emphasis here will be on the definition of the fruit, what the opposites might be and additional ways in which the Holy Spirit develops the fruit to maturity.

Love

All Christians worth their salt covet this priceless character trait. So just knowing where love comes from is very reassuring. It takes us out from under the guilt trip that we must somehow muster up love by our own stripes.

Paul, under divine inspiration of the Holy Spirit, penned this revelation of love to the church at Rome. He wrote: "God has poured out his love into our own hearts by the Holy Spirit, whom he has given us" (Romans 5:5, NIV).

Through the Holy Spirit, God gave us His love, not man's kind of love. This love is in our spiritual hearts, not necessarily in our feelings. That is *why* we begin to love God and one another differently. Let it flow! Allow love to spring forth from the Source within you.

What do we mean by God's love? Here is 1 Corinthians 13 somewhat paraphrased. God's love is patient, kind, not jealous or envious, never boastful or proud, never haughty, selfish or rude. His love is not irritable, or touchy, does not withhold forgiveness, keeps no record of wrongs, does not think evil or rejoice in unrighteousness, but exults in truth. God's love is encouraging, protective, faithful, hopeful, strong and loyal—always.

It takes a long time to put God's love into words, and still the half is never told. So perhaps it could be said an easier way. God's love is the fruit of the Spirit in our hearts.

Jesus taught us how to keep ourselves in God's love: the same way He did. Obey. "If ye keep my commandments, ye shall abide in my love; even as I have kept my Father's commandments, and abide in his love" (John 15:10).

Jesus' two commandments are both about love. Love God and love your neighbor. Whoever keeps this word, in him the love of God is perfected. For the commandment of love has never been revoked and never will be.

The opposite of love is hate. Scripture says anyone who hates his brother walks in darkness and is a murderer. Hate is a fruit of the devil, who was a murderer from the beginning. For the Christian there is enough love to love God and our neighbors with plenty left over for ourselves. There is enough love to cover a multitude of sins. We need to use it.

Joy

Joy is a fruit *of* the Spirit, *by* the Spirit and *for* the spirit. As long as we can be filled with the Holy Spirit, we can be filled with joy. Conversely, without the Holy Spirit it is impossible to be filled with this precious fruit.

Joy should be distinguished from happiness and pleasure. Happiness is in the soul; pleasure is in the body. Happiness and pleasure are temporary but joy in the Spirit is eternal.

The joy of the Holy Spirit springs from knowing God in the inner man of the heart. It is not affected by circumstances, nor by feelings, nor by the works of the devil. True joy is rooted in something that never changes: a direct, personal, continuing relationship with God, in whose presence is fullness of joy.

Jesus Himself *is* joy—the "good tidings of great joy for all people" that the angels announced. The seventy disciples were filled with joy when they ministered deliverance to the people (see Luke 10:17). The Kingdom of God had come into full view and the joy of the Lord had strengthened them to bear the infirmities of the weak. It was a new day!

Jesus was full of joy, too—with their joy. He said, "Rejoice, because your names are written in heaven. In that hour Jesus rejoiced in spirit, and said, I thank thee, O Father, Lord of heaven and earth, that thou hast hid these things from the wise and prudent, and hast revealed them unto babes" (Luke 10:20–21).

The Lord ordained that we should share His joy and that no one could take it away. When Jesus was leaving the earth, He prayed to His Father for us. Our joy was His main concern as He told His Father, "Now I am coming to You. I say these things while I am still in the world, so that My joy may be made full and complete and perfect in them—that they may experience My delight fulfilled in them, that My enjoyment may be perfected in their own souls, that they may have My gladness within them filling their hearts" (John 17:13, AMPLIFIED).

His prayer was answered. This newfound joy in ministry was repeated time and time again for the disciples after Jesus went to be with His Father (see Acts 13:52, NIV).

The fruit of joy is prolific. Nothing can stop it. It blossoms in the midst of suffering and ripens as the Gospel is preached and souls are harvested. Joy is a privilege of the redeemed of the Lord!

Peace

Peace is a state of quietness, rest and harmony. With this fruit of the Spirit we remain steadfast in the Spirit in the midst of turmoil, strife and temptations.

Before Jesus came to earth a war raged because of sin. The battle was fought in heaven and earth, against God and against one another. To understand this, picture both a horizontal and a vertical conflict. Scripture speaks of the vertical aspect as hatred against God, and the horizontal as lack of peace and goodwill to men. When Jesus appeared on earth, He brought the offer of peace from God to stop both wars.

How could victory be won? The cross. As hostage for us, Jesus took upon Himself our war crimes. His punishment paid the price in full and bought peace. Through the cross, we are reconciled to both God and men. It was "our grief he bore, our sorrows that weighed him down. And we thought his troubles were a punishment from God, for his own sins! But he was wounded and bruised for our sins. He was chastised that we might have peace; he was lashed—and we were healed!" (Isaiah 53:4–5, TLB).

Jesus signed the peace treaty with God in His own blood. God accepted it in heaven and whosoever will may accept it on earth. It is the only armistice for mankind. For those who receive it Jesus has given them His own perfect peace. "Peace I leave with you, my peace I give unto you: not as the world giveth, give I unto you. Let not your heart be troubled, neither let it be afraid" (John 14:27).

Peace is the everlasting Gospel in one word. "'How beautiful are the feet of those who preach the Gospel of peace with God and bring glad tidings of good things.' In other words, how welcome are those who come preaching God's Good News!" (Romans 10:15, TLB).

God's Kingdom news of righteousness, peace and joy is shared with us and through us by the work of the Holy Spirit. It is our birthright, which supersedes our reasoning and keeps our hearts and minds in perfect peace.

Love. Joy. Peace.

Against such there is no law!

Holy Spirit,
thank You for Your love, joy and peace,
which make me like Christ—fruitful in
every good work to do my Father's will.

100
LONGSUFFERING, GENTLENESS, GOODNESS

The fruit of the Spirit is . . . longsuffering, gentleness, goodness. . . .

GALATIANS 5:22

Longsuffering

he word *longsuffering* means what it says—suffering long; with frailties, offenses, injuries, insults and aggravation of others and ourselves. All this without murmuring, discontentment or resentment.

Longsuffering is a fruit grown in us by the Holy Spirit. A person who has this fruit operating in his or her life is slow to anger and slow to avenge wrong. It produces patience, perseverance and endurance.

Most people get excited about the fruit of love, joy and peace but do not want to hear about longsuffering. It is a hard sell. But the fruit of longsuffering is necessary because of sin. If there were no sin, it would not be needed.

As Christians we are not asked to die *for* sin as Jesus did, but we are asked to die *to* sin. Through the Holy Spirit, we have the privilege of saying no to sin with all its evil consequences so that the nature of Christ might be produced in us. For this very purpose we were chosen and ordained. "To this you were called, because Christ suffered for you, leaving you an example, that you should follow in his steps. When they hurled their insults at him, he did not retaliate; when he suffered, he made no threats. Instead, he entrusted himself to him who judges justly" (1 Peter 2:21, 23, NIV).

Jesus was led like a lamb to the slaughter and opened not His mouth. In fact, He did at least four things in demonstrating the fruit of longsuffering.

- He kept silent.
- He trusted Himself to the Lord by letting God plead His case.
- He did not yield to sin.
- He prayed for His enemies and forgave them.

Jesus is our pattern. So often we could begin with keeping our mouths shut and praying in the Spirit.

Paul spent considerable time writing to Christians about how to behave. He let us know we should be ready to suffer long. "[Give] no offence in any thing, that the ministry be not blamed: but in all things approving ourselves as ministers of God, in much patience, in afflictions, in necessities, in distresses, in stripes, in imprisonments, in tumults, in labors, in watchings, in fastings; by pureness, by knowledge, by longsuffering, by kindness, by the Holy [Spirit], by love unfeigned" (2 Corinthians 6:3–6).

The fruit of longsuffering is grown so that we do not put a stumbling block in anyone's way and the ministry is not discredited. In other words, "We try to live in such a way that no one will ever be offended or kept back from finding the Lord by the way we act, so that no one can find fault with us and blame it on the Lord" (2 Corinthians 6:3, TLB).

The fruit of longsuffering, born through the Holy Spirit within, enables us to be patient with sinners, with one another and with ourselves. Will we ever produce perfect longsuffering fruit of the Spirit? In this day of fast fixes and ready mixes that sounds impossible. We have gotten caught up in a "right now" culture. Indeed, longsuffering and patient endurance would be impossible if not for the grace of God.

Yes, it is possible to bring forth fruit that will remain. For once again, God has provided the essential ingredient: *Himself*. "He has given us his very great and precious promises, so that through them you may participate in the divine nature and escape the corruption in the world caused by evil desires" (2 Peter 1:4, NIV).

How does the Holy Spirit minister the fruit of longsuffering to us? Those who are in Christ Jesus slowly begin to understand its value. The fruit becomes sweet to our taste and irresistible. A willingness to yield to the Holy Spirit emerges. With the help of the Holy Spirit, the old way of doing things dies. Life springs forth from the new nature of Christ within, blossoming into spiritual fruit. We find ourselves behaving just like Him.

Gentleness

Gentleness is demonstrated by being soft-spoken, kind, even-tempered, cultured, refined in character and conduct, calm and soothing. In some versions of Scripture the word *kindness* is used for *gentleness*. Gentleness is kindness in action. It is treating others the way you want to be treated.

Jesus taught these actions—"Be-attitudes," called the Beatitudes—several times: "Love your enemies. Do good to those who hate you. Pray for the happiness of those who curse you; implore God's blessing on those who hurt you. If someone slaps you on one cheek, let him slap the other too! If someone demands your coat, give him your shirt besides. Give what you have to anyone who asks you for it; and when things are taken from you, don't worry about getting them back. Treat others as you want them to treat you" (Luke 6:27–31, TLB).

Someone has wisely observed that kindness is enlightened self-interest, because what we sow, we reap. Those who plant kindness live in harmony with the spiritual laws that govern the Kingdom of God. "Don't be misled; remember that you can't ignore God and get away with it: a man will always reap just the kind of crop he sows! If he sows to please his own wrong desires, he will be planting seeds of evil and he will surely reap a harvest of spiritual decay and death; but if he plants the good things of the Spirit, he will reap the everlasting life which the Holy Spirit gives him. And let us not get tired of doing what is right, for after a while we will reap a harvest of blessing if we don't get discouraged and give up. That's why whenever we can we should always be kind to everyone, and especially to our Christian brothers" (Galatians 6:7–10, TLB).

Jesus' spirit is kind and gentle. Even when we sin we do not need to be afraid of Him. He understands. He talked to the woman caught in adultery with a calm, soothing voice. Then with a word of wisdom He spoke to her religious accusers. "He that is without sin among you, let him cast the first stone." Who would? Who could?

How welcome the fruit of gentleness is! When we are willing, this gentleness of the Spirit comes forth from us, too, to be enjoyed by others. O, Lord, "You have given me the shield of your salvation; Your gentleness has made me great" (2 Samuel 22:36, TLB).

Goodness

The dictionary defines *goodness* as "virtue, excellence, the quality of being good." But the fruit of goodness, in the strictest sense, applies only to God. It is based on the high standard of who God is and what He does.

Therefore, goodness as a fruit of the Spirit is complete uprightness, moral excellence, true goodness, perfect honesty, perfect justice, perfect mercy. In a word: *perfection.*

Who could be really *good* but God? Jesus, in His humanity, recognized this ultimate perfection of God's goodness. He was quick to make this point to the rich young ruler who called Him "Good Master." Jesus said, "Why callest thou me good? there is none good but one, that is God" (Matthew 19:17).

Only by the work of the Holy Spirit can we bring forth goodness. He alone reproduces God's perfect, everlasting goodness in us so that we may be like Him.

The fruit of goodness shows the world what God is really like. Being good bears witness to God. When His goodness is lived out through us, the world cannot deny there is a God. It may be all some people ever see of the Father.

Our own self-initiated "good" is not a substitute for the fruit of goodness. Adam and Eve ate the fruit of the tree of the knowledge of good and evil, but its fruit brought sin and death. The fruit only looked good. It did not make them wise nor did it impart life. They lost God and the power to do good and found their nakedness and the power to do evil.

This "good" was the sham Jesus recognized in the Pharisees, Sadducees, scribes and lawyers of His day. He pronounced many "woes" upon their outward show of perfection. They meticulously tithed herbs and boasted of their goodness, while omitting mercy, faith and just judgment. "Woe to you, teachers of the Law and Pharisees, you hypocrites! You are like white-washed tombs, which look beautiful on the outside but on the inside are full of dead men's bones and everything unclean. In the same way, on the outside you appear to people as righteous but on the inside you are full of hypocrisy and wickedness" (Matthew 23:27–28, NIV).

Hypocrisy is a pretense of virtue and goodness. Jesus saw through their "good works" of tradition, which had a form of godliness but were void of the Holy Spirit's power. Instead of the woes we can avail ourselves of the wooing of the Spirit, and glorify our Father with fruit that remains.

Evil is the opposite of good. Therefore, we are admonished, "Do not repay anyone evil for evil. Be careful to do what is right in the eyes of everybody. . . . Do not be overcome by evil, but overcome evil with good" (Romans 12:17, 21, NIV).

Since we are commanded to overcome evil with good, then good is more powerful than evil. That is exactly what Jesus demonstrated. He used the power of God's goodness to overcome evil. Everything Jesus did was good.

The fruit of goodness is powerful enough to perform every work of godliness, if we will yield to it. Otherwise, Jesus never would have encouraged us to overcome and be perfect by saying, "Be ye therefore perfect, even as your Father which is in heaven is perfect" (Matthew 5:48).

It is possible for the goodness of God to be perfected through us. God recreated us in His likeness and image and gave us His Spirit. He is our *birthright*.

Paul gave the Gentiles in Rome this encouragement in his day, and the word is the same for us now: "I myself am convinced, my brothers, that you yourselves are full of goodness, complete in knowledge and competent to instruct one another" (Romans 15:14, NIV).

Let us therefore do good, not just to our enemies but especially to the household of faith. We need to encourage one another to bring forth this fruit of the Spirit, as Paul did. For God is working in us to will and to do of His *good* pleasure.

Longsuffering. Gentleness. Goodness.

Against such there is no law!

Precious Holy Spirit,
Your fruit is sweet to my taste and
brings glory to God. Reproduce
it in me, in season and out of season.

101

FAITH, MEEKNESS, TEMPERANCE

The fruit of the Spirit is . . . faith, meekness, temperance. . . .
GALATIANS 5:22–23

Faith

Faith is a fruit of the Spirit that manifests itself in faithfulness. This faith fruit is a living substance created from within by the Holy Spirit. It is demonstrated in a quiet, steady, continuing dependence upon God.

Faith supplied by the Holy Spirit does not doubt God, get frustrated, think of turning back or giving up, panic, fret, murmur or worry about proving God.

Faith is spiritual reality. It goes beyond the realm of the physical senses. Faith is "the assurance (the confirmation, the title-deed) of the things [we] hope for, being proof of things [we] do not see and the conviction of their reality—faith perceiving as real fact what is not revealed to the senses" (Hebrews 11:1, AMPLIFIED).

It is by faith that we respond to the atonement. Because I know I share in the benefits of Christ's crucifixion I can now say, "Christ liveth in me." And "the life which I now live in the flesh [body] I live by the faith of the Son of God, who loved me, and gave himself for me" (Galatians 2:20).

The same faith Jesus lived by on this planet is the same faith we receive as fruit of the Spirit.

Why would the Son of God need faith, you ask? Because He lived as a man.

When did Jesus most vividly demonstrate the personal faith He lived by? On the cross. It was there He trusted His Father to raise Him from the dead. That is why Paul could say, "Now God can bless the Gentiles, too, with this same blessing he promised to Abraham; and all of us as Christians can have the promised Holy Spirit through this faith" (Galatians 3:14, TLB). Yes, Abraham saw Christ's day by faith and was glad (see John 8:56).

The bottom line is that Jesus did His works and produced fruit by the same Spirit He gave to us. Therefore, He has a right to expect His followers to behave like Him and to arrive at the same destination. Having begun in the Holy Spirit, we continue to be made perfect through the same Holy Spirit.

More than any other fruit, faith is essential this side of eternity. Everything we have from God is received by faith. Without faith it is impossible to please God. Without faith, we sin. But *with* faith, we have the victory that overcomes the world, the flesh and the devil.

Faith is so important that the Holy Spirit equips us with it as both a *gift* and a *fruit*. The contrast between the nine gifts and the nine fruit is worth noting.

- The Spirit *gives* the gifts.
- The Spirit *grows* the fruit.
- The gifts are given as needed but are *temporary*.
- The Spirit supplies fruit *permanently*.
- Gifts are for signs and wonders to *act* like Jesus.
- Fruit is Christ's character to *be* like Jesus.

In spite of these facts, many Christians still believe faith is something they must produce. How deceived we are to believe we can do anything on our own to please God. Without the Holy Spirit, we offer God "strange fire" like Nadab and Abihu, and die. Without the Holy Spirit we can do nothing that counts for eternity. Without the Holy Spirit we cannot bring forth fruit that will remain.

Meekness

A meek spirit is quiet, gentle, mild, kind, humble, yielding. Such a spirit is submissive to authority, balanced in mind and heart, temperament and passions. A meek spirit is patient in suffering without a spirit of revenge.

The ultimate example of perfect meekness is Jesus. He was never proud or haughty. Zechariah described Jesus' modest entrance into Jerusalem on Palm Sunday five hundred years before it happened when he prophesied, "Rejoice greatly, O Daughter of Zion! Shout aloud, O Daughter of Jerusalem! Lo, your King comes to you . . . triumphant and victorious; patient, meek, lowly and riding on a donkey, upon a colt, the foal of a donkey" (Zechariah 9:9, AMPLIFIED).

As Messiah, Jesus rode humbly into Jerusalem upon a donkey when He could have been transported on a celestial throne by twelve legions of angels.

Paul describes Jesus' meekness from beginning to end, admonishing us to have the same attitude. Jesus, "being in very nature God, did not consider equality with God something to be grasped, but made himself nothing, taking the very nature of a servant, being made in human likeness. And being found in appearance as a man, he humbled himself and became obedient to death—even death on a cross!" (Philippians 2:6–8, NIV).

Do you know that Christ described Himself as meek? He said: "Take my yoke upon you, and learn of me; for I am meek and lowly in heart: and ye shall find rest unto your souls. For my yoke is easy, and my burden is light" (Matthew 11:29–30).

Jesus' yoke is not merely given *by* Him for us to take, but it is shared *with* Him. Just as He was willing to be yoked together with His Father in complete submission, He invites us into His yoke, too.

Meekness is the spirit in which we learn to accept God's will for us, for there is promise of great reward. It is then that we experience rest for our souls. Rest for the troubled mind, will and emotions. A calm, peaceful, worry-free life.

Do you know why Jesus could afford to be so humble? For one thing, He knew who *He* was. He knew who His *Father* was. He also knew He had the infinite resources of the Godhead at His command. So when Satan tempted Him with the questions "Who are you?" or "If you really are God's son" Jesus did not need to prove His identity. And neither should we. You see, spiritual meekness is not spiritual weakness. It is the mighty strengthening power of the Holy Spirit known in the inner man.

As God's elect, we are to "put on" meekness as if it were underwear—and walk in it. With the spirit of meekness we are to instruct those who oppose the truth. With the spirit of meekness we are to restore our wounded brothers. Paul urges us to "walk worthy of the vocation wherewith ye are called, with all lowliness and meekness, with longsuffering, forbearing one another in love; endeavoring to keep the unity of the Spirit in the bond of peace" (Ephesians 4:1–3).

Notice this passage includes four fruit of the Spirit: meekness, longsuffering, love and peace. It is a special blending of the Holy Spirit's work.

In the sight of God a meek and quiet spirit is of infinite value, for the meek attain everything. Yes, blessed are the meek, for they shall inherit the earth!

Temperance

A more up-to-date word for temperance is *self-control*. This fruit manifests itself in mastering one's actions and reactions in all areas of life.

With this fruit of the Spirit our appetites and passions are safely under His control.

The fruit—self-control—is not "will worship." Will worship is self doing something apart from the Holy Spirit—that is, doing something by the strength of self-will, which emanates from the soul, not the Spirit. The spiritual fruit of temperance is not "touch not," "taste not" or "see not" behavior regulated by law or the traditions of men. Neither is it self-imposed legalism or religion. "These rules may seem good, for rules of this kind require strong devotion and are humiliating and hard on the body, but they have no effect when it comes to conquering a person's evil thoughts and desires. They only make him proud" (Colossians 2:23, TLB).

How then do we conquer our evil thoughts and desires? By declaring war on the old nature—the flesh, the carnal mind. This was the war Paul faced inside himself. Jesus' death had freed him from the *power* of sin in the old nature, but not from the *presence* of sin. Therefore, controlling the old sinful nature had to be a *choice* he made of using the power over sin already given to him. It was a choice he made in the *mind*. "O wretched man that I am! who shall deliver me from the body of this death? I thank God through Jesus Christ our Lord. So then with the mind I myself serve the law of God, but with the flesh the law of sin" (Romans 7:24–25).

In a word, conquering evil thoughts and desires means dealing with the *soul*. Many people "put on the whole spiritual armor of God" in Ephesians 6. But they are not well dressed if they have eliminated the first item of preparation: the carnal mind. "Though we walk in the flesh, we do not war after the flesh: (for the weapons of our warfare are not carnal, but mighty through God to the pulling down of strongholds;) Casting down imaginations, and every high thing that exalteth itself against the knowledge of God, and bringing into captivity every thought to the obedience of Christ" (2 Corinthians 10:3–5).

We need the fruit of self-control operating in our lives because the rights granted us by our Creator are capable of abuse. What abuse? Scripture lists many. Adultery, fornication, homosexuality, lesbianism, eagerness for lustful pleasure, gluttony, sodomy, incest, evil thoughts, covetousness, idolatry, witchcraft, spiritism, sorceries, heresies, bitterness, hatred, fighting, jealousy, greed, envy, anger, wrath, violence, murders, strife, rebellion, hypocrisy, stubbornness, laziness, complaining, criticisms, arguments, cursing, coarse jokes, foul talk, foolishness, confusion, lying, stealing, drunkenness, wild parties, orgies, philosophy, vain imaginations, pride, boasting, arrogance, unmercifulness, unforgivingness, gossip, slander, disobedience to parents, hatred of God, cowardice, fearfulness, unbelief, love of money, love of self—every evil work.

There are spiritual laws against these fruits of the flesh. They lead to slavery, condemnation and death. Those who practice such things will not inherit the Kingdom of God.

But there are *no laws* against the fruit of the Spirit: love, joy, peace, long-suffering, goodness, gentleness, faith, meekness and self-control. When you are led by the Spirit you are never in conflict with God's laws. There is no condemnation.

I am convinced there are two natures inside of Christians, and we decide whom we will serve by yielding to one or the other. How do we yield to the Spirit? By making a decision similar to the one Joshua gave the children of Israel: "Choose for yourselves this day whom you will serve. . . . But as for me and my house, we will serve the LORD" (Joshua 24:15, NKJV).

How awesome the power of *nine* fruit of the Spirit compared with the many works of the flesh! By choosing the *fruit of the Spirit* we can overcome the *fruit of the flesh,* the world and the devil. The fruit of the Spirit is stronger than the fruit of the flesh. It perfects God's image and likeness in us!

The focus here is on the work of the Holy Spirit, not on our failures. We have been enabled to run the race set before us. We *shall* lay aside every weight and the sin that so easily trips us up. We *shall* reap fruit unto holiness in due season if we faint not.

It seems that every fruit of the Spirit is the fruit I need most of all. The good news is that, unlike Aladdin's lamp, I do not have to choose two or three. By virtue of the power that works in us as children of the Most High God, we are blessed with them all: love, joy, peace, longsuffering, gentleness, goodness, faith, meekness, temperance.

O come, Holy Spirit,
and breathe upon my garden, that the
sweet-smelling spices may flow out.
Let my Beloved come into
His garden and eat His pleasant fruits.

102

SEALING US

After that ye believed, ye were sealed with that holy Spirit of promise.

EPHESIANS 1:13

t the time a person believes God's Word and accepts the finished work of Christ as his personal payment for sin, a divine transaction takes place. The believer is stamped, identified, marked or sealed as belonging to Christ, by the Holy Spirit. "Having believed, you were marked in him [Christ] with a seal, the promised Holy Spirit, who is a deposit guaranteeing our inheritance until the redemption of those who are God's possession" (Ephesians 1:13–14, NIV).

Why is this sealing work of the Holy Spirit so vital? Because God never intended to lose His sheep by forfeiting His down payment. Consider the facts from His viewpoint: For us to be paid for with the blood of Jesus, and then not fully redeemed to be with Him, would be utter foolishness. Why should the Son of God die in vain? To prevent this, God proved we are genuinely His by depositing His Holy Spirit within us as the down payment of that promise while we wait and He waits—to possess what is ours.

J. B. Phillips translates the verse: "After you gave your confidence to him you were, so to speak, stamped with the promised Holy Spirit as a guarantee of purchase, until the day when God completes the redemption of what he has paid for as his own." The Holy Spirit's sealing works both ways. God's repossession of us is consummated and our inheritance of God is confirmed. God's Holy Spirit is both the *seal* and the *sealer*.

Just as God the Father sealed the Son (see John 6:27) and the Holy Spirit seals the Son's heirs, there is another sealing yet to come. Revelation 7 reveals an instantaneous sealing of 144,000 servants of God on their foreheads. They will all be blameless Jews from the twelve tribes of Israel who have never lied or "defiled themselves by relations with women, for they are [pure as] virgins. These are they who follow the Lamb wherever He goes. These are they who have been ransomed (purchased, redeemed) from among men as the first fruits for God and the Lamb" (Revelation 14:4, AMPLIFIED).

How can we be sure that we have been sealed *by* the Holy Spirit and *with* the Holy Spirit? Is there some outward mark of identification made in our flesh like circumcision in the Old Covenant? No, under the New Covenant our mark, or certainty of being accepted by God, comes through the Holy Spirit in our hearts. As we sing about Jesus we also can sing about the Holy Spirit: "You ask me how I know He lives, He lives within my heart." God "has put his brand upon us—his mark of ownership—and given us his Holy Spirit in our hearts as guarantee that we belong to him, and as the first installment of all that he is going to give us" (2 Corinthians 1:22, TLB).

What is God going to give us? Jesus left no doubt in our minds. He said, "I give them eternal life and they shall never perish. No one shall snatch them away from me, for my Father has given them to me, and he is more powerful than anyone else, so no one can kidnap them from me" (John 10:28–29, TLB).

Thus it can be said, the blood of Jesus bought us and the sealing of the Holy Spirit guarantees our delivery. Think of this as a certified letter. Believers are the contents of the letter, stamped, sealed and addressed to God in heaven where Jesus Christ opens the seal. This ensures we will not end up in the dead letter office.

Yes, the Lord always knows those who are His. The Holy Spirit's seal is a finished transaction so well recognized in the spirit world that what God has joined together no powers of darkness can put asunder. This work of God's Holy Spirit is just one more reason for us to praise our glorious God. "This is too glorious, too wonderful to believe! I can never be lost to your Spirit! I can never get away from my God!" (Psalm 139:6–7, TLB).

Thank You, sweet Spirit of promise.
You sealed the deal, and now I know
that I am my Beloved's and He is mine.

103
ACCESS TO THE FATHER

We both [Jew and Gentile] have access by one Spirit unto the Father.

EPHESIANS 2:18

*B*efore the death and resurrection of Jesus Christ, to be born a Gentile was disastrous.

Gentiles, meaning anyone not born a Jew, were worse than second-class citizens. In Israel they were not counted as citizens at all. Gentiles had no share in the covenants God made with Israel and no promise of ever being included in them. These uncircumcised heathens were considered lost, without hope and without God in the world.

This racial and religious enmity was so evident that Gentiles were shunned as "unclean" and denied access to God. In the Temple a wall of partition separated the court of Israel from the court of the Gentiles, where a posted warning forbade Gentiles from trespassing—on pain of death.

Jesus changed all this, radically and permanently. He put an end to the Gentiles' hopeless condition by eliminating the spiritual wall that separated them from God. He offered to all nations, kindred and tongues the same blessings Israel had—by faith in Him.

Times were changing. In a letter, Jewish Paul explained to the Gentile Ephesians what the blood of Jesus had done for them. "By his death he [Jesus] ended the angry resentment between us, caused by the Jewish laws which favored the Jews and excluded the Gentiles. . . . Then he took the two groups that had been opposed to each other and made them parts of himself; thus he fused us together to become one new person, and at last there was peace" (Ephesians 2:15, TLB).

Do not miss the point of the peace. Jesus made peace between Jews and Gentiles in order to create something *new*. As part of the same body with Jesus, both Jews and Gentiles were mystically embodied into a new creation, one that never existed before. One that shared Jesus' holy nature, His eternal Spirit and a new name: Christ's ones. "Each of us is a part of the *one* body of Christ. Some of us are Jews, some are Gentiles. . . . But the

Holy Spirit has fitted us all together into one body . . . and [we] have all been given that same Holy Spirit" (1 Corinthians 12:13, TLB).

The Holy Spirit not only fashions us together into one body, but He is like the neck that maintains the vital connection between each member of the body and Christ, the Head.

This integration of one Head with one body united through one Holy Spirit had one eternal purpose: access to God. At last it was possible for "both have an introduction (access) by one (Holy) Spirit to the Father— so that we are able to approach Him" (Ephesians 2:18, AMPLIFIED).

Access to God is our highest calling. Having the right to approach such a holy God is good news, for the way to the King of kings is narrow and carefully guarded.

Persian court life in the Book of Esther illustrates this protocol. Even though Esther was the queen, she could not come unbidden into the king's presence. She had to be summoned by the king first, who would then hold out his golden scepter for her to touch, indicating permission to approach his throne. To draw near to the king without permission meant sure death. Knowing this, when Esther approached the king unannounced to plead for mercy for her people (the Jews), she trembled with fear. What if the king would not extend his scepter?

As it happened, the king did extend his scepter, granted her grace and gave her the desires of her heart.

Today, in like manner, there is only one way of access to God. The King of Glory has willingly summoned us and held out His scepter of right-eousness, Jesus Christ, to all those who approach Him through one Holy Spirit.

Who shall ascend into the hill of the Lord
and who shall stand in His holy place?
Those who have joined the union
of the Holy Spirit!

104
BUILDING GOD'S HOUSE

Ye also are builded together for an habitation of God through the Spirit.

EPHESIANS 2:22

Not only do both Jews and Gentiles have access to God through one Holy Spirit, but God has access to them. That is, these Spirit-sealed people become God's holy house. God finds in them a dwelling place for His Spirit as together they are "being built up [into this structure] . . . to form a fixed abode (dwelling place) of God in (by, through) the Spirit" (Ephesians 2:22, AMPLIFIED).

Jesus envisioned this dwelling place when He explained the consequences of His death to the hostile Jews. He challenged them by saying, "Destroy this temple, and in three days I will raise it up" (John 2:19, NKJV).

By "this temple" Jesus meant His body: the temple of God. And when His tomb was vacated in three days, Jesus arose to begin building this vast spiritual household.

Jesus was the first Rock in place. The stones were not adequately prepared until the Holy Spirit entered into the believers at Pentecost. Then it was possible for the building to take shape "upon the foundation of the apostles and prophets with Christ Jesus Himself the chief Cornerstone. In Him the whole structure is joined (bound, welded) together harmoniously; and it continues to rise (grow, increase) into a holy temple in the Lord—a sanctuary dedicated, consecrated and sacred to the presence of the Lord" (Ephesians 2:20–21, AMPLIFIED).

The emphasis here is on the *quantity* of the spiritual house. When we consider that heaven is God's throne and earth His footstool, the enormity of God's house is measureless, beyond human understanding. Surely the exponential vision of Christians as "living stones" being built up into such a dwelling where God lives is unthinkable.

The house Moses built on earth for God to dwell in was only a pattern of this true tent erected in heaven. Even Peter wanted to make a dwelling place for the Master on the Mount of Transfiguration, but Jesus knew His Father desired a spiritual house—a tabernacle created by and for Him by the Holy Spirit. A dwelling not made with human hands but with the spirits of just men and women made perfect. A dwelling furnished throughout with gladness, for it is there that God inhabits the praises of His chosen ones. "How greatly to be envied are those you have chosen to come and live with you within the holy tabernacle courts! What joys await us among all the good things there" (Psalm 65:4, TLB).

Who but the Holy Spirit could build God such a home? He is the faithful Architect who has raised the house upon Jesus, the apostles and prophets. For He supplies His Spirit, enabling this great cloud of witnesses to increase with the increase of God.

Even while we are still at home in these earthly bodies God has access to us in heavenly places through the Spirit. There we bow before His Majesty, worshiping Him together in the beauty of holiness. In heaven and in earth we are God's house.

Those of us who are His dwelling place should cherish this fact. "Don't you realize that all of you together are the house of God, and that the Spirit of God lives among you in his house?" (1 Corinthians 3:16, TLB).

Yes, by His power we are "God's temple, the home of the living God" (2 Corinthians 6:16, TLB).

*Spirit of Holiness
thankYou for making us
a living sanctuary of praise to God.*

105
REVEALING MYSTERIES

The mystery . . . now revealed . . . by the Spirit.
EPHESIANS 3:3, 5

God purposely kept secret some of His foreordained plans in Old Testament times. These hidden things are referred to as "mysteries" in the New Testament. Revealing these mysteries is the exclusive work of the Holy Spirit.

For example, one of the most surprising mysteries of God in the New Testament is not Jewish salvation but Gentile salvation. Paul illustrates this *mystery* of Christ, "which was not made known to men in other generations as it has now been revealed by the Spirit to God's holy apostles and prophets. This mystery is that through the gospel the Gentiles are heirs together with Israel, members together of one body, and sharers together in the promise of Christ Jesus" (Ephesians 3:5–6, NIV).

This revelation of truth may be familiar to us now, but when Paul boldly preached it as doctrine, it landed him in a Roman jail. Why? Because it was something *new*.

The Old and New Testaments bear witness to the fact that God has divided His program into more than one time period. The difference is obvious. The old is old and the new is new. The old is superseded by the new. To consider the old new or the new old would only cause problems. Remember the proverb? New wine should not be put into old wineskins. Therefore, identifying the current *time* of the Lord not only prevents us from being ignorant but permits us to preserve both the old and the new wine.

Did God change His mind and reject the old for the new? No, He chose the nation of Israel and brought them through long centuries of Old Testament history to bless *all* nations through their Messiah. The mystery revealed to the apostles and prophets by the Holy Spirit was how and when the others were to be included. The answer was found in one new word: the *Church*. Paul told the believers at Ephesus that "you Gentiles are a part of God's house . . . (you) will have (your) full share with the Jews in all the riches inherited by God's sons; both are invited to belong to his church" (Ephesians 3:1, 6, TLB).

Think back to the first time Jesus mentioned the Church to His disciples. He gave them very little detail. He waited until Peter knew who He really was before He drove home the point, saying, "I will build my church; and the gates of hell shall not prevail against it" (Matthew 16:18).

Jesus began to build His Church with the souls of redeemed men, and this was something new. The gates of hell rattled from the start. Satan had to get adjusted. The angels had to get adjusted. The Jews had to get adjusted. The Gentiles had to get adjusted. And the whole system of religious tradition had to reinvent itself all because Jesus Christ had placed both Jew and Gentile into one Church.

What is the Church? Christ's body. In Scripture it is referred to as "the mystery of God's will." It is another mystery the Holy Spirit reveals in Ephesians 1:19–23. Although God chose the Church *before* the foundation of the world, it was kept secret until there was a Head. This mysterious new creation is destined to become one perfect Man because it is "His body, the fullness of Him Who fills all in all—for in that body lives the full measure of Him Who makes everything complete, and Who fills everything everywhere [with Himself]" (Ephesians 1:23, AMPLIFIED).

The Church, filled with Christ Himself, is a living organism, not an empty cathedral.

Who is the Church? Anyone who respectfully subjects himself to the Lord Jesus Christ. To better understand the relationship of this remnant to one another and to the Head, the Holy Spirit used this simile of married life. "Wives, submit to your husbands as to the Lord. For the husband is the head of the wife as Christ is the head of the church, his body. . . . Now as the church submits to Christ, so also wives should submit to their husbands in everything. Husbands, love your wives, just as Christ loved the church and gave himself up for her. . . . 'For this reason a man will leave his father and mother and be united to his wife, and the two will become one flesh.' This is a profound mystery—but I am talking about Christ and the church" (Ephesians 5:22–25, 31–32, NIV).

When is the Church? Now. Of the twenty-plus mysteries revealed in the New Testament the Church is revolutionary. It is the new wine put into new wineskins. But the Church has a time limit, a beginning and an ending. What began at Pentecost will end when the "called out ones" *(ekklesia)* have been *called out* from this world in newly resurrected bodies. This is another previously hidden mystery revealed by the Holy Spirit in 1 Thessalonians 4:13–17.

It is important to understand that God did not introduce the "church age" to *replace* His everlasting covenant with Israel but only to *interrupt* it for a season until the full number of Gentiles has been called in. When will that be? Yet another mystery revealed by the Holy Spirit in Romans 11:25–26.

Where is the Church? Everywhere. In heaven and in earth. It is true the Body of Christ is not visible to the naked eye, even as the Head is not now visible. But when Jesus comes to greet the Church in the air, we shall be united with Him in a twinkling of an eye. In a moment we shall be with Him and like Him forever. Bone of His bone and flesh of His flesh, made for Him and from Him as Eve was for Adam.

Why is the Church? God purchased this "one pearl of great price" so that "He might clearly demonstrate through the ages to come the immeasurable (limitless, surpassing) riches of His free grace (His unmerited favor) in kindness and goodness of heart toward us in Christ Jesus" (Ephesians 2:7, AMPLIFIED).

Is it any wonder that when Paul pondered the Church he bowed his knees to the Father, overwhelmed by God's goodness and mercy? For although men in Old Testament times had seen God's miracles, signs and wonders, no eye had seen, nor ear heard, nor mind conceived the exceeding riches of God's *grace* that appeared to all men. Jesus Christ.

Nor did the angels understand this mystery. For God's saving grace does not belong to them. Jesus is not their Savior; He did not come to save them. Jesus is not their Lover; He did not come to woo them. Yet the angels are curious. They desire to look into this *amazing grace* and learn what saved a wretch like me. For this reason, the fullness of God's grace reaches beyond this world so that "now, through the church, the manifold wisdom of God [is] made known to the rulers and authorities in the heavenly realms, according to his eternal purpose which he accomplished in Christ Jesus our Lord" (Ephesians 3:10–11, NIV).

God's eternal purpose is the reason you exist. You were born to be an unbroken wineskin filled with Christ's glory.

Holy Spirit,
continue to reveal mysteries to the
Church so that we might understand
and grow up quickly into the fullness
of the Godhead bodily.

106
STRENGTHENING

Strengthened with might by his Spirit in the inner man.

EPHESIANS 3:16

he Holy Spirit strengthens the waiting Church in its long journey through time.

To comprehend this unique work it is helpful to contrast the Holy Spirit's strengthening of the *outer man* with His strengthening of the *inner man*. For example, in the Old Testament the account of Samson's physical strength was clearly demonstrated in the "outer man" by the feats he performed against the enemies of God. Without the supernatural strengthening of Samson's *body* by the Holy Spirit, he would not have been able to accomplish God's will against His enemies.

However, the New Testament describes a *spiritual* strengthening of the Holy Spirit in the "inner man," which remains hidden. Without His work we would be unable to accomplish God's will in our lives. Paul recognized the need for a strong heart and wrote to the Ephesians, "I pray that out of his [God's] glorious riches he may strengthen you with power through his Spirit in your inner being, so that Christ may dwell in your hearts through faith" (Ephesians 3:16–17, NIV).

Why do we need the Holy Spirit's strengthening of the inner man? If left to our own understanding, sooner or later we would lack the strength to believe He abides there continuously. Our foolish hearts would be darkened and our faith would eventually fail.

Believing Christ dwells within us is the beginning of our inner strengthening, "For it is by believing in his heart that a man becomes right with God; and with his mouth he tells others of his faith, confirming his salvation" (Romans 10:10, TLB).

There is no end to the Holy Spirit's glorious strength for it flows forth from the limitless riches of God. We live from strength to strength. And as our faith is more and more empowered by the Holy Spirit, that which may have started out in the heart as blind faith becomes no longer blind but *seeing*. When the *heart* sees by faith, the proof of Christ's indwelling becomes a permanent, personal, powerful reality. "That is why we never give up. Though our bodies are dying, our inner strength in the Lord is growing every day" (2 Corinthians 4:16, TLB).

Only the heart strengthened by the Holy Spirit can grow strong enough to reach maturity, that is, to attain the perfection ordained by God for us to be "filled (through all your being) unto all the fullness of God—[that is] may have the richest measure of the divine Presence, and become a body wholly filled and flooded with God Himself!" (Ephesians 3:19, AMPLIFIED).

Truly, the joy of the Lord's presence inside is our strength. Therefore, be strong in the Lord and the power of His might! Be wondrously filled with His Spirit; this is the will of God for you.

It is by might!
It is by power!
It is by Your Spirit,
that I avoid heart failure!
Thank You, mighty Strengthener.

107
UNITY

Keep the unity of the Spirit . . .
EPHESIANS 4:3

The Holy Spirit gives the Church His full unity and orders us to keep it. "Be eager and strive earnestly to guard and keep the harmony and oneness of [produced by] the Spirit in the binding power of peace" (Ephesians 4:3, AMPLIFIED).

Note: It is the Holy Spirit's unity, not man's. It originated in heaven, not on the earth. And, as such, it is not subject to change, nor will it ever cease to exist. Therefore, two questions need careful study: What exactly is the Holy Spirit's unity, and how do we successfully keep it?

The sevenfold unity of the Holy Spirit is defined in the following Scriptures. There is "one body and one Spirit . . . one hope of your calling; one Lord, one faith, one baptism; one God and Father of all" (Ephesians 4:4–6, NKJV).

Checking the list to find out if we keep these seven seems simple enough. It is even easier than observing ten commandments. We must all acknowledge:

1. One Body: the Church
2. One Spirit: the Holy Spirit
3. One hope: of our future calling
4. One Lord: Jesus Christ
5. One faith: the Gospel
6. One baptism: into Christ's body by the Holy Spirit
7. One God: the Father of us all

Maintaining the unity of one Holy Spirit, one Lord Jesus Christ and one God is not a problem in the Christian Church today. But what about agreeing on one faith and one hope? Can we get together on those? And one body and one baptism? A little bit harder, perhaps. So is total accord possible? If we will not receive the precise unity of one body, Spirit, hope, Lord, faith, baptism and God, then we disagree with the Holy Spirit and our unity with Him is broken.

Another consideration. What unity do we have if we *add* something or someone to the list? Or *subtract* some from the total? To add or subtract from the Holy Spirit's nature of unity would foster denominations and dilute His complete fullness. We would be guilty of losing the same unity Jesus prayed about, saying, "Holy Father, keep them in your own care . . . so that they will be united just as we are, with none missing. . . . My prayer for all of them is that they will be of one heart and mind, just as you and I are, Father" (John 17:11, 21, TLB).

Keeping the unity of the Spirit protects our identity with one Father, Son and Holy Spirit and with one another. It ensures our birthright as Christians, promised to us through John the Baptist when Jesus came. "Of His fullness we have all received, and grace for grace" (John 1:16, NKJV).

Just as His strength is multiplied into everlasting strength, and His faith is multiplied into still more righteousness by faith, even so the unity of the Spirit explodes into ever-increasing unity with the Godhead the more we practice keeping it. Fullness is the issue here. That's what Jesus meant when He said, "Whoever has, to him more will be given, and he will have abundance; but whoever does not have, even what he has will be taken away from him" (Matthew 13:12, NKJV).

How do we successfully keep what we have received lest it be taken away from us? Adam did not *keep* the garden given to him. The Israelites did not *keep* the Law of Moses given to them. Will we, of this generation, be able to *keep* the unity of the Spirit by being at peace with one another?

It is our choice and our responsibility to hold fast the Spirit's unity without murmuring and complaining. Paul pleaded with us to do so. "Dear brothers, I beg you in the name of the Lord Jesus Christ to stop arguing among yourselves. Let there be real harmony so that there won't be splits in the church. I plead with you to be of one mind, united in thought and purpose" (1 Corinthians 1:10, TLB).

To be of one mind and one accord in one place is not automatic. It demands a willingness on our part. But when we come into agreement with the Holy Spirit we know it, and peace flows like a river.

The first church began that way, and it can be that way again. For Jesus anticipated our dilemma and did something about it. He died and went to hell and back in order to heap upon us gifts of grace designed to bring us into unity. These abilities were given "to each of us individually . . . but in different ways" (Ephesians 4:7, AMPLIFIED).

Some were called to be "apostles (special messengers), some prophets (inspired preachers and expounders), some evangelists (preachers of the Gospel, traveling missionaries), some pastors (shepherds of His flock) and teachers" (Ephesians 4:11, AMPLIFIED). All of us, however, were called to use the gifts given to us individually until "we all reach unity in the faith and in the knowledge of the Son of God and become mature, attaining to the whole measure of the fullness of Christ" (Ephesians 4:13, NIV).

We do not mature alone. The whole body is designed to multiply and grow together. For God's love, injected through spiritual gifts, begets more love the way grace, strength and faith do, until we *all* attain full growth in the Lord together.

Peace is the catalyst that keeps this process in motion. Therefore, if all the apostles, prophets, pastors, evangelists and teachers are obedient to do what they were gifted to do by Christ, there should be an incentive for all body members to respond with unity. If not, then we will remain self-centered, immature babies tossed to and fro by every wind of doctrine—with seven different creeds, or another Jesus, or another spirit, or unknown gods, or different gospels. This is what Paul feared when he warned the church not to be corrupted from the *simplicity* of Christ, saying, "If a man comes and preaches another Jesus than the One we preached, or if you receive a different spirit from the [Spirit] you [once] received, or a different gospel from the one you [then] received *and* welcomed" (2 Corinthians 11:4, AMPLIFIED)—you are deceived.

Oh, "how good and pleasant it is when brothers live together in unity! It is like precious oil poured on the head, running down on the beard, running down on Aaron's beard, down upon the collar of his robes. It is as if the dew of Hermon were falling on Mount Zion. For there the Lord bestows his blessing, even life forevermore" (Psalm 133:1–3, NIV).

True unity at last with great "recompense of reward." May it ever be!

Holy Spirit,
thank You for Your unity.
How good and pleasant it is to keep.
Blessed are the peacemakers.
Make us one!

108
BEING SO SENSITIVE

Grieve not the Holy Spirit.
EPHESIANS 4:30

Since the warning "grieve not the Holy Spirit" is plainly written in Scripture, it must mean that grieving Him *is* possible.

At first glance, we might assume that grieving the Spirit is done by those who willfully reject God by believing that men are gods instead. This is the original lie, called *humanism,* that produces antichrists. But notice, the admonition is clearly written to Christians who know better. "Do not grieve the Holy Spirit of God, by whom you were sealed for the day of redemption" (Ephesians 4:30, NKJV).

Having been sealed by the Holy Spirit, Christians *know* their God, for they have been enlightened. They have a personal relationship with Jesus Christ, share the indwelling presence of the Holy Spirit, experience the goodness of God and His Word, and taste the mighty powers of the age to come.

How then could these "sealed ones" possibly grieve the Holy Spirit? We grieve the Holy Spirit by grieving one another.

Grieving the Holy Spirit is not a matter of lacking reconciliation with God but of lacking reconciliation with our brethren. It is not a vertical problem but a horizontal one. For "whoever is angry with his brother without a cause shall be in danger of the judgment. . . . Therefore, if you bring your gift to the altar, and there remember that your brother has something against you, leave your gift . . . and first be reconciled to your brother, and then come and offer your gift" (Matthew 5:22–24, NKJV).

It becomes our responsibility to stop "a mere flesh wound" before it results in quenching the Holy Spirit. The letters written to the churches are weighted heavily with plain talk about how we should treat one another, lest we mistreat the Holy Spirit. When we inflict pain upon one another, or on ourselves, we hurt the Holy Spirit who joins us together. To deny our calling, by acting like fools, prevents us from enjoying His intimacy.

Each one of us knows when we are grieved in our own spirits, let alone in our souls, which scream with feelings. We cannot play dumb any longer. Yet so often we do not care whether or not we bite and devour one another. But we can no longer ignore the fact that when we do, the Holy Spirit is saddened—to our shame.

True Christianity is a religion of right relationships. The Father and the Son lovingly relate to one another through one Holy Spirit, and so should we. The Holy Spirit tells us how *not* to grieve Him: "Get rid of all bitterness, rage and anger, brawling and slander, along with every form of malice. Be kind and compassionate to one another, forgiving each other, just as in Christ God forgave you. Be imitators of God . . . and live a life of love, just as Christ [did]" (Ephesians 4:31–32; 5:1–2, NIV).

So for me, this puts a different light upon my actions and reactions. While I might not care about whether or not I provoke Susie Q, I certainly do care about distressing the Holy Spirit. I do not want to tempt Him to leave me. He intercedes for me. Nor do I want to quench His mighty power to help me. He cannot be replaced. Neither do I want to vex the Holy Spirit and have Him turn against me. Suddenly I am aware that it truly *grieves me* to *grieve Him,* and I am extremely uncomfortable until I repent of my wrong attitudes and behavior. Thankfully, when I do, His presence once more assures me of victory over *myself.*

But wait. Victory over myself is not enough. I hear that still, small voice saying, "Why do you persecute Me?" I realize that I insult the Spirit when I wound you. You flee from me and there is a void. An emptiness. For no one is designed to take your place. I miss your sweet expression of grace. I need you. You need me. We belong together in one body. The Holy Spirit yoked us together and made us dependent upon one another. When you are sorrowful, I am also sad. When you suffer, I suffer, too. I want you to be honored so I may be honored with you. I am glad when you can rejoice, so I may rejoice, too. Now it *grieves me* to *grieve you* because I truly desire to hold *all things* in common with you. I love you and I am sorry. Please forgive me and restore the unity of the Spirit we shared, for I am less than whole alone. I am beginning to understand what the Holy Spirit meant when He said, "Who makes a mistake and I do not feel his sadness? Who falls without my longing to help him? Who is spiritually hurt without my fury rising against the one who hurt him?" (2 Corinthians 11:28, TLB).

There are occasions, however, when we are our own worst enemies and hurt ourselves by not loving ourselves as we should (let alone our neighbors). Our bodies are to be *living* sacrifices for God. But when we criticize His handiwork by not accepting the bodies and souls He gave us, we are rejecting them—despising the temples in which the Holy Spirit chooses to live. "You have formed my inward parts; You have covered me in my mother's womb. I will praise You, for I am fearfully and wonderfully made; marvelous are Your works, and that my soul knows very well" (Psalm 139:13–14, NKJV).

The Holy Spirit is also grieved when we will not forgive ourselves (let alone others). If I have not practiced forgiving myself seventy times seven, is it any wonder that I do not know how to forgive others?

Lord, You did not come to condemn us but to save us. You forgave our sins, gave us Your righteousness and told us to go and sin no more. Since You have already accepted us, why should we frustrate Your work of grace by falling prey to the accuser of the brethren? God forbid. You did not die in vain!

Holy Spirit,
we choose to stop grieving You.
Help our unbelief and rightly relate us to
one another and to ourselves.

109

HIS SWORD

The sword of the Spirit . . .
EPHESIANS 6:17

Peculiar to the Holy Spirit is His almighty sword. This He powerfully wields in every direction to execute the righteous judgments of God.

The first appearance of His sword was to keep Adam from eating of the Tree of Life in God's Garden. The Lord God "drove out the man; and He placed cherubim at the east of the garden of Eden, and a flaming sword which turned every way, to guard . . . the tree of life" (Genesis 3:24, NKJV).

- Joshua beheld a drawn sword in the hand of the Commander of the Lord's army (Joshua 5:13).
- Balaam's donkey saw the sword (Numbers 22:23).
- King David experienced the sword (1 Chronicles 21:16).
- Daniel beheld the flaming sword (Daniel 7:9–10).
- Jesus used the sword in the wilderness (Matthew 4:4, 7, 10).
- Mary's soul was pierced by the sword (Luke 2:35).
- Jesus baptized with the sword (Luke 3:16).
- Those of Judea and Jerusalem repented when the sword "pricked their hearts" (Acts 2:37).
- The Sanhedrin council rebelled when their hearts were cut by the sword (Acts 5:33).
- The Jews were furious when they were cut to the quick by the sword (Acts 7:54).
- The sword fell on those in Cornelius' house (Acts 10:44).
- Demons shudder at the sword (James 2:19).

And today we either live or die by His sword.

What is the Holy Spirit's sword? Scripture plainly tells us that "the sword of the Spirit . . . is the word of God" (Ephesians 6:17).

God's Word and the Spirit's sword are the same. They work together as one. The Spirit's sword originates in the breath of God. The psalmist paints a vivid picture by saying His voice divides the flames of fire (see Psalm 29:7, NKJV). It is as if the breath coming from God's mouth separates the fire into fiery tongues, multiplying every word God utters. It is so majestic and powerful that it can never return to Him void of carrying out His will. Nothing or no one is able to prevail against God's omnipotent sword.

Yet Satan has dared to try. He tried with Adam. He tried with Israel. He tried with Jesus. He tries with the Church. And he tries with you and me. He seeks to destroy us with *his* word. His lies. His evil. His doctrines of demons. His doubts. And his perdition. Satan's sword is unholy.

So how do we "take the sword of the Spirit" against the devil's stronghold? The same way Jesus did. He spoke the Word of God and through His mouth wielded the Spirit's sword: the right word, at the right time, the right number of times. "It is written . . . it is written . . . it is written," He proclaimed to His tempter. And the devil's arguments were overruled by the Law and the testimony from His mouth.

The devil never even questioned the authority of the two-edged sword Jesus used from Deuteronomy, but he did try to counterfeit the meaning of the Word. Perhaps the Son of Man could be tricked into obeying him if he quoted Scripture, too. If the devil tried this with Jesus, no wonder he unceasingly hounds you and me.

Jesus encourages believers to use the sword of the Spirit. It is not necessary to thrust forth the entire Bible to wound the adversary. Declaring what the Word says the blood of Jesus does for us causes the enemy to fall like lightning.

God's terrible swift sword is both good and severe. It strikes each one at the point of his or her need. Some with conviction, some with conversion, some with condemnation, and all with life-or-death decisions. It blesses those who yield to its correction of "what is true and . . . make[s] us realize what is wrong in our lives; it straightens us out and helps us do what is right. It is God's way of making us well prepared at every point, fully equipped to do good to everyone" (2 Timothy 3:16–17, TLB).

Spirit of the living God,
I stand in awe of Your sword.
Thank You for using it on me.
I would have perished without it.

110
SETTING US APART

Sanctification of the Spirit . . .
2 THESSALONIANS 2:13

The Holy Spirit has the task of making saints out of sinners. This patient, holy process is called sanctification.

The Holy Spirit sanctifies us in two different ways: by separating us *from sin* and separating us *to God.* A person who is "set apart to God" is separated from sin and partakes of God's holy nature. He is a "sanctified one" or saint. Because God is holy, everything belonging to Him must be most holy. Free from sin. Perfect. Pure.

Our personal sanctification is needed because of the sin of our first parents. So the history of our sanctification began long before we were born. Before we had done anything good or evil, God ordained us to belong to Him and be like Him. How? "From the beginning God chose you to be saved through the sanctifying work of the Spirit and through belief in the truth" (2 Thessalonians 2:13, NIV).

Our sanctification is the ultimate intention of the Godhead. It is Their delight. Their good pleasure. Their expectation! It was preordained and *conceived* in the will of God, *consummated* by the obedience of Jesus and *confirmed* through the work of the Holy Spirit. We were "chosen and foreknown by God the Father and consecrated (sanctified, made holy) by the Spirit to be obedient to Jesus Christ, the Messiah" (1 Peter 1:2, AMPLIFIED).

Jesus consummated the will of God for our sanctification by dying on the cross. In so doing, He did away with the daily sacrifices and offerings for sin under the Law, setting aside the first will of His Father to establish the second. And "by that [second] will we have been made holy through the sacrifice of the body of Jesus Christ once for all" (Hebrews 10:10, NIV).

The emphasis is on Jesus' sacrifice once. And to prove this point, when He had purged our sins, He sat down at the right hand of the Majesty on high. Contrast this with Old Testament priests, who never could sit down because their daily sacrifices for sin were never finished. With Jesus, "when sins have once been forever forgiven and forgotten, there is no need to offer more sacrifices to get rid of them" (Hebrews 10:18, TLB).

Scripture tells us that "by the one offering of Jesus He perfected forever those who are being sanctified," which indicates the continuing present tense. Once Jesus justified us before God, the progressive work of sanctification was set free to operate in our lives. Jesus gave His body and blood; God gives His Spirit. Jesus' work is done; the Holy Spirit's work goes on cleansing us daily from sin by that blood. We *have been* perfected forever by Jesus' sacrifice for sin, yet we *are being* sanctified moment by moment by the Spirit, because nobody can obey God without the Holy Spirit. He is the one who enables us "to be obedient to Jesus Christ, the Messiah, and to be sprinkled with [His] blood" (1 Peter 1:2, AMPLIFIED).

Because the Holy Spirit is the only agent who can sprinkle the blood of Jesus, it is not under man's control. Realize that the blood in the basin in the Old Testament, or at the foot of the cross in the New Testament, would not have cleansed anyone from sin. The blood had to be applied for the effects of sin and death to "pass over."

The pattern has always been there. Moses instructed the children of Israel to "drain the lamb's blood into a basin, and then take a cluster of hyssop branches and dip them into the lamb's blood, and strike the hyssop against the lintel above the door and against the two side panels, so that there will be blood upon them" (Exodus 12:22, TLB).

Applying the blood is the work of the Holy Spirit. He is the Hyssop of the New Covenant—the representative of the Godhead who sprinkles the Passover blood of Jesus on the door.

- Where? Upon our hearts.
- Why? To purify them from sin—something the blood of bulls and goats could never do (Hebrews 10:22).
- When? Every time we confess our sin (1 John 1:9).

The Holy Spirit, however, does not sprinkle the blood of Jesus on the disobedient. If those under the Old Covenant were not willing to apply the blood of bulls and goats shed for their trespasses, they would have perished. How much more shall we be damned if spiritually we have "trampled underfoot the Son of God and treated his cleansing blood as though it were common and unhallowed, and insulted and outraged the Holy Spirit who brings God's mercy to his people?" (Hebrews 10:29, TLB).

We, too, must be obedient to Jesus Christ and take God seriously. For the devil comes in to undermine our faith in the sufficiency of that *one* sacrifice. He tells us our sins are too big or too many to forgive. And if we believe him we lose our confidence in the perfect work of Jesus and substitute our own works—which are never finished. Bottom line: Nothing qualifies us for true holiness except the blood of Jesus sprinkled by the Holy Spirit. And Satan knows that better than we do.

Praise God, we have been forgiven and are being forgiven. We are holy and we are being made still more holy by the work of the Holy Spirit.

Therefore, "seeing ye have purified your souls in obeying the truth through the Spirit" (1 Peter 1:22), give thanks always for your sanctification, which made you saints of the Most High God.

Ah, the beauty of holiness!
How little I know; how much I owe.
Thank You, Holy Spirit, for being my hyssop
and "sainting" me.

111

SPEAKING TO US

The Spirit speaketh. . . .
1 TIMOTHY 4:1

Yes, the Holy Spirit speaks! And to those who hear, faith comes. For not only does He have a voice, but He quickens (makes alive) what He says. He is outspoken in His speech so that Scripture says, "The Spirit speaketh expressly" (1 Timothy 4:1). There is no uncertainty in His rhetoric. He does not speak in riddles or use ambiguous language. His words are easily understood, leaving no doubt about what is truth. Neither does He speak in parables as Jesus sometimes did. The Holy Spirit speaks as the oracle of God.

The oracles of God were spoken first to the nation of Israel. So awesome was God's voice that Moses asked the people, "Did any people ever hear the voice of God speaking out of the midst of the fire, as you have heard, and live? Out of heaven He let you hear His voice, that He might instruct you" (Deuteronomy 4:33, 36, NKJV).

But even though they heard the Lord speaking to them, they became dull of hearing and soon forgot. So Moses warned them again and again to "take heed and listen, O Israel . . . you shall obey the voice of the Lord your God, and observe His commandments and His statutes" (Deuteronomy 27:9–10, NKJV).

They saw His glory, received the covenants, the Law, the Temple service and the promises. To them belonged the patriarchs, the ancestors of Christ. And when Christ came He too spoke as the oracles of God and validated the Holy Spirit's message saying, "When He, the Spirit of truth, has come . . . He will not speak on His own authority, but whatever He hears [from the Father] He will speak; and He will tell you things to come" (John 16:13, NKJV).

The Holy Spirit, having access to the councils of the Godhead, speaks what He hears to those prepared to listen. He speaks in an explicit way and for a specific purpose: to reveal what was, what is and what is yet to come.

Concerning future events, it is extremely important to know the voice you are listening to. In this Scripture, written in the first century, the Holy

Spirit warns of the apostasy now in progress: "The Spirit expressly says that in the latter times some will depart from the faith, giving heed to deceiving spirits and doctrines of demons [occult], speaking lies in hypocrisy [humanism], having their own conscience seared with a hot iron [rebellion], forbidding to marry, and commanding to abstain from foods which God created to be received with thanksgiving by those who believe and know the truth" (1 Timothy 4:1–3, NKJV).

The Holy Spirit leaves nothing unsaid. Everything that pertains to life and godliness, as well as everything pertaining to death and perdition, is made clear in the Old and New Testaments. As a result all men can know the difference between right or wrong and good or evil.

We are not responsible for what happened before our times, but we are responsible for ourselves today lest we deny the power of the Holy Spirit and refuse Him who is still speaking. Yes, "the Holy Spirit says: 'Today, if you will hear His voice, do not harden your hearts as in . . . the wilderness, where your fathers tested Me and proved Me, and saw My works forty years'" (Hebrews 3:7–9, NKJV).

The Holy Spirit communicates with the whole world through the mouths and pens of the Scripture writers. This Gospel of the Kingdom will be preached to all nations before the end comes.

Beloved, listen with the ear of faith and you will *hear* the Holy Spirit speaking to you.

Spirit of holy truth,
continue speaking to me
so that I too
may speak the oracles of God.

112

KEEPING US

Keep by the Holy [Spirit]...
2 TIMOTHY 1:14

*T*he Holy Spirit has "keeping power." He keeps, guards, watches over, protects, preserves and holds fast spiritual things.

In Scripture the "keeping power" of the Holy Spirit functions in two ways: for man and for God. For man, the Holy Spirit keeps all that God gives to the saints. For God, the Holy Spirit keeps all that the saints give to God.

Paul explained this important work of the Holy Spirit to Timothy, "his own dearly beloved son in the faith," who was the son of a pagan Greek father and a devout Jewish mother. As a child, Timothy was nurtured in the Old Testament Scriptures by his grandmother Lois and his mother, Eunice. Thus, he was a knowledgeable Israelite when Paul met and converted him.

Paul's fatherly love for Timothy caused him to disciple him diligently. By the laying on of Paul's hands and the hands of the presbyters, Timothy was set apart to do the work of an evangelist and became Paul's faithful companion on his second missionary journey.

Observing Timothy to be timid and overwhelmed by the responsibilities of ministering church doctrine at such a young age, Paul exhorted Timothy to be bold and not let anyone despise his youthfulness. Nor should Timothy permit a spirit of fear to worry him about the trials and hardships that might come his way. He counseled, "Take your share of the suffering [to which the preaching] of the Gospel [may expose you, and do it] in the power of God" (2 Timothy 1:8, AMPLIFIED).

Paul knew it took the power of God to overcome the persecutions of those who hate the Gospel message. Having been through his own share of suffering, Paul understood how Timothy might need to "stir up" the gift of God that was in him to preach. Paul encouraged Timothy with the "keeping power" of the Holy Spirit, telling him to hold on to the truth of the Gospel the same way he had done: by the help of the Holy Spirit. "What you heard from me, keep as the pattern of sound teaching. . . . Guard the good deposit that was entrusted to you—guard it with the help of the Holy Spirit who lives in us" (2 Timothy 1:13–14, NIV).

Paul knew the Holy Spirit, who deposited the gift in Timothy in the first place, would help him keep it pure and undefiled. Not only for Timothy's sake but for the other men and women of faith who would follow in his footsteps.

As Timothy took more responsibility for the churches, he faced the same problems pastors of this century face. The apostasy of the Church had already begun, as Paul confirmed when he penned his last letter to Timothy from a Roman prison cell. Having been brought before the emperor Nero, who took fiendish delight in making martyrs out of Christians, the aging apostle knew his days on earth were numbered. Even then, his love and prayers still focused on Timothy, whom he longed to see once more so he could tell him why he was not ashamed to suffer. Writing to him Paul said, "I know whom I have believed and am persuaded that He is able to keep what I have committed to Him until that Day" (2 Timothy 1:12, NKJV).

Every Timothy needs a Paul and every Paul needs a Timothy. Timothys need to keep what Pauls commit to them and Pauls need to commit their Timothys to God.

The charge Paul gave to Timothy for the Church is still good today. And so is the assurance that the Holy Spirit keeps and watches over all God deposits in us. The Holy Spirit is able to hold everything God commits to us in His word and everything we commit to God by our word of faith.

"He will not allow your foot to be moved; He who keeps you will not slumber. Behold, He who keeps Israel shall neither slumber nor sleep. The LORD is your keeper" (Psalm 121:3–5, NKJV).

O, blessed Keeper,
into Your hands I
gladly commit my spirit.

113
RENEWING US

Renewing of the Holy [Spirit].
TITUS 3:5

The faithful work of the Holy Spirit renews us day by day, hour by hour, moment by moment.

Once we are born again, spiritual renewal is the essential part of life we cannot do without. Not only is our *spirit* quickened and regenerated by the Holy Spirit, but our *soul* is transformed as well. Paul reviews the salvation process from God's point of view saying, "He saved us, through the washing of regeneration and renewing of the Holy Spirit, whom He poured out on us abundantly through Jesus Christ our Savior" (Titus 3:5–6, NKJV).

Our souls, which house our minds, wills and emotions, must continually be reeducated by the Holy Spirit for us to have Christ's mind. As we yield to the conversion power of God's Word, we come under the Holy Spirit's influence: thinking God's thoughts and doing His will. At the same time, we come out from under the influence of Satan, the god of this world, who blinds the minds of those choosing *not* to retain God in their knowledge. Their minds become incurably sick. Only believers heed Paul's admonition "not [to] be conformed to this world, but be transformed by the renewing of your mind, that you may prove what is that good and acceptable and perfect will of God" (Romans 12:2, NKJV).

The good, acceptable and perfect will of God is an awesome thing to put in your mind. Only the mind renewed by the Holy Spirit is truly able to comprehend it. The unrenewed mind can never understand God's will—that Jesus Christ gave Himself for our sins "in order to rescue and deliver us from this present wicked age and world order, in accordance with the will and purpose and plan of our God and Father" (Galatians 1:4, AMPLIFIED).

The Holy Spirit's restoration of our mind does even more. It enables us to shed our old nature and be clothed with a new divine nature: the character of Christ. Paul encouraged us to "be renewed in the spirit of your mind, and . . . put on the new man which was created according to God, in righteousness and true holiness" (Ephesians 4:23–24, NKJV).

What makes the new man new? The knowledge of Christ. Just as Jesus used the Scriptures to open the minds of the men on the road to Emmaus, the new man's mind is "renewed in knowledge after the image of him that created him" (Colossians 3:10) by the Holy Spirit. The Greek meaning of the word *knowledge* is very emphatic here. It does not refer to mere intellectual knowledge but to spiritual knowledge. It is an advanced recognition of God not perceived by natural instincts. This knowledge is a true and comprehensive awareness of God that perfectly unites the subject with the object.

Scripture indicates this knowledge is superimposed upon us by the Holy Spirit as He renews our minds about the one who created us. Thus we become intimately acquainted with our heavenly Father and our Lord Jesus.

Yes, minds made new again can *know* their Creator and *love* Him as they learn to trust the changing work of the Holy Spirit, who is not a Spirit of fear, "but of power and of love, and of a sound mind" (2 Timothy 1:7).

Our minds become calm, self-controlled and disciplined, for we are renewed by the Holy Spirit inside. His strength and power are secretly at work restoring the inner man with faith, hope and love. That is why "we do not become discouraged—utterly spiritless, exhausted, and wearied out through fear. Though our outer man is (progressively) decaying and wasting away, yet our inner self is being (progressively) renewed day after day" (2 Corinthians 4:16, AMPLIFIED).

In the believer, the inner man is the sanctuary of the Godhead. Those who *know* the true God and Jesus Christ whom He has sent have eternal life present in them already. While the body may die, the inner man of the Spirit lives on to worship the One who so fearfully and wonderfully made him.

How true it is, Holy Spirit,
that to know God is to love Him.
Thank You for restoring my soul.

114
ETERNAL SPIRIT

Through the eternal Spirit [Christ] offered himself....

HEBREWS 9:14

The most important revelation about the Holy Spirit occurs deep within the book of Hebrews. There He is introduced as the "eternal Spirit," without beginning or ending. Understanding the significance of His eternal nature is imperative, for it is His permanence that we seek for ourselves.

The word *eternal* does not mean just existing for a long period of time, it means "out of time," in a different order of being. And because this is true, the works of the Holy Spirit are timeless—from everlasting to everlasting.

Everything done or said "in the Spirit, by the Spirit or through the Spirit" never dies. It is not subject to the limitations of time or place.

If you have ever questioned how the death of Jesus Christ two thousand years ago could take away the sins you have committed in your lifetime, this is the Scripture that gives the answer. It is because Jesus' blood was offered "through the eternal Spirit" (Hebrews 9:14) and not through the Law of carnal commandments. The Law made nothing perfect, nor could it change the heart. It was only a schoolmaster to bring us to Christ, who superseded the law and "obtained eternal redemption for us" (Hebrews 9:12).

In the same way, if you have ever wondered how the blood of bulls and goats, sacrificed fifteen hundred years *before Christ's death,* could possibly redeem the transgressions of those under the Law of Moses, the same answer applies. It was "by the help of the eternal Holy Spirit, [that] . . . Christ . . . died to rescue them from the penalty of the sins they had committed while still under that old system [of law]" (Hebrews 9:14–15, TLB).

It also applies to those who lived from Abraham to Moses, five hundred years *before* the Law was introduced. Abraham obeyed God and by faith shed blood in circumcising himself and his male descendants. By faith he obeyed God by taking his only son, Isaac, to sacrifice as a burnt offering, believing God would raise him from the dead. It was then that he saw God offering His Son afar off while he waited for Messiah's resurrection and his own. Abraham and his seed were still living by faith when they died, not having received the things promised them, but fully persuaded they would come to pass. God counted it to them as righteousness.

Take one more step back in time to the beginning. Was eternal redemption also applied to those who offered blood sacrifices to God from Adam to Abraham? I believe it was, for God Himself covered the nakedness of Adam and Eve with the skins of animals whose blood He shed for their clothing. And Abel's lamb offering by faith was acceptable to God.

What took place on the cross transcended the limits of time and place. Since the blood of Jesus Christ was offered in the eternal realm to God through the Holy Spirit, He bore the sin and guilt of all people, of all ages: past, present and future. This means that now, through the eternal Holy Spirit, Calvary can become as real to you and me as though it happened five minutes ago. Jesus' blood has eternal consequences that benefit our spirits, souls and bodies the moment we touch Him. And when you experience the blood of the everlasting covenant, ministered by the Holy Spirit, you should have no more trouble with a guilty sin conscience. Nothing is held against you in the records of heaven. There is now no condemnation for you who belong to Christ Jesus. God says that "the blood of goats and bulls and the ashes of a heifer sprinkled on those who are ceremonially unclean sanctify them so that they are outwardly clean. How much more, then, will the blood of Christ, who through the eternal Spirit offered himself unblemished to God, cleanse our consciences from acts that lead to death [useless rituals], so that we may serve the living God!" (Hebrews 9:13–14, NIV).

Understanding the eternal significance of this transaction makes our eternal salvation an eternal reality for which we are eternally grateful.

God so loved the world
that He gave His only begotten Son
through the eternal Holy Spirit,
that whosoever believes in Him
should not perish, but have eternal life.

115

GRACE

The Spirit of grace . . .
HEBREWS 10:29

*I*t is not possible fully to comprehend the work of the "Spirit of grace," for it is the vast theme of time and eternity. In spite of this, the answer to three questions is in order here. Who is grace? What is grace? How do we receive and keep grace?

The Spirit of grace is the Holy Spirit. We met Him in the Old Testament prophecies of Zechariah as the Spirit of Grace and Supplications who would be poured out upon the house of David and the inhabitants of Jerusalem sometime in the near future. As a result of His work the people will *look upon* Messiah Yeshua with recognition and repentance. Grace is a Spirit.

One aspect of grace is the way we *look* at one another. In the Old Testament we read that Jacob gave gifts to his brother, Esau, hoping to find grace in his sight. Esther found grace and favor in the eyes of the king, and he made her a queen. Ruth asked Boaz why she had found grace in his eyes. Grace is undeserved favor.

God's grace is also found in the way He chooses to *look* at people. When He looks in their direction it means the blessing and favor of His glory begins to shine upon them, changing their destiny. For example, God looked at Noah with grace in His eyes and saved his household. God looked at Moses with grace in His eyes and saved a nation. God looks at all mankind with grace in His eyes and saves a multitude no one can number. Grace is God's choice. Grace saves.

The grace of God is also found in the adjectives of His names. "The LORD, the LORD God, merciful and gracious, longsuffering, and abounding in goodness and truth, keeping mercy for thousands, forgiving iniquity and transgression and sin, by no means clearing the guilty" (Exodus 34:6–7, NKJV).

In the wilderness thousands received God's promise of grace by faith, and their sins were forgiven; just as many refused His grace and partook of His wrath. Grace is forgiveness of sins. Grace is God's justice.

It is helpful to think about grace as light. When Scripture begins, a mysterious darkness and chaos cover the earth. How long this lasted no one knows. But into that morbid scene of death and destruction God spoke

His light, and the Holy Spirit flooded the blackness with the radiance of God's presence. Not the light of the sun, the moon or the stars, but the brightness of God's face. Grace is the absence of darkness. Grace is the light of God's shining countenance.

The same God who said, "'Let there be light in the darkness,' has made us understand that it is the brightness of his glory that is seen in the face of Jesus Christ" (2 Corinthians 4:6, TLB). Our human souls, hopelessly darkened by sin and death, were revived by the light of Jesus' coming. His glorious face enlightens every soul born into the world. And like His Father, Jesus forgives the sins of all who are willing to humble themselves by admitting their need of Him.

The fullness of grace and truth embodied in Christ Jesus was not received by men until the coming of the promised Holy Spirit. Since then, "this precious treasure—this light and power that now shine within us—is held in a perishable container, that is, in our weak bodies. Everyone can see that the glorious power within must be from God and is not our own" (2 Corinthians 4:7, TLB).

The power of grace within helps us overcome every weakness and temptation we encounter so we can be Christlike. There is no temptation common to man that resists grace. The Lord says, "My grace is sufficient for all your needs."

My love is grace for your hate.
My rest is grace for your works.
My life is grace for your death.
My joy is grace for your sorrow.
My purity is grace for your lust.
My peace is grace for your worry.
My faith is grace for your doubts.
My beauty is grace for your ashes.
My healing is grace for your hurts.
My courage is grace for your fears.
My wealth is grace for your poverty.
My humility is grace for your pride.
My gentleness is grace for your anger.
My goodness is grace for your cruelty.
My praise is grace for your heaviness.
My wisdom is grace for your ignorance.
My strength is grace for your weakness.

My acceptance is grace for your rejection.

My submission is grace for your rebellion.

My self-control is grace for your addiction.

My obedience is grace for your stubbornness.

My longsuffering is grace for your impatience.

My righteousness is grace for your sinfulness.

My grace has no ending. My grace is greater than all your sins. Grace is My throne.

The wonderful works of God are received and kept through the Spirit of grace. For this reason we are given strong warning to be careful how we "look" at the Holy Spirit lest we despise His work and become guilty of having "insulted the Spirit of grace" (Hebrews 10:29, NKJV).

He is offended when we:

- Frustrate the grace of God by treating Christ's death as if it were meaningless (Galatians 1:6–8; 2:21).
- Receive God's grace in vain by failing to come under the teaching and discipline of grace (2 Corinthians 6:1; Titus 2:11–14).
- Turn God's grace into a license for immorality by deliberately sinning (Jude 4; Romans 6:1–2; Hebrews 10:26).
- Fail to find God's grace because we allow a root of bitterness to spring up between family members (Hebrews 12:15–17; Ephesians 4:30–32).
- "Fall from grace" by slipping back from the law of faith to be cursed by the law of works (Galatians 3:10; 5:4; Romans 11:5–6).

Grace can be lost. While we cannot crucify the Holy Spirit, we can quench His ministry of imparting Christ's glory. When this happens the grace of Jesus is never completely experienced or appreciated, resulting in some people being saved by a stranger. They are converted and turn away from sin but never really know the One who saved them. Nor, perhaps, do they care. They know their church rules and work diligently, yet they miss the blessing of an intimate relationship with their Savior.

A true story illustrates this point. One day at the hospital my husband, who is a surgeon, was waiting for an elevator to take him to the operating room. A woman rushed up to him crying uncontrollably because her baby was dead. My husband took the lifeless infant, laid him on a nearby table, and began to massage his heart and administer artificial respiration. The baby gasped for air. Eventually he began to breathe and regain some color.

The mother retreated to the emergency room for further help while Rudy, late for his surgery, rejoiced in God's mercy.

Thirty-two years later in the same hospital, at the same elevator, a man came up to my husband inquiring, "Are you Dr. Hecksher?"

"Yes, I am," he replied.

"I've been looking for you for some time."

The man continued to speak as he reached to shake Rudy's hand. "You probably don't remember me, but over thirty years ago my mother brought me into this hospital dead, and you saved my life. I've been looking for you for a long time to say thank you."

Without the Spirit of grace we would not be acquainted with the stranger who saved us, nor could we acknowledge Him by name to say, "Thank You, Lord Jesus, for saving my life!"

Be blessed, beloved. The grace of our Lord Jesus Christ be with your spirit always. Amen.

> *Spirit of grace, no longer a stranger,*
> *Spirit of grace, no longer a Ghost,*
> *Spirit of grace, oh, how I need You,*
> *Spirit of grace, come be my Host.*

116
INSPIRING THE PROPHETS

Holy men of God spake as they were moved by the Holy [Spirit].
2 PETER 1:21

he Holy Spirit inspires men to express the mind of God in understandable words. He directs their speech and provides the message. Therefore, "prophecy came not in old time by the will of man: but holy men of God spake as they were moved by the Holy [Spirit]" (2 Peter 1:21).

In the Old Testament period God purposed not to do anything without first telling His servants, the prophets. This was His way of communicating His plans to Israel so they could be blessed by obeying Him.

The prophets' words did not originate with the men themselves. It was not something they invented. When they prophesied they were not hypnotized, in a trance, in a daze, or controlled by spirits. These holy men of God were moved by the Holy Spirit not only to speak God's mind, but to be in the right place, at the right time, among the right people.

God spoke to the prophets either in an audible voice, in a whisper or a "still, small voice." The prophets heard the revelation in much the same way they would hear any other voice.

The prophet Samuel illustrates the point. He needed to know whom to anoint as the first king of Israel. "Now the LORD had told Samuel in his ear the day before Saul came, saying, 'Tomorrow about this time I will send you a man from the land of Benjamin, and you shall anoint him'" (1 Samuel 9:15–16, NKJV).

Micah is also a good example of a prophet who was moved upon by the Holy Spirit. He confessed this fact: "As for me, I am filled with power, with the Spirit of the Lord, fearlessly announcing God's punishment on Israel for her sins" (Micah 3:8, TLB).

Although the prophets disclosed God's intention of judgment, it did not mean the people would listen or repent. Often, "they hardened their hearts like flint, afraid to hear the words that God, the Lord of Hosts, commanded them—the laws he had revealed to them by his Spirit through the early prophets. That is why such great wrath came down on them from God" (Zechariah 7:12, TLB).

Because the prophets did not choose what they were going to say, they not only divulged the severity of God but the goodness of God as well. Isaiah spoke for God about His favor upon His covenant people saying, "'My spirit who is upon you, and My words which I have put in your mouth, shall not depart from your mouth, nor from the mouth of your descendants, nor from the mouth of your descendants' descendants,' says the LORD, 'from this time and forevermore'" (Isaiah 59:21, NKJV).

If all the messages of the prophets were printed in red, we would have very red Old and New Testaments. All Scripture, whether written or spoken, has been given to us by the Holy Spirit—through men—so that we may know what is true, what is false and how to live pleasing to the Lord. The fact that the Holy Spirit is the one who directed the prophets' speech should encourage our acceptance of what is recorded.

Are there still prophets today? Are there still holy men and women of God moved by the Holy Spirit to speak God's messages? Yes! Today we have both prophets and preachers. But the divine Author of inspiration is the same; only the mouthpiece has changed. And so the question really is, "Are you called to preach? Then preach as though God himself were speaking through you" (1 Peter 4:11, TLB). For "if God has given you the ability to prophesy, then prophesy whenever you can—as often as your faith is strong enough to receive a message from God" (Romans 12:6, TLB).

Be like Paul, who did not take the credit for being a brilliant preacher, but freely acknowledged, "the Holy Spirit's power was in my words, proving to those who heard them that the message was from God. I did this because I wanted your faith to stand firmly upon God, not on man's great ideas" (1 Corinthians 2:4–5, TLB).

All the prophets, including Jesus, have spoken the truth. As Peter prophesied, "You will do well to pay close attention to everything they have written, for like lights shining into dark corners, their words help us to understand many things that otherwise would be dark and difficult. But when you consider the wonderful truth of the prophets' words, then the light will dawn in your . . . hearts" (1 Peter 2:19–20, TLB).

The darker it grows the more
I see You, Spirit of prophecy.
Yes, You light up my life—with Jesus!

117

BEING A WITNESS

The Spirit . . . beareth witness, because the Spirit is truth.

1 JOHN 5:6

he Holy Spirit is the official "expert witness" to the coming of Jesus Christ in the flesh. And since the Spirit of God cannot lie, His testimony is far greater than that of men or angels. This is the reason "it is the Spirit who bears witness because the Spirit is truth" (1 John 5:6, NKJV).

Jesus said the Spirit of truth would comfort us by telling us all about Him—and He did. But not as we would have expected. The Holy Spirit verified Jesus' humanity by using two five-letter words: "This is the one who came by water and blood—Jesus Christ. He did not come by water only, but by water and blood" (1 John 5:6, NIV).

Water and blood emphasize the earthly nature of Jesus as well as all mankind. The adult male consists of about five quarts of *blood* while sixty percent of his body weight is *water*. These two elements more than anything else are part of Jesus' body and His ministry.

How wonderful then to know Jesus came as a man and not as an angel or a god. He knew who His father and mother were. He grew from childhood to manhood in a poor Jewish family with other brothers and sisters. He matured physically and mentally with grace pouring from His lips. He was subject to His parents and learned a trade. Before the age of thirty He worked as a carpenter, then left home to be about His Father's business of building the Church.

Jesus experienced human nature in every aspect. Fatigue, frustration, hunger, thirst, compassion, joy, zeal, anger, love. He wept, groaned in His spirit, took responsibility for His mother and was tested in every way we are. He even learned obedience by the things He suffered—yet in all these circumstances He never once sinned in thought, word or deed.

Scripture further testifies that the second Person of the Godhead was of the human race. Jesus is known as the son of Abraham, the son of David, the son of Mary, the Root of David and the Lion of the tribe of Judah.

The Holy Spirit bears witness to the fact that Jesus was not ashamed to be called our brother. He purposely called Himself "the Son of Man" more than eighty times in the gospels, saying such things as:

The Son of Man has nowhere to lay His head.

The Son of Man has power on earth to forgive sins.

The Son of Man is Lord of the Sabbath.

The Son of Man came eating and drinking.

The Son of Man came to save that which was lost.

The Son of Man is betrayed with a kiss.

The Son of Man goes as it is written of Him but woe to that man by whom the Son of Man is betrayed.

The Son of Man shall rise from the dead.

The Son of Man shall come in an hour that you think not.

The Son of Man shall come in his glory, and all the holy angels with Him.

And eventually He asked the haunting question we all must answer, "Who do you say that I the Son of Man am?"

In Scripture the article *the* always precedes *man* when it is used of the flesh and blood nature of Christ. To illustrate, Pilate said of Jesus, "Behold the Man." Stephen declared, "I see the heavens opened, and the Son of Man standing on the right hand of God." Paul testified, "There is one Mediator between God and men, the Man Christ Jesus." John recorded seeing a vision of "One like the Son of Man, clothed with a garment down to the feet and girded about the chest with a golden band" (Revelation 1:13, NKJV).

Jesus' coming to earth as the Son of Man was the legal issue that frustrated Satan, for only another *Man* could undo what the first man had done. So that when Jesus met the requirements of an eye for an eye, a tooth for a tooth and an Adam for an Adam, He restored man's original dominion ordained by God and guaranteed Satan's defeat.

Why is it of such importance that the Holy Spirit bear witness that Jesus Christ was a human being like we are? Because if Jesus was not born as a man—lived, died and was resurrected as a man—*how can we be?*

Jesus was born right the *first* time, making it possible for us to be born right the *second* time. He was born of a woman but was not the seed of a man. As such, He is the *second Adam,* displacing the first. He is also the *last Adam,* replacing the need for any other. That is why "every spirit that confesses that Jesus Christ has come in the flesh is of God, and every spirit that does not confess that Jesus Christ has come in the flesh is not of God. . . . This is the spirit of the Antichrist, which you have heard was coming, and is now already in the world" (1 John 4:2–3, NKJV).

Ever since the birth of Jesus, the spirit of Antichrist in the world has been lying about Christ. This "spirit of error" denies two truths: that Jesus is the Christ and that He actually came in the flesh by water and blood. The name *Jesus,* as well as the name *Christ* (Greek) or *Messiah* (Hebrew), does not refer to the *deity* but to the *humanity* of God's Son. "If anyone doesn't believe this, he is actually calling God a liar, because he doesn't believe what God has said about his Son" (1 John 5:10, TLB).

Suddenly David's penetrating question to God in the Psalms is made clearer. "What is man, that You are mindful of him, and the son of [earth-born] man, that You care for him? Yet You have made him but a little lower than God [or heavenly beings], and You have crowned him with glory and honor" (Psalm 8:4–5, AMPLIFIED).

Yes, we behold *the Man!* Now see Jesus, "who was made a little lower than the angels for the suffering of death, crowned with glory and honour; that he by the grace of God should taste death for every man . . . bringing many sons unto glory" (Hebrews 2:9–10).

Thank You for Your witness, O Spirit of truth.
Your testimony confirms the Man, Christ Jesus,
so that the Antichrist cannot rob me of my inheritance.
I am one of those He died for.

118

PREPARING THE CHURCH

The Spirit saith unto the churches . . .
REVELATION 2:7, 11, 17, 29; 3:6, 13, 22

I, Jesus, have sent My angel to testify to you these things in the churches" (Revelation 22:16, NKJV).

The fact that Jesus' last words were directed to the churches should demand our immediate attention. Even though spoken to seven churches in Asia Minor existing in John's day, the Spirit of truth "speaking to the churches" is the same yesterday, *today* and forever.

John wrote the things that concerned those churches before he was caught up into heaven to see and record "things that shall be here after the church is gone."

He wrote differently to each church, but one warning is the same for every church. They are admonished to hear what the Holy Spirit is saying to *them*. "He who has an ear, let him hear what the Spirit says to the churches" (Revelation 2:7, 11, 17, 29; 3:6, 13, 22, NKJV).

The Church, made possible through the work of Christ on earth, was a *new creation,* not written about in the Old Testament. It was made up of men and women from every nation, kindred, tribe and tongue on earth.

What was the last will and testament to be carried out by the "living stones," that we might do the will of God?

To answer this question, the Holy Spirit addressed the right things and the wrong things about the churches, for no two were the same. Each had different strengths and weaknesses.

One church was already falling away from her first love for Jesus. Another church was poor, persecuted and afraid. The third was endangered because it allowed truth to be compromised with error. The fourth church permitted spiritual fornication through Jezebel-type spirits to seduce the servants of God. The fifth church was a sleeping giant, almost in a coma.

But the sixth church was one of a kind. Although it was not strong, it was obedient to Christ and not ashamed of His name. In fact, this is the *only* church that did not incur any disapproval by the ever-watchful Holy Spirit.

The seventh church, however, was just the opposite. It had *nothing* to commend it. Everything was wrong. They existed in a state of spiritual denial. Totally deceived. God called them "lukewarm" and promised He would vomit them out of His mouth. This last church was so carnal that John saw Jesus standing outside the door of the church knocking to get in, pleading for someone to hear His voice and open the door to Him. Jesus was not welcome in His own Body, the Church.

Why should these churches need to hear what the Spirit was saying? It had to do with their longevity. To survive the dark ages of time, until Christ would come for her, the Church would need the Holy Spirit's direction and correction to be victorious over the world, the flesh and the devil. Not only could the Holy Spirit tell these churches what God *liked* or *hated* about them, but how to fix it by repenting. If they heard what the Spirit was saying to their churches, they would know the rewards for being overcomers.

The question for us today then is, Which one of the churches do we belong to? The Holy Spirit knows and can reveal it to us. But do we have spiritual ears to listen and do what the Spirit is saying to our church? Is Jesus welcome in our assembly, or are we deaf, unable to hear Him outside knocking to get in?

The problem is not with the Holy Spirit, beloved, it is with us—clamoring over who is worthy to open the door.

Wise Holy Spirit,
speak! For we covet ears to hear Your
words to our church
before it is too late for the wedding.

119

PREPARING THE LAMB

A Lamb . . . having . . . the seven Spirits of God . . .
REVELATION 5:6

he Holy Spirit caught John up into heaven through an open door. There he witnessed mysteries Paul was not allowed to utter—inexpressible things taking place at the throne of God.

John was captivated by the scene. The dazzling brightness of the one who dwells in unapproachable light was like the Sun of Righteousness shining through myriads of diamonds and rubies. Around the throne an endless rainbow exploded into a halo with the brilliance of a transparent emerald.

The floor of the throne room was a vast firmament, clear as crystal, upon which stood seven golden lampstands aflame with fire. These are "the seven Spirits of God [the sevenfold (Holy) Spirit]" (Revelation 4:5, AMPLIFIED).

Surrounding the throne, 24 smaller thrones were occupied by 24 elders dressed in pure white gowns with golden crowns upon their heads. Heaven was alive with the beauty of holiness emanating from the glory of the "Lord God Almighty, who was and is and is to come" (Revelation 4:8, NKJV).

Nor was heaven silent. "Holy, Holy, Holy" sang the multitude of angelic hosts while all heaven reflected the glory, honor and praise due to Him who sits on the throne. John inhaled incense and heard the music of the spheres played on harps before watching the 24 elders cast down their golden crowns at His feet. And from the throne came lightning and loud peals of thunderous voices in reply.

What John beheld in heaven was the excitement of "things to come." Yet, in spite of all this grandeur, his eyes were riveted upon one thing, the Lamb—standing in the midst of the assembly with wounds that once caused His death.

John knew Him immediately. The Passover Lamb of Moses' day. The gentle Lamb Isaiah foresaw who was led to the slaughter without opening His mouth. The Lamb wounded for our transgressions and bruised for our iniquities.

John the Baptist had correctly named Him "the Lamb of God, who takes away the sin of the world!" (John 1:29, NKJV).

Yes, this was the one and only Lamb of God, but questions flooded John's thoughts. What was He doing taking the scroll out of the right hand of the one who sat on the throne? The scroll, with writing on the front and back, sealed with seven seals. Could this be the scroll Daniel wrote centuries ago? The one Gabriel told him to "close up and seal . . . until the time of the end?" (Daniel 12:4, NIV). Had the scroll been in the Father's hand all this time? And if the Lamb opened those seals would it mean that the time of the end had finally come?

Then it happened. John heard heaven erupt three times with new songs to the Lamb.

- The guardian angels and elders sang, "You are worthy to take the scroll, and to open its seals; for You were slain, and have redeemed us to God by Your blood out of every tribe and tongue and people and nation" (Revelation 5:9, NKJV).
- Heavenly hosts, in number like the stars of heaven, sang this seven-fold blessing to the Lamb: "Worthy is the Lamb who was slain to receive power and riches and wisdom, and strength and honor and glory and blessing!" (Revelation 5:12, NKJV).
- And finally, every creature in *heaven* and in *earth* and in the *sea* responded, "Blessing and honor and glory and power be to Him who sits on the throne, and to the Lamb, forever and ever!" (Revelation 5:13, NKJV). Amen.

John witnessed the Lamb upon whom rested the "seven horns and seven eyes, which are the seven Spirits of God sent out into all the earth" (Revelation 5:6, NKJV). The Holy Spirit had prepared Him for this time, this day, this very hour—known only to the Father. And the Lamb was willing. Not to be slain, but to finish the work He began on earth—by opening the seals in heaven. What John saw, and recorded for us, was the Spirit's anointing upon His Lamb to consummate "the day of vengeance of our God" (Isaiah 61:2, NKJV).

Yes, Church, "Blessed is he who reads . . . and those who hear . . . for the time is near" (Revelation 1:3, NKJV).

Sevenfold Spirit of holiness
thank You for preparing the Lamb to prevail
from the foundation of the world
and to comfort all those who mourn in Zion.

120
YOUR INVITATION

The Spirit [says] Come. . . .
REVELATION 22:17

The Spirit and the Bride
take pleasure in inviting you
to come quickly to the throne of God
and the Lamb
to drink the water of life freely.

Attire: white linen raiment
Place: New Jerusalem

R.S.V.P.

SUBJECT INDEX

SCRIPTURE INDEX